THE ACCOMPLISHED ART

Gold and Gold-Working in Britain and Ireland during the Bronze Age (*c.* 2300–650 BC)

George Eogan

Oxbow Monograph 42
1994

Published by
Oxbow Books, Park End Place, Oxford OX1 1HN

© George Eogan 1994

ISBN 0 946897 72 7

This book is available direct from
Oxbow Books, Park End Place, Oxford OX1 1HN
(Phone: 0–865–241249; Fax: 0–865–794449)

and

The David Brown Book Company
PO Box 5605, Bloomington, IN 47407, USA
(Phone: 812–331–0266; Fax: 812–331–0277)

Printed in Great Britain by
The Information Press, Eynsham, Oxford

Contents

For Charles Haughey and Christopher Hawkes (†)
who in their disparate yet complimentary ways
enriched our understanding of Bronze Age gold.

Acknowledgements

I wish to record my gratitude to a wide range of people and institutions for assistance received. I am especially grateful to Ms Helen Roche for so much help during the preparation of the text. Dr Elizabeth Shee Twohig read the manuscript and improved it with her suggestions. In the National Museum of Ireland Dr Patrick Wallace and Ms Mary Cahill cooperated in every way, in addition Ms Cahill offered helpful comments on the text and information on specific objects. That institution also provided illustrations. Mr Richard Warner provided information about the gold collection in the Ulster Museum. Likewise in the British Museum Dr Ian Longworth and Dr Stuart Needham were most generous with facilities and information and in addition provided illustrations. At the National Museum of Scotland Mr Trevor Cowie and Dr Alison Sheridan freely gave much of their time to answering my queries and assisted in every way my research in their Department and provided illustrations. In the Ashmolean Museum, Oxford my thanks are due to Mr Arthur MacGregor for his assistance. I am also grateful to the Ashmolean's Librarian Mr Brian McGregor for placing the facilities of the library at my disposal.

A considerable amount of comparative investigation was carried out in the Prehistoric Department at the National Museum of Denmark and I am very grateful to the Director Professor Olaf Olsen and members of the staff of that Department, in particular the Keeper, Dr Poul Otto Nielsen and Mr Christian Adamsen for so much help. My stay in Copenhagen was facilitated by the Danish National Bank who provided accommodation in their centre for visiting scholars.

Throughout the facilities of the Department of Archaeology, University College Dublin were of enormous assistance and did so much to make the work possible. Ms Mary Cuthbert prepared the distribution maps and set out the entire range of illustrations while the late Albert Glaholm helped with photographic and related issues. For assistance with research and improving the text the work of Ms Róisín Barton and Ms Fiona Dillon is much valued and appreciated.

The finalisation of the work was completed in All Souls College, Oxford, to whom I am most grateful for research facilities and to Miss Deborah McGovern for so much assistance with the preparation and checking of the typescript.

The assistance of Mrs Gabriela Canseco, Oxbow Books, in seeing the manuscript through the press is much appreciated.

Invaluable financial contributions to the cost of publication were made by the National University of Ireland, University College, Dublin, and Mr Malachy McCloskey, Drogheda.

List of Illustrations

37. Hoard. Tooradoo, Co. Limerick, decorated thick penannular rings (1-4), plain solid bronze rings (5-8), rings with lateral buffer-shaped perforated projections (9-10), lignite bead (11) and amber necklace (12). (After Eogan, 1983a).
38. Distribution of British type penannular bracelets with expanded terminals.
39. Distribution of Irish type penannular bracelets with expanded terminals.
40. Distribution of 'dress-fasteners'.
41. Distribution of 'lock-rings'.
42. Distribution of 'hair-rings'.
43. Distribution of 'sleeve-fasteners', striated rings, heart-shaped bullae and decorated thick penannular rings.
44. Distribution in Ireland of sheet-gold objects of the Dowris Phase. (Collars, gorgets, boxes, bowls, discs and disc mounts).

Black and White Plates

1. Discs. No locality, Ireland (1-2). Cloyne, Co. Cork (3-4). *Photo:* National Museum of Ireland.
2. Details of lunulae horns. Nairn, Co. Donegal [Unaccomplished] (No. 1), Trillick, Co. Tyrone [Classical] (No. 2), nr. Killarney, Co.Kerry [Classical] (No. 3). *Photos:* National Museum of Ireland.
3. Hoard. Kerivoa, Côtes-du-Nord, Brittany. *Photo:* Musée des Antiquitiés Nationales, Saint Germain-en-Laye.
4. Hoard. Lanrivoaré, Finistère, Brittany. *Photo:* Musée des Antiquitiés Nationales, Saint Germain-en-Laye.
5. Disc. Lansdown, Avon (Somerset). Surviving remains (top); Reconstruction (bottom). *Photo:* British Museum.
6. Reconstruction of Mold cape, Flintshire. (After Powell 1953).
7. Gold ornaments from Sporle, Norfolk (1-3); bracelets and rings, Duff House, Banffshire (4-8); bracelets from Briglands, Kinross (9) and Bonnyside, Stirling (10). *Photos:* Norfolk Museum Services (top) and National Museum of Scotland (remainder).
8. Hoard No. 1. Bexley Heath, Kent (1-8). *Photo:* British Museum.
9. Hoard No. 2. Bexley Heath, Kent (1-9). *Photo:* British Museum.
10. Gold bracelets, part of hoard from Beachy Head, Sussex (1-5). *Photo:* British Museum.
11. Hoard. Tisbury, Wiltshire (1-6). *Photo:* British Museum.
12. Bracelets. Cottingham (Wanlas) area, Yorkshire (1-4). Hoard. Little Chart, Kent (5-7). *Photos:* Ashmolean Museum and British Museum.
13. Hoard. Caister-on-Sea, Norfolk. Vertical (top) and oblique view of each object (1-4). *Photo:* Norfolk Museum Services.
14. Hoard, bronze except for 'hair-rings', 'lock-rings' and beads. Balmashanner, Angus. *Photo:* National Museum of Scotland.
15. Hoard. Stonehill, Lanark (1-3), single bracelet, Penningham, Wigtownshire (4), hoard Kirkhill, Berwickshire (5-6). *Photo:* National Museum of Scotland.
16. Hoards of bracelets. Ormingdale, Arran (1-4); Alloa, Clackmannan (5-6). *Photo:* National Museum of Scotland.
17. Hoards of bracelets. Hillhead, Caithness (1-2) and Kilmallie, Inverness-shire (3-4). Individual bracelets. Tomnavien, Morayshire (5) and Islay, Argyll (6). *Photo:* National Museum of Scotland.
18. Hoard. West of Scotland (1-3). Individual bracelet. No location, Berwickshire (4). *Photo:* National Museum of Scotland.
19. Hoard. Tullich, Glenaray, Argyll (1-3). *Photo:* National Museum of Scotland.

viii

ENGLAND/ WALES	SCOTLAND/ NORTHERN ENGLAND	IRELAND	PROVISIONAL DATE B.C.
Bell beakers	Bell beakers	Bell beakers (Knocknague)	2300
Wessex I	Migdale-Marnoch	Frankford-Ballyvalley/ Bowl food-vessel	2000
Wessex II	Gavel Moss	Omagh (Derryniggin)/ Urns	1700
Acton Park/ Deverel-Rimbury	Auchterhouse	Killymaddy	1500
Beerhackett-Taunton (ornament horizon)/ Deverel-Rimbury	Glentrool	Bishopsland	1300
Penard	Poldar	Early Roscommon	1150
Wilburton	Poldar/Wallington	Late Roscommon	1050
'Carp's-tongue'/Ewart Park	Duddingston	Dowris	900–950
Llynfawr (Hallstatt C) (earliest Iron Age elements)	Adabrock (Hallstatt C elements)	Athlone (Hallstatt C elements)	700–600

Guide to terminology (mainly metal stages) and suggested chronology used for Bronze Age Britain and Ireland.

Chapter I

Introduction: The Natural and Historical Setting of British and Irish Gold

APPROACHES TO STUDY

From the dawn of the metal ages until today, gold has been valued and prized by societies and peoples in different places in the world. This is partly due to its rarity which makes it a valuable commodity, and to its properties which are different from other metals, for instance, unlike copper it is malleable, flexible and homogeneous. It can be worked by hammering, that is cold-working without the necessity of casting, annealing or soldering, although these techniques could be and were subsequently used. The manufactured object is enduring because it does not corrode but above all gold possesses intrinsic beauty and objects made from it may have had a symbolic as well as a decorative function in early times.

In Europe natural gold occurs in the Carpathian region, in Iberia, in south-western France, Brittany and in Britain but especially in Ireland which has been called the ancient *El Dorado* (Hawkes 1961a, 138). In Ireland gold was the commonest material used for making ornaments during the Bronze Age, those of bronze or other materials such as amber and jet being rare. Amber is the only other material that comes close to gold in colour but apart from the Wessex "culture" of the Early Bronze Age it was rarely used in Britain during the Bronze Age (Beck and Shennan 1991) while in Ireland widespread use was confined to the final (Dowris) stage (MacWhite 1944; Feeney 1976).

Many thousands of gold objects were made and used in Britain and Ireland during the Bronze Age and today about one thousand five hundred survive in collections, approximately one thousand from Ireland and five hundred from Britain. There are various ways of studying these such as the compilation of a catalogue or *corpus* based on visual examination, and scientific studies notably analysis of the metal (Hartmann 1970; 1982). Various techniques, such as optical emission spectroscopy have been used but scientific analysis is a complex undertaking as the work on the bar torc from the Bracks Farm, Soham, Cambridgeshire, England has shown (Taylor 1980, 8–13). Furthermore, analysis has to be followed up by statistical studies to assist in the interpretation of the results and establish groupings, clusterings and possibly even the source of the gold used.

This study offers an evaluation and interpretation of the material in social terms. It is based on wide-ranging studies of the objects. This is backed up by a number of distribution maps and illustrations of typical examples of each class or sub-class of object. This present work is not a *corpus* or catalogue and the results of metal and statistical analysis are only treated in general terms as is also the case with measurements and weights. Being an individual craft each piece is unique, indeed many are accomplished and outstanding works of art and craft and provide evidence for highly developed toreutic skills at four main periods during the Bronze Age. As such they constitute vital documents that will aid our understanding not only of the work of craftsmen and technicians but of the broader aspects of society such as social stratification, trade, commerce and ritual.

1

DISCOVERIES

Records of the finding of Bronze Age gold ornaments in Britain and Ireland go back for more than three hundred years. Very few objects have been discovered as a result of controlled archaeological investigation, the vast majority having come to light by chance, usually as a result of agricultural activities or peat-cutting. From early accounts it appears that a vast number of such finds were melted down or otherwise lost. In Britain the losses have been greatest in Scotland where only slightly over half the recorded finds of penannular bracelets survive but the greatest losses have been in Ireland (p. 144–5).

(i) Grave-Finds

Britain provides the best evidence with most coming from the limited geographical area of Wessex and dating to the Bell Beaker and Early Bronze Ages. For the Bell Beaker stage there are at least eight finds (Table 1) but the largest number can be assigned to the Early Bronze Age of Wessex. There are fifteen find places in that region with another five or so outside it (Piggott 1938). The Wessex finds came to light as a result of a series of excavations that were carried out during the initial years of the nineteenth century. These investigations were part of a study of ancient Wiltshire undertaken in collaboration by Sir Richard Colt-Hoare (1758–1838), a wealthy landowner with a banking background, and William Cunnington (1754–1810), a wool-merchant and draper. The excavations were the responsibility of Cunnington while surface field-work was carried out by Colt-Hoare. Cunnington's excavations concentrated on round barrows on Salisbury Plain, about a dozen of which produced gold artefacts (*cf.* Annable and Simpson 1964, 1–6). Outside the Wessex area graves containing gold objects are rare, Little Cressingham, Norfolk being the richest of these (Piggott 1938, Fig. 22). Gold objects also occurred in graves at Rillaton, Cornwall and Pendleton, Lancashire (Longworth 1984, 220). Scotland has produced a couple of finds, the Knowes of Trotty, Orkney and Broughty Ferry (Barnhill), Angus (Taylor 1980, 89, 94). During the next main stage of Bronze Age gold-working, *c.* 13th century, there are only three grave-finds, the Mold cape, the Lansdown disc and the Duff House bracelets and rings (p. 51,64–5). Grave-finds of gold are not known from the third main gold-using stage, the 'carp's tongue'-Ewart Park stage, *c.* 8th century.

It was not the practice to place gold objects in burials in Ireland. There are only two definite grave-finds, a 'hair-ring' from a cremation burial at Rathgall, Co. Wicklow (information from Prof. Barry Raftery) and a small band from the pommel of a dagger hilt from Topped Mountain, Co. Fermanagh (*cf.* Taylor 1980, 105). It is possible that the Ballyshannon discs (p. 5) and the plaque from Carrick-na-Crump, Castlemartyr, Co. Cork also came from graves but as the finds were made many years ago one has to be careful about fully accepting the accounts of those discoveries (*cf.* Case 1977, 30; Armstrong 1933, 3, 42–3, 92, No. 398). Rathgall dates from the end of the Bronze Age; the other pieces can be assigned to the Early Bronze Age.

(ii) Habitations

In England, finds from habitation sites are confined to the final phase of the Bronze Age. 'Lock-rings' have been discovered on the hill-fort sites of Harting Beacon, Highdown Hill and Portfield (Eogan 1969, 129–30, 137) and part of a penannular bracelet at Cadbury Castle, Somerset (Alcock 1971, 5). Two bracelets and a fragment of another came from a settlement at Brean Down, Somerset (Needham 1990a). The Sculptor's Cave, Covesea, Morayshire yielded ten pieces of 'hair-rings' (Benton 1930–31, 181–4).

In Ireland habitation finds are also limited. These are the disc from the Beaker phase settlement, Site D, Knockadoon, Lough Gur (Ó Ríordáin 1954, 410–11, Pl. 46; b. 31), the Late Bronze Age hoard, part of which consisted of three thick gold penannular rings, from a crannóg at Rathtinaun (Lough Gara), Co. Sligo, found by Dr Joseph Raftery (*cf.* Eogan 1983a, 151), a piece of 'hair-rings', two beads and a strip of wire from Rathgall, Co. Wicklow (information from the excavator, Prof. Barry Raftery). The Downpatrick hoards were found within a hill-fort but it is not possible to establish a chronological relationship between them and the use of the earthwork (Proudfoot 1955; 1957).

(iii) Isolated Finds

Apart from the already-mentioned habitation and grave finds, all the other objects have been found by chance, in some cases only coming to scientific notice years after discovery and hardly any attempts have been made to thoroughly examine the find place by excavation or other methods.

There is a small number of exceptions such as the Heights of Brae hoard (Ross and Cromarty), Portfield (Lancashire) and Downpatrick (Co. Down) but generally precise details of the actual spot in which the find was made are limited. The position was that objects were simply deposited either in dry land or damp, wet places. They were placed singly or much more rarely were associated with one or more objects of the same class, or with objects of a different class and of different material. The reason for deposition varies, it need not be "that in general gold articles were hidden in haste and possibly at a time when the foe or the invader pressed hotly upon the heels of the fugitive" (Wilde 1862, 4; Wood-Martin 1895, 486). This problem will be discussed more fully below (p. 78).

During the Early Bronze Age in *Britain* isolated finds and hoards are rare, only about eighty to ninety objects, but these increase substantially during the Beerhackett-Taunton and 'carp's tongue'-Ewart Park stages. Practically all were found by accident, usually in the course of work in fields and bogs. These objects have been found at different times over the centuries. One of the earliest finds, 1782, is the disc from Kirk Andrews, Isle of Man. During the early part of the 19th century, in 1806, the Beachy Head (Sussex) hoard which contained bracelets was discovered. The Hilton hoard (Dorset) was found in 1825, Hampton (Cheshire) in 1829 and Boyton (Suffolk) in 1835. The hoards from Stretham (Cambridgeshire), Morvah (Cornwall) and Beerhackett (Dorset) turned up in 1850. Three bracelets were found near Aylesford, Kent in 1861 and that county also produced the richest finds, two hoards of bracelets found during gravel extraction respectively in 1906–1907 at Bexley, one contained nine bracelets; the other contained eight (p. 91). In 1931 the Towednack hoard (Cornwall) came to light and there have been several subsequent finds such as the bar torc from the Croxton hoard, Norfolk (Needham 1990b). The mid 1950's saw the discovery of two hoards, Llanwrthwl and Heyope in mid-Wales, while in 1975 the Capel Isaf hoard was discovered (Savory 1958, 1977). The most recent find, a hoard of three torcs, is considered to have been made at Tiers Cross near Fishguard in 1991.

In *Scotland* the earliest find of Bronze Age gold appears to have been the ribbed hilt-band of a dagger which was found at Monikie, Angus in 1620 (Anderson 1886, 66, Figs. 76–7). For the 18th century only a small number of finds are known. These include a 'dress fastener' and 'armlet' found in a loch in Galloway before 1732 but the largest was a hoard of at least thirty six penannular bracelets from Coul, Islay in 1780. A considerable number of finds were recorded in the 19th century. Coincidentally, the three hoards of ribbon torcs from Lower Largo (Fife), Law Farm (Moray) and Belhelvic (Aberdeen) were all discovered within a few years in the middle of the century (Anderson 1886, 61–7, 208–23). During the 20th century a number of finds have also turned up including 'hair-rings' from the 1930 excavations in the Sculptor's Cave at Covesea, Morayshire (Benton 1930–31, 181–4) and the Late Bronze Age hoard from Heights of Brae, Ross and Cromarty, part of which was found about 1967 and another part in 1979 (Clarke and Kemp 1984).

COLLECTIONS AND PUBLICATIONS

One of the first objects to reach a public collection in Britain was the Ballyshannon disc (p. 5), which was presented to the Ashmolean Museum, Oxford in 1696 and this museum has added considerably to its insular gold collection since then. The earliest gold item to be acquired by the British Museum was also a disc, the previously-mentioned piece from Kirk Andrews, Isle of Man in 1782. Due to the implementation of the laws of Treasure Trove and especially since the introduction of new regulations in 1837, the British Museum has acquired most of the gold finds from England. However, the important collection of objects from the Wiltshire barrows was originally kept by William Cunnington at Heytesbury but after his death they passed to his collaborator, Richard Colt-Hoare, in 1818. After Colt-Hoare's death in 1838 they remained in the possession of the family at Stourhead until 1878 when they were deposited in the museum of the Wiltshire Archaeological Society at Devizes and were acquired outright in 1883 (Annable and Simpson 1964, 5–6). A small but important collection has been formed, principally since the 1930s, by Norwich Castle Museum while the University Museum of Archaeology and Ethnology in Cambridge has a number of pieces. All recent finds from Wales have been acquired by the National Museum under Treasure Trove laws. The whereabouts of a large number of finds from Scotland is not known, several appear to have been melted down. An indication of the loss is provided by the fact that out of approximately thirty finds of penannular bracelets, the present whereabouts of only a little over half is known. Most of these are in the National Museum of Scotland in Edinburgh which also acquires all finds under Treasure Trove law.

One of the earliest publications of a British Bronze Age gold item appeared in 1789 in Vol. II of Camden's *Britannia*. This concerned a flange-twisted bar torc from Fantley Hill, Puttingham, Staffordshire. The Wiltshire barrow gold was initially published in Richard Colt-Hoare's *The Ancient History of South Wiltshire* which appeared in London in 1812. Subsequently the gold objects were included in wider studies of the Early Bronze Age in Wessex such as that of Stuart Piggott in 1938. The Beachy Head, Sussex hoard was published in *Archaeologia* Vol. 16, 1812 and since then there has been a fairly steady stream of publications such as Little Cressingham in *Norfolk Archaeology* Vol. III, 1852, the Harlyn Bay lunula in the *Archaeological Journal* in 1865, Towednack in *Man* (1932) down to the Brean Down bracelets and the Croxton torc (Needham 1990a and b).

Most of the Welsh gold has been published within recent years by Savory (1958; 1977) while Anglesey finds, originally published in the *Archaeological Journal* XIII, 1856, have been included by Lynch (1970) in her study of the prehistory of that island.

Scotland has a long history of publications. Foremost amongst these in the last century were the surveys by Daniel Wilson *(The Prehistoric Annals of Scotland*, 1863) and Joseph Anderson's *Scotland in Pagan Times* 1886. In his study of Bronze Age hoards Callander (1922–23) included gold objects. A number of individual finds and hoards have been published in the *Proceedings of the Society of Antiquaries of Scotland* such as the Knowes of Trotty discs in Vol. III, 1857–60, the lunulae from Southside, near Coulter in Vol. IV, 1861–62, 'hair-ring' from Galloway, Vol. XXVI, 1891–92, the Kirk Hill bracelets, Vol. LXVI, 1931–32 and the Heights of Brae hoard, Vol. 114, 1984.

The first comprehensive study of Bronze Age gold from Britain and Ireland was carried out by Dr Joan Taylor (1980). This broadly-based evaluation of the material was accompanied by lists of finds and other data.

For *Ireland* accounts of the discovery of Bronze Age gold objects go back to the 17th century. One of the earliest (an unpublished account in MS F.1 20, ff. 71–2 in Trinity College, Dublin) concerns the finding of a hoard of gold objects at Ballymacmorrish, "in Ye King's County" about the end of May 1670 (Smith 1858; Wright 1900, 10–11; Herity 1969b, 2; Eogan 1983a, 39–40 with find-place assigned to Co. Laoghais) but Aideen Ireland (1989) thinks that the find-place was Ballymacmorris, parish of Kilbeggan, Co. Westmeath. This find is also of interest from the point of view of the history of Irish archaeology as it is an early example of the use of the laws of Treasure Trove. The objects were found by Farrell McMorris of Ballickmorish apparently on his property; this was subsequently confiscated and granted by Queen Elizabeth I to Owen M'Hugh O'Dempsie in the thirteenth year of her reign. Consequent to the finding, two depositions were made before a magistrate in January 1673 apparently to determine the ownership of the treasure. The result of the inquisition and subsequent fate of the objects is not known.

Although not recorded in print until 1723 (in Dermot O'Connor's translation of Geoffrey Keating's *History of Ireland*) the gold object from Bearnán Eile (Devil's Bit), Co. Tipperary, possibly a bowl (see p. 91), was found in 1692. In the latter half of the 17th century "not too many years" before 1695, two sun-discs were found near Ballyshannon, Co. Donegal under unusual circumstances. A local landowner, Mr Edward Whiteway, was entertaining the Bishop of Derry, Dr Hopkins, formerly Bishop of Raphoe in which diocese Ballyshannon is situated. During the course of the dinner a harper sang a song in Irish which named a spot where a man of "gygantick stature lay buried" with plates of gold on his breasts and rings of gold on his fingers. As the place was exactly described in the song, Mr Whiteway's brother-in-law, Mr Foliot, and the Bishop's steward, Mr Nevill, dug at the place mentioned and found the two discs apparently the same evening and though digging recommenced the next morning nothing further was discovered (Case 1977, 30).

During the course of the 18th century, recording and collecting of finds became more common. An important source is the Minute Books of the Society of Antiquaries of London, especially from 1720 to late in the century (Herity 1969b). Amongst these are accounts of a sun-disc found in 1718 near Baltimore, Co. Cork on the estate of Sir Piercy Freake, Bart. (communicated 29 December 1724). A letter dated 26 May 1747 from James Simon, a Dublin merchant and Secretary of the Physico-Historical Society to the Vice-President of the Society of Antiquaries of London, Martin Folkes, mentions several antiquities. These were a lunula from Rehey or Rey Hill, Co. Clare, an associated find of a 'dress-fastener' and 'sleeve-fastener' from an unrecorded location in County Galway and three unlocalised objects at least two of which, possibly all, were 'dress-fasteners' (Herity 1969b, 4–8).

An important collector of gold and objects of other material was Dr Richard Pococke, Archdeacon of Dublin and subsequently Bishop of Ossory and later of Meath. He published a paper on Irish antiquities in *Archaeologia* Vol. 2, 1773 but his activities started well before then. At a meeting of the Society of Antiquaries of London on 5 December 1750 he exhibited a hoard consisting of a 'dress-fastener' and a number of 'hair-rings'. On 6 February 1755 Pococke presented drawings of four Later Bronze Age swords and a purse-shaped chape which were "found near Tipperary in Ireland". Herity (1969b, 9, pl. 9) suggested that these were probably some of the finds from the Bog of Cullen. The Cullen finds were the subject of a paper by T. "Governor" Pownall in Volume 3 of *Archaeologia* which was published in 1775. Obviously this "golden bog" yielded a huge assemblage of gold and also bronze objects but even an approximation of the actual numbers is now impossible (Wallace 1938; Eogan 1983a, 154–56) but it appears to have been more than one hundred. The first published account of the discovery of a gold object in the bog appeared in Sylvester O'Halloran's introduction to his *History and Antiquities of Ireland* (1722, 147), which was published in Dublin. This refers to the purchase by Joseph Kinshalloe, a Limerick jeweller, from John Clery a shopkeeper in the village of Cullen of an "irregular cone-like object of gold", which he melted down. It is not known for how long objects were turning up in the bog. The lists in Pownall's paper of 1775 refer to finds made between 1731 and 1773. It does not appear that finds were being made after the latter date but how much before 1722, the year of publication of O'Halloran's *History*, is unknown. The only extensive information is provided by Pownall. This was based on lists sent to him by a Tipperary clergyman, Rev. Mr Armstrong. The first part (1731–53) was compiled by a young man from Cullen, Mr Nash, who was for a time a student in Dublin and this was fairly detailed. The second and less comprehensive part was compiled by a Mr Cleary, perhaps the John Cleary already mentioned. The objects came to light during the cutting of turf but some were found afterwards in the dried sods or the turf mould. It appears that the objects were found in different parts of the bog but most of them around the centre where, according to Nash, "they lay very deep". This might imply that they were at the bottom. However, as some pieces were in the turf these might have been at a higher level but that cannot be proved as such sods could have come from the basal spit. There is also the human side to some of the discoveries such as that of the "fool" who found three rings in 1750. He put one on the end of a walking-stick but when his father realised it was gold he took it from him. The boy hid the other two but could not remember where. Then, there was the "clever" thirteen year old boy who, when out playing with his friends, noticed an object in the bank of a drain, he quickly gathered his wits together and called to the other boys, "I see two rabbits" and ran towards the nearby hill with the boys following him. When they went home he returned with his mother and uncovered the object, "a plate of gold, five inches broad at one end, four at the other, and almost six long" which was sold to a goldsmith. After discovery most of the objects were sold or given to pedlars, tinkers or merchants but some were acquired by the local landlord, John Damer of Shronell. Despite the large number of objects found, it is incredible that the whereabouts of only one is known. This is the terminal of a 'dress-fastener' now in Birmingham City Museum (Reg. No. 283'64) which was acquired in 1964 at the sale of property of Winnafreda, widow of the sixth Earl of Portarlington, a descendant of John Damer (Eogan 1983a, 154–5).

Moving into the 19th century it is recorded that "rather more than the contents of half a coal box of gold" was found with an inhumation burial during quarrying operations in a cave or rock cleft at Carrick-na-Crump, near Castlemartyr, Co. Cork in 1805. These consisted of gold plaques and other objects as well as amber beads. Only one item, a plaque, survives (Case 1977, 25, No. 5). Another important find was made by a peasant boy about 1810 "in a mound or bank, near the church yard", Ráth na Seanad, on the Hill of Tara, Co. Meath. This consisted of three flange-twisted torcs (Herity 1969a, 21–25). Two were purchased by Alderman Matthew West, jeweller, Skinner Row, Dublin; the third by Dr William Knox, Bishop of Derry, who sold it in London probably before 1815, its subsequent fate is unknown. Indeed, there was a danger that the other two would also be taken out of the country. The Turkish Ambassador to London brought them to St Petersburg for display and later they were sold to the Duke of Sussex in whose possession they remained for some years. They were again sold, this time to Mr Jones West, probably a relation of the original buyer. There was now a possibility that the torcs might be "sent out of the country a second time, and forever" (Wright 1900, 21). To prevent this a subscription was organised in order to secure them and as a result they were purchased and presented to the Royal Irish Academy where they formed part of the nucleus of the National Collection which the Academy was then establishing (Herity 1969a, 21–25, 30–1).

If Cullen was the richest gold find of the 18th century that of the 19th was clearly the "great Clare find" (Armstrong 1917; Eogan 1983a, 69–72). This huge find may have consisted of around two hundred objects and it is the largest associated gold find in Ireland and indeed probably for Bronze Age Europe. It was brought to light about mid-March 1854 by labourers who were working on the construction of the Limerick to Ennis railway. The find-place was low ground between Loch Ataska and Mooghaun Lake and it appears that the objects were found behind a large stone in a cavity or chamber, whether natural or artificial is not known. On discovery, the objects were hastily gathered by the finders and out of the many dozens found only the whereabouts of twenty-nine are now known, fifteen in the National Museum of Ireland and fourteen in the British Museum. The find was quickly brought to scientific notice and on 7 April, Dr J. H. Todd gave an account to a meeting of the Archaeological Institute of Great Britain and Ireland. Soon afterwards, on 26 June, Dr Todd exhibited several ornaments – listed as six gorgets, two torcs, one hundred and thirty-seven bracelets or related objects weighing 5.43 kilogrammes – to a meeting of the Royal Irish Academy. The bulk of the objects was dispersed and unfortunately like so many others were probably melted down. Discovery of individual items and also hoards continues down to the present time but as has been the case in the past, it still remains likely that many discoveries are not reaching museums or even being reported.

It seems that Ireland has lost more gold objects than any other European country. To quote Sir William Wilde (1862, 3) a "lamentable dispersion, or destruction, of the golden treasures found beneath the surface of the soil of Ireland" has taken place. As a result there is a considerable quantity of Irish gold abroad, some in private collections but principally in public collections not only in Britain but further afield, notably in Canada and the USA. Only one piece survives from the previously mentioned large Early Bronze Age find from Castlemartyr, Co.

Cork. It is stated that the Late Bronze Age find from Askeaton (Co. Limerick), contained "bucket fulls of gold" but only one piece has survived (*cf.* Eogan 1983a, 102). Most of the Bog of Cullen objects and a number of those from Mooghaun have vanished. One will never know how many gold objects disappeared after finding but it may be worth mentioning that for a period of some decades before the publication of Wilde's *Catalogue* in 1862 it appears that jewellers and goldsmiths purchased about £10,000 worth of gold at an average purchase price of between 65 and 70 shillings per ounce (Wood-Martin 1895, 480–86). That would suggest that about 3,000 ounces of gold were purchased and as very few lunulae or penannular bracelets with evenly expanded terminals weigh over 2 ounces (62.207 grammes), one arrives at the extraordinary figure of at least one thousand objects, all of which could have been found during the first half or so of the 19th century. Such an estimate cannot be precise, nevertheless it is clear that hundreds of gold objects which were discovered within recent centuries, most of which would be of Bronze Age date, cannot be accounted for and therefore it may be assumed that they have been destroyed.

It was as late as the end of the 18th century that private collections developed. One of the earliest was that formed by Major Henry Charles Sirr, a Town-Major of Dublin who achieved notoriety through his arrest of the patriot, Lord Edward Fitzgerald, on 19 May 1798. After his death in 1841 the collection, which contained some Bronze Age gold ornaments, was purchased by the Royal Irish Academy. The building up of private collections continued during the 19th century, such as those of the Rev. Henry Richard Dawson who was Dean of St Patrick's Cathedral, Dublin from 1828 to 1840, Redmond Anthony of Piltown, Co. Kilkenny and later in the century Robert Day of Myrtle Hill House, Cork, a local merchant who died in 1914.

From the end of the 1830s the Royal Irish Academy was becoming the national depository for antiquities and was quickly building up its own collection of artefacts including those of gold. Its purchase of the two Tara torcs has already been mentioned but it also purchased private collections such as those of Major Sirr and Rev. Dean H. R. Dawson, the latter in 1840 for £1,000. Within the following twenty years or so it had the largest collection of Bronze Age gold in Europe. This was further helped on 16 August 1860 when the Treasury sanctioned an annual expenditure of £100 by the Receiver of the Irish Constabulary "in paying the finders of treasure-trove the intrinsic value of the articles found which articles were then sent to the Royal Irish Academy" (Wright 1900, 16).

With the growth of the collection the Academy quickly realised the need for a Catalogue and as early as 1851 it was decided to commence such an undertaking. For a short time this work was undertaken by Dr George Petrie but soon the task passed to Sir William Wilde whose first volume on the stone antiquities was published in 1857. The final volume dealing with the gold appeared in 1862. In it Wilde listed 310 objects, of which about 250 date to the Bronze Age, with a small number of Iron Age objects and a larger number of medieval finger rings. In the catalogue a number was assigned to each object with a brief description and details and in addition there was a discussion on the various types and on other aspects of gold including analysis. For the first time the study of Irish prehistoric gold was put on a secure footing. A year or so before the publication of the *Catalogue*, the Curator of the Academy, Edward Clibborn, published a "record of the opinions on the gold antiquities expressed by intelligent strangers, from various countries" who had visited the Academy's collection. The notes were accompanied by line illustrations of some of the pieces (Clibborn 1860a and b). In the second half of the 19th century new finds reached the Academy largely as a result of the Treasure Trove law. Accounts of some were published and works of synthesis were also beginning to be published. Amongst these were William Frazer's papers (1897, a-b) on lunulae, and on the origin of the gold and its composition. Indeed, analysis of gold has a long history in Ireland. In 1853 J. W. Mallet published the analysis of some pieces (*cf.* Hawkes, in Hawkes and Clarke 1963, 207). In 1895 W. G. Wood-Martin devoted practically the whole of Chapter XI of his book, *Pagan Ireland* to gold antiquities.

In the early part of this century, George Coffey (1909) published a definitive study of lunulae. Research was continued by E. C. R. Armstrong, Coffey's successor as Keeper of Irish Antiquities in the National Museum, who became the leading expert for his time. In 1917 he published a study of the Mooghaun find and in 1920 his *Catalogue of Irish Gold Ornaments in the Collection of the Royal Irish Academy* appeared. The number of Bronze Age gold specimens in the Academy's collection had doubled, amounting to about 500 pieces. The acquisition of the Arboe/Killycolpy (or Killycolp) and Killymoon hoards from Co. Tyrone in 1967 (Raftery 1970) initiated a new phase of acquisition of Bronze Age gold by the State, which happily is continuing, as is demonstrated by the most recent acquisition in 1990 of a hoard of eight itiems from Ballineskar, Co. Wexford, a lunula from an unrecorded locality and twelve objects from the collection of the Duke of Northumberland, Alnwick Castle, Northumberland (Sotheby 1990, 54–63). Another notable event was the discovery of two hoards from Downpatrick Hill, the investigation of the find-place and the publication of the objects (Proudfoot 1955; 1957). A number of other finds, especially hoards, were also published and there have been a number of papers dealing both with specific and wider issues such as those of Eogan (1957, 1967, 1969, 1972, 1981a and b), Hawkes (1961a and b, 1963 [with Clarke], 1971) and Taylor (1970). As already mentioned the Irish finds were also included in Joan J. Taylor's (1980) important study. On the Continent a significant event was the finding in 1936 at Gahlstorf, near Bremen, Germany, of an Irish thick penannular bracelet and its subsequent comprehensive publication by Ernst Grohne and a study of its metal composition by Helmut Otto (1939).

Another new development was the programme of gold analysis being carried by the *Arbeitsgemeinschaft für die Metallurgie des Altertums* under the direction of Dr Axel Hartmann (see p. 11). His first volume which appeared in 1970 contains the results of analyses of a large number of Irish pieces together with interpretation of the results; volume II extends this and also includes some British as well as continental objects (1982).

Studies of continental gold also have a long history, this century seeing notable advances. In 1913 Gustaf Kossinna published the then recently-discovered gold hoard of 81 pieces from Messingwerk, close to the town of Eberswalde in Brandenburg (Pl. XX). Another, but independent, publication of the hoard also appeared the following year by Carl Schuchhardt (1914). The year 1916 saw the publication of the gold objects of the Swedish Bronze Age by Oscar Montelius, while the following year Kossinna (1917) published the east German 'oathrings'. From the 1950s the rich Carpathian area of Hungary-Romania has been the subject of several studies by Amalia Mozsolics, firstly with a detailed account of the important find from Velem-Szentvid, not far from Szombathy, in western Hungary (1950), and subsequently with the range of finds from the Hajdúsámson (1965; 1967) and Forró-Opályi (1973) horizons. Important finds were also being published from west-central and northern Europe, such as those from Midskov in Denmark (Broholm 1948) and Ezelsdorf-Buch near Nürnberg, Germany (Raschke 1954). A significant event in German gold studies was the exhibition in the Germanisches Nationalmuseum, Nüremberg in 1977 and the accompanying short but most useful catalogue, *Magisches Gold*, by Dr Wilfried Menghin and Dr Peter Schauer. Subsequently, in 1985 and 1986, Dr Schauer published the Ezelsdorf and other gold "cones"; these works also considered those objects in their comparative setting. The great Villena treasure in Spain was published by Soler García in 1965 while in 1974 (a and b) Martín Almagro Gorbea reviewed the Iberian treasures of the Late Bronze Age. A comprehensive study of the Spanish and Portugese gold-work by Volker Pingel appeared in 1992. The gold of the French Bronze Age has been evaluated and published by Christiane Eluère (1982).

LOCATION AND EXTRACTION

There is evidence for native gold, that is gold "found in the metallic state and which is not produced from ores by smelting" (Tylecote 1962, 1), in different parts of Britian and Ireland (Fig. 1). In Cornwall small nuggets have been found while in Wales there is limited evidence from such sites as Dolaucothy, Carmarthen (Tylecote 1962, 2–4). The evidence from Scotland is more widespread (Scott 1951, 37, 71, Fig. 1). In the south-west, on the Firth of Forth above

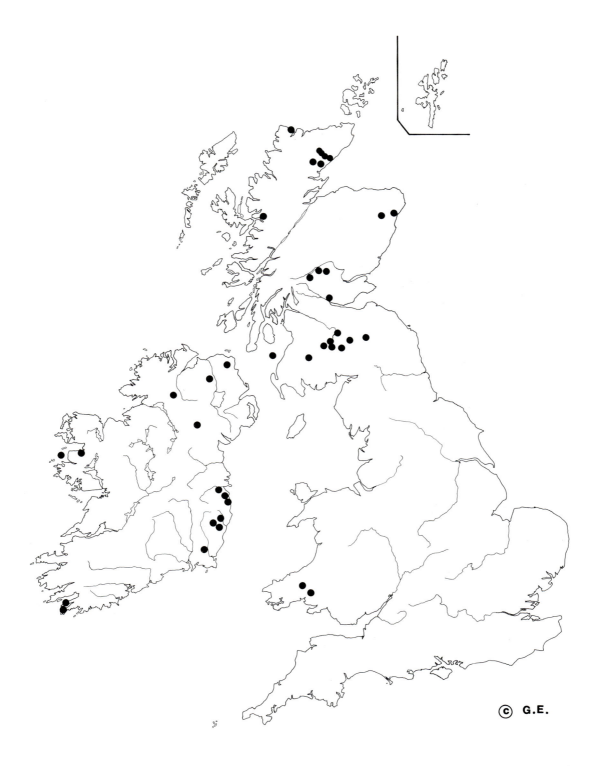

Figure 1. Location of native gold in Britain and Ireland.
(Based on Jackson, 1979, Tylecote, 1962, and Scott, 1951).

Dunfermline, the upper Tweed, Lower Nith and Ayrshire coast there is evidence for gold. Inland, between the headwaters of the rivers Clyde and Nith, streams running down from Leadhills were auriferous. To the east gold has been recorded in Perthshire in the neighbourhood of Lough's Tay and Earn and in the Isla valley. Another prolific source is in the north-east in Sutherland and Caithness in from the coast between Strath Brora and Helmsdale where the gold rush took place in the 19th century. It cannot be established that British gold sources were exploited during the Bronze Age. However on the grounds that some gold objects were found in Leadhills area Scott (1951) suggested that these deposits might have been exploited.

As in Britain, there is no clear evidence from Ireland for gold deposits *in situ* that could have been worked in prehistoric times (Fig. 1) but as gold has, within recent centuries, been found in secondary positions in the auriferous gravels from rivers and streams, those alluvial deposits were the possible sources for the gold used during the Bronze Age. The number of surviving ornaments provide a clear indication of the extensive use of gold. As previously pointed out, we will never know what percentage of the whole these represent but it is clear that considerable quantities of gold were used in Ireland during the Bronze Age. There are a number of locations where native gold has been found – Wicklow, Cork, Wexford, Tipperary, Galway, Monaghan, Derry, Dublin, Antrim, Tyrone and Donegal (Reeves 1971). As original deposits do not exist, the gold is from placer deposits within fluvio-glacial gravels. This was probably dissolved out of a *lode* in quartzite or related rocks. For instance in Wicklow, Croghan Kinshelagh is in an area where Silurian shales have been altered and mineralised by volcanic rocks and this might be a source of gold. In the gravels the gold generally occurs as small flakes (placer gold) and can be recovered by sieving, or panning as it is called. Pebbles or small nuggets occur on rare occasions. Small quantities of gold have within recent decades been found by panning, notably by James Brennan in the Moyola River, Co. Derry (Briggs, Brennan and Freeburn 1973, 20) but the best evidence comes from the glacial deposits of the Wicklow Mountains. In particular, at the end of the 18th century gold was discovered in quantity in the rivers which flow off the northern and north-western flanks of Croghan Kinshelagh mountain, the Aughatinavought, or Gold Mines river, being the richest (Reeves 1971).

This modern phase of searching for gold in Wicklow started about 1770 and during the following hundred years one can estimate that between 7,400 and 9,390 ounces were discovered (Armstrong 1933, 4). Initially the quantities were small but from early in September 1795 knowledge of gold in the sands and gravels became general and in 1795 there was a veritable "rush" with about 300 women as well as men and children frantically digging up the gravels in their search. This activity continued until 15 October when the Government ordered in the Kildare militia to possess the area. Before the cessation of the scrabble it appears that at least 2,500 ounces of gold were found, this including two nuggets, one weighing twenty-two ounces and the other nine ounces (Wood-Martin 1895, 479). The following year, on 12 August 1796, controlled exploitation commenced, with the systematic washing of the sands and gravels in the townland of Ballinvalley. This work, which produced 555 ounces of gold, continued until the outbreak, on 26 May 1798, of an insurrection in the neighbouring county of Wexford to the south, when a number of the workers left and joined the Insurgents. At the same time the military returned to collect as much as possible of their material and equipment that had survived but a little later the Insurgents moved into the area and burnt what remained. With the suppression of the insurrection, work resumed on 8 September 1800. This broadened out to trenching on the northern slopes of Croghan Kinshelagh although this failed to produce gold. However simultaneous work on the river gravels and sands which continued until 1803 produced 388 ounces bringing the total of this official work to about 943 ounces. Some time later the search was unofficially resumed by local people and gold was still being found down to 1840 when a company, Messrs Crockford and Company, were granted a 21-year lease but for reasons unknown work terminated after four months. During the remainder of the last century and during most of this century sporadic exploitations have been under way (Reeves 1971).

As gold was found in rivers in different parts of Ireland within recent times it is, therefore, likely that gold from these sources was also available, possibly in even greater quantities, during the Bronze Age. It has generally been accepted that Irish gold ornaments were worked by Irish smiths from native material. However, Hartmann (1970) has questioned this assumption (see also Raftery 1971b). Analyses of 507 Irish objects have been published and as a result, in particular of chemical trace element analysis, Hartmann isolated six groups and a small miscellaneous group. Group L has a high percentage of silver, an average 12.5%, a copper average of 0.1 to 0.25% and usually less than 0.1% tin. Group M has a silver content that ranges from 7% to 21%, copper averages about 1.1% and that of tin around 0.16%. Group OC has a tin content above 0.28%. The average for silver is 16%, for copper 6-7%, and for tin 0.4%. Group MC/NC consists of gold that contains silver to an average maxima of 21%, 15% copper but tin is under 0.28%. Group PC is characterised by 0.012% platinum, 30% silver and 0.03% tin. It resembles gold used in the Rhineland during La Tène times but Scott (1976, 23) has argued on evidence proved by Mallet's analysis (1853), that PC gold could have been produced in Wicklow. Group N has only one specimen. Finally, there was a *Restgrupe*, a miscellaneous alloy found in a small number of objects.

Subsequently, Hartmann (1979; 1982, 4–22) modified his earlier conclusions. He isolated a B Group which is tin free and is frequently used in the Balkans and also in Iberia. A number of Irish lunulae are now assigned to this group. His S Group is characterised by a low copper content, at most 0.08% but having a tin percentage of 0.005% and a tiny silver presence. Ten Irish lunulae and the Mere (England) disc were manufactured from this gold. According to Hartmann this alloy was initially used in Iberia when Beaker material was current; he further suggests that both B and S Groups spread to Ireland and Britain via Brittany. These two groups contain objects that were formerly assigned to Hartmann's Group L, and this group is now seen to consist of two species characterised with a smaller copper maxima and two further species characterised by a relatively higher maxima (L1 and L2). This alloy was also used for the production of lunulae and Wessex gold. Hartmann also sees L1 as Iberian and L2 as Irish or British and being equivalent to Q1 and Q2 gold in Central Europe. Group M gold, Bishopsland phase, has 1.17% copper, 0.16% tin and 10% silver but Group N (or NC if alloyed with copper) was coming into use. For Hartmann the gold-copper alloying commenced at the beginning of the Dowris phase and in his view the technique could have been Central European in origin.

Taking a broad view, the groups tend to fall into a chronological pattern. Lunulae and sun-discs predominate in Group L which, therefore, must be Early Bronze Age. The objects in the Derrinboy hoard and some torcs were made from M metal, these are Bishopsland phase in date (p. 74). Groups OC and MC/NC mainly consist of objects of Dowris Phase date although a number of torcs, including the bar torcs from Tara belong to the OC Group. The PC Group mainly consists of La Tène objects.

Regarding the place of origin of the gold, in composition Group L has affinities with the composition of some nuggets of Wicklow gold and could therefore be native although as Briggs (Briggs *et al.* 1973, 22) remarked, not one analysis from Wicklow is comparable to those of the analysed lunulae. Hartmann concluded that the gold from which the vast majority of objects were made had no connection with Wicklow and might have been imported. However, this view has been challenged in a critical way especially by Harbison (1971) and by Briggs *et al.* (1973). As has been pointed out by these scholars not enough analysis of *native* gold has been carried out, neither should it be assumed that Wicklow gold was the only gold used in prehistory, as we have seen gold occurs naturally in several places (Fig. 1). There can be variation in gold composition over a small area, for instance gold from the surface of lodes can be different from that in the lower zone. All traces of some deposits could have disappeared due to the exhaustion of the source through panning in antiquity but there is also the possibility that undetected gold may be buried underneath the gravels of some rivers. As Briggs states, basing too much on the relative percentages of silver and copper with gold is unwise, as silver can dissolve out of weathered gold. Consequently the further from source, the more battering the particles would have received, with the result that samples from the same river could have had different silver percentages. Copper might also occur in a stream but then dissolve due to action of water which might explain why Group L has a larger copper content than M. If the bulk of the gold analysed does not resemble the small selection of natural gold from Wicklow neither does it "correspond to natural gold from any source outside Ireland" (Harbison 1971, 159).

As there are many imponderables one cannot say that the bulk of the gold ornaments of the Irish Bronze Age was made from imported material. It is clear that as the potential exists in Ireland for the presence of natural gold in sufficient bulk and quantity to meet the needs of the native goldsmith, it is most likely that it was these sources that provided the material which led to the blossoming of great periods of manufacture. In this connection one may, for instance, compare the extensive use made of gold in Ireland during the three main stages of the Bronze Age with its more limited use in Britain during the approximately chronologically equivalent and otherwise industrially related stages. In the main, Britain was a non-gold producing area, this can explain why a considerable percentage of its ornaments were made from bronze. The opposite is the case in Ireland where natural gold was present.

Chapter II

Gold-Working in an Age of Social and Ritual Change: Beaker Societies and the Earliest Insular Gold Objects

Close to two hundred and fifty gold objects survive from the insular Earlier Bronze Age, *c.* 2300–1500 BC, about eighty-three from Britain and one hundred and sixty-five from Ireland. As will be shown the main period of production and use was during the "middle" stage of that period, for instance during the Frankford-Ballyvalley (Bowl food vessel) stage in Ireland and Wessex I in England. Lunulae, with close to one hundred examples, the vast majority coming from Ireland, are by far the most common (Pls. IV–VI; 2; Figs. 11–13). Next come discs with over thirty examples (Pl. VII top, 1), again mainly Irish, followed by other types in smaller numbers. These include basket-shaped earrings, sub-rectangular plaques, broad bracelets and also the finds of plaques, pendants, beads and other objects from Wessex "Culture" and related graves. In the Wessex "Culture" gold was used in association with other materials but there and elsewhere sheet-gold was the technique used. This involved the hammering of an ingot into shape but as most of the objects were made from thin foil or sheet their manufacture required care and skill. After the initial hammering the piece would have been placed on a firm but not solid surface such as a piece of timber or a slab of resin, this would prevent puncturing of the foil by the hammer. For decoration a sharp tool was used to incise patterns into the surface but faint repoussé, the pushing out of the surface from one side so that the design would stand in relief on the opposite surface, was also used. The art was linear and consisted of straight lines, angular lines or rows of dots.

PRIMARY BELL BEAKER GOLD-WORK IN BRITAIN

The Beaker complex arose in the area of the Low Countries-Rhineland close to 2500 BC – but also flourished in Central Europe, France and Iberia (Harrison, 1980). A common feature of the various continental complexes was the presence of crouched inhumation burials under a round mound and a distinctive range of artefacts of which the most notable were fine, highly decorated, pottery vessels, barbed-and-tanged flint arrowheads, archers' wristbracers, V-perforated buttons and stone 'battle-axes'. The evidence from archaeology is that Beaker-using communities were the earliest metallurgists in Britain and Ireland, the produce included copper artefacts such as tanged daggers but also gold objects as well as the use of gold for embellishment. Therefore, gold items were amongst the earliest insular metal objects to be produced. The variety of objects produced initially was limited but they are significant for they represent the beginnings of a tradition that went on to produce notable pieces.

THE GOLD OBJECTS *(Table 1)*

Stone wristbracer with gold-capped rivets (Pl. II; Figs. 2–3). In two examples, Driffield (Kellythorpe), Yorkshire and Culduthel Mains, Inverness-shire the bracer had a pair of holes at

County	Find place	Burial (all barrows)	Sex	Beaker type	Gold disc	Gold basket-shaped earrings	Gold bead	Stone wrist-bracer with gold capped rivets	Stone wrist-bracer	Barbed and tanged flint arrowhead	Flint flakes and beads	Whet-stone	Stone rubber	Tanged copper knife/dagger	Bone or antler spatula	Bone toggle	Bone belt-ring	Copper pendant	Shale bead
Berkshire	Radley	inhumation	M	E		2			4										
Cambridgeshire	Barnack	inhumation	M	W/MR				1						1				1	55
Hampshire	Chilbolton	inhumation	M	W/MR		4	1				9			1	1				
Northumberland	Kirkhaugh	-	-	AOC		1				1	9+	1	1						
Wiltshire	Fairleigh Wick	inhumation	Two persons	W/MR W/MR	1					4	1						1		
Wiltshire	Mere	inhumation	M + young person	W/MR	2				1					1	1				
Yorkshire	Driffield (Kelly-thorpe)	inhumation	M	N2				1		8				1					
Inverness-shire	Culduthel Mains	inhumation	M	N2				1			1					1			

Table 1. Beaker graves in Britain containing gold objects and their associated contents.

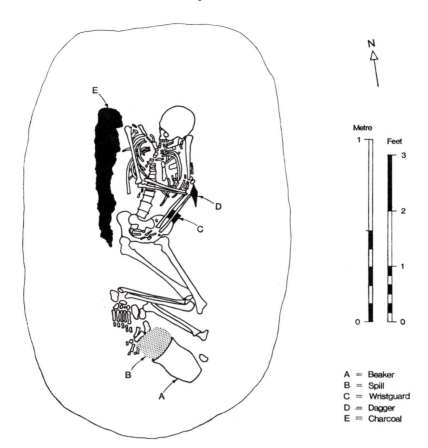

N

Metre

Feet

A = Beaker
B = Spill
C = Wristguard
D = Dagger
E = Charcoal

Figure 2. Beaker burial (Grave 28) Barnack, Cambridgeshire. (After Donaldson, 1977).

each end, each of which held a rivet (Class C_1, Clarke 1970, 261, 570, Note 39). The Barnack, Cambridgeshire example had eighteen rivets (Donaldson 1977; see Fig. 2)

Basket-shaped earrings (Fig. 4). These objects are usually considered as earrings although Sherratt (1986, 1987) suggests that they were hair ornaments that could have been slid on to plaits. Ten examples from five find-places are known. Each consists of a flat oblong plate curved longitudinally with a hook projecting from the centre of one side. Decoration is in the form of transverse ridges formed by faint repoussé work near the hook or parallel to the edges. Dot ornament also occurs, e.g. the surviving Orbliston, Moray, piece has a prominent band of dot decoration parallel to the edges. Basket-shaped earrings made from copper are also known in Britain (Coles 1968–9, Fig. 39:13). Taylor (1979, 237) suggests that the earliest examples were of simple form, Radley for instance (Pl. I, top), subsequent evolution producing a larger form such as the piece from Orbliston, Morayshire. The background for the basket-shaped earrings made from both gold and bronze is known from Early Bronze Age contexts on the continent. (*cf.* Gimbutas 1965, 39–40, 44, 50).

Discs. There are three examples from four find-places. All are small and average 30 mm in diameter. Those with Beaker associations (Mere and Farleigh Wick) have two perforations in the centre.

Decoration consists of a central cruciform-shaped motif and a band consisting of a ladder pattern bounded by a line on each side parallel to the edge. The disc from Kirk Andrews, Isle of Man, 50 mm in diameter, is decorated with three concentric rings of repoussé-formed dots parallel to the edge. At one point, on the inside of the innermost ring, there are two closely-set perforations. This is not paralleled on any other insular disc, a fact that caused Butler (1963, 169) to have reservations about accepting it as British, however repoussé dot ornament is also found on basket-shaped earrings.

Discs of gold or copper were amongst the first metal objects used on the continent. The earliest examples occur in Chalcolithic contexts in east-central Europe such as the Bodrogkeresztúr culture of Hungary (Butler 1963, 168–9; *cf.* Bognár-Kutzián 1963, 483–4) but they are also known at an early date in Denmark. The copper disc from Rude in east Jutland may date from the late 4th or early 3rd millennium BC (Randsborg 1970).

Bead. The single example (from Chilbolton) is tubular and was made by rolling a rectangle of sheet gold.

BURIAL 1

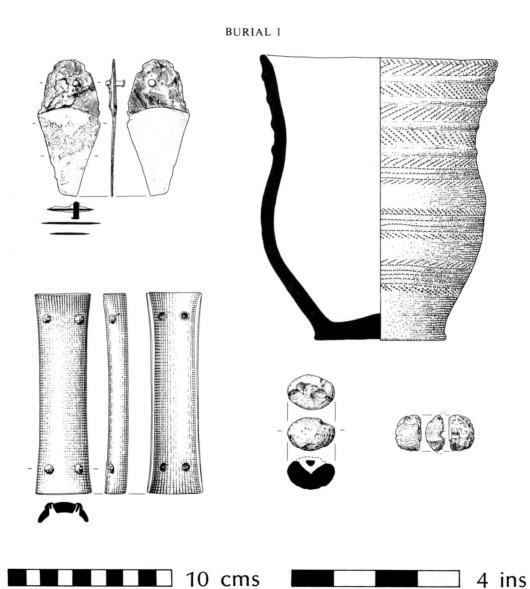

10 cms   4 ins

Figure 3. Beaker burial (No. 1), Driffield (Kellythorpe), Yorkshire.
(*After* British Bronze Age Metalwork, *British Museum (1985), series A, no. 11).*

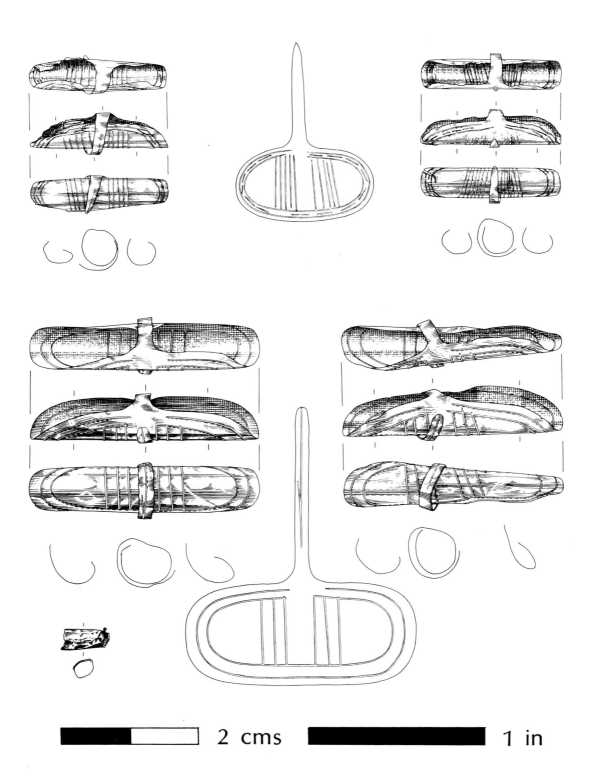

Figure 4. Basket-shaped gold earrings from Beaker burial, Chilbolton, Hampshire.
(After Russel, Proceedings of the Prehistoric Society, *56 (1990), fig. 7).*

Assessment

The number of gold objects that one can assign to the primary (Bell) British Beaker phase is not large, only twenty or so, nevertheless, they form a homogeneous group and when taken in conjunction with other metal types demonstrate that a new technology was introduced. Some of the gold objects, the Boltby Scar, Yorkshire basket earrings for instance, do not show great skill in manufacture but amongst the other pieces are examples of skilled craftsmanship such as the Chilbolton earrings (Fig. 4). An accompanying copper industry also got under way; this is represented by tools (broad-butted axes, knives, tanged daggers and awls). The material used was an arsenic-copper alloy (Case 1966). Stone-work was represented by 'battle-axes', bracers for the wrists of archers and barbed-and-tanged arrowheads; the latter objects also highlight the importance of the bow-and-arrow in hunting. V-perforated buttons demonstrate the use and fashioning of jet but this is of further significance as it probably shows that a change in personal costume took place. The buttoned garment was now the main form of dress. The highly-decorated fine wares demonstrate skills in pottery manufacture not hitherto seen in Britain. Ritual played a significant role, as is clear not only from the burials but also from the extensive use of enclosures, especially the henge monuments. Due to their large size the construction of henges, and also barrows, involved extensive labour forces. It is clear that the Beaker phase was a time when a new society with a wide range of novel trappings emerged in Britain. Its initiation can be attributed to the arrival of people from the continent, especially the lower Rhineland and the Low Countries. External contacts no doubt remained but local development was a feature and this gave rise to the emergence of regional groups. One of the key areas was Wessex, especially the Salisbury Plain. Stonehenge during its early stages of development was a focal point for, what Clarke (1970, 84–107) called, the Wessex-Middle Rhine group as about 60% of all significant associations are found within an 80 km radius of that site (Megaw and Simpson 1979, 181). These include the rich grave groups from Roundway, Winterslow (Wiltshire), and Dorchester in Oxfordshire (Case 1966, Fig. 9). It is this area that also has the already-mentioned significant gold associations at Mere, Radley (Case 1966, Fig 10, top) and Chilbolton (Table I).

The Beaker-using people may also have introduced new agricultural techniques and certainly they utilized to the fullest the rich lands of Wessex, Yorkshire, Aberdeenshire and elsewhere, lands that had already been successfully exploited by Neolithic farmers. Areas such as the Salisbury Plain became core centres for living but also for burial and for other aspects of ritual. The rich content of grave-goods in some burials indicated that certain families or individuals had access to wealth. Where evidence has survived from graves that contained gold objects the remains were those of men (Table 1). Therefore, Beaker society in Britain may have been stratified with male leaders.

The Beginnings of Gold-Working in Ireland

There was an extension of aspects of the British Beaker complex to Ireland and this may explain the appearance of some items like basket-shaped earrings and discs but there may also have been contacts with other areas such as Iberia and possibly Brittany.

The Gold Objects

Basket-shaped earrings are represented by two specimens (both unlocalised). The bodies are undecorated and are now flat. In size both can be compared to the Orbliston piece. Another item that may have been an earring (although Taylor (1979, 235) wondered if it could be an imitation pinhead) comes from Dacomet, Co. Down. It is made from thin gold and consists of a flat, somewhat spoon-shaped head and short pointed tang. The outer edge has been slightly damaged but parallel to it is decoration consisting of three rows of dots. This object is very close in form to the two gold earrings from Ermegeira and Cova da Moura in the Estremadura region of Portugal where they occur in late Beaker contexts (Savory 1968, 189). In view of the similarity of shape and decoration plus the fact that the Dacomet piece, with its low silver content and a lead trace, is made from a composition that is different from the other Irish Early Bronze Age types all goes to suggest that it may have been imported from Portugal.

Plaques, Band. A find from the bed of a stream at Beleville, Co. Cavan consists of three plaques with rounded ends and decorated with transverse bands each of which consists of three raised lines. In the centre of each there are two perforations. A similar plaque together with a band with rounded ends was found in the same county (Cavan) but the locality has not been recorded. In view of its similarity to the other three could it, also, have been part of the same deposit? The band has ornamentation consisting of equally spaced transverse rows of dots; Case (1977, 27) suggested that this might be a diadem comparable to examples from Iberia (Hernando Gonzalo 1983, 100–3). For the plaques Taylor (1979, 237) would see a connection between their ornament and that on the British basket-shaped earrings.

Discs (Pl. VII top; 1). The Irish group consists of twenty-one specimens which vary in size from 11 mm to 114 mm. They are discussed together but this need not imply that they constitute a chronologically homogeneous group. Apart from the Knockadoon (Lough Gur) piece all the others are decorated, the motifs consisting of concentric lines, concentric rows of dots, crosses, triangles and zigzags. Case (1977, 21) divided the discs into two main groups, A and B, on the presence or absence of a ladder patterned cruciform motif.

In the Ballina pair, the Kilmuckridge and the unprovenanced examples the arms of the cross connect with the enclosing band. There is another similar band parallel to the edge. All have a ladder pattern. In addition, the Castle Treasure and W.270 (? Corran) pieces have a dot and simple line ornament. Ballyshannon has added a two member triangle extending in from the centre of the edge of each quadrant formed by the cross. The two discs that have been given a Co. Wexford location by Armstrong (1933, Nos. 328–9) have dots instead of a ladder in the cross and also dot as well as line and zigzag ornament between the end of the cross and the edge. A Maltese Cross with ladder pattern characterised the Co. Roscommon pair and also the Ballydehob disc but the latter has a much more elaborate design with a herring-bone pattern on the arms and a ladder pattern in the voids between. There is also a band of ladder pattern parallel to the edge. The most elaborately decorated cruciform discs are the Tedavnet (Co. Monaghan) pair; their art is far removed from the simple cross-design and, in addition, there is greater emphasis on repoussé work (Pl. VII, top). A major falling-off in design is evident on the Baltimore, Co. Cork disc. The elimination of the cross and ladder ornament but with an elaboration of the area near the edge characterises the Cloyne and one of the Ballyvourney discs. Except for the absence of the cruciform motif the art composition on these discs is close to the decoration on the Co. Wexford discs. The plainest and smallest decorated disc is an example from Knockadoon, Lough Gur, which is 11 mm in diameter (Ó Ríordáin 1954, 410–11).

As is the case in England, Irish discs also have Beaker associations. The Knockadoon disc was found on Site D "amongst stones which supported the uprights of the lower terrace wall". When found it was folded over along the line of the perforations (Ó Ríordáin 1954, 384–6; 410–11). The terrace wall and a hut ("House 1") "represented the latest phase of activity on the site" although the terracing appears to predate the house. As pieces of clay and stone moulds and crucible fragments were associated with the house the occupants were "evidently engaged in bronze working" (p. 401). From identifiable pieces the moulds were for casting base-looped spearheads and palstaves, types that were current around the end of the second millenium, i.e. Bishopsland Phase (Herity and Eogan 1977, 170). However, Ó Ríordáin (p. 390) considered that the terrace wall can be assigned to the earlier Beaker period, and a striking feature of the site is the large quantity of Beaker pottery which it yielded. "The number of vessels here represented is larger than on any other site at Lough Gur" (Ó Ríordáin 1954, 394). In the main the sherds

George Eogan

Figure 5. Distribution of Beaker graves containing gold objects in Britain.

seem to have come from vessels of Clarke's (1970) Wessex-Middle Rhine or Northern-Middle Rhine groups. Incidentally, a penannular bracelet of (copper/bronze) with slightly tapering terminals and body of rounded cross-section was found in the material of the lower terrace wall and at least one of the three awls found (No. 1) at a low level on the site was "evidently associated with an early stage in the occupation". A somewhat similar bracelet came from the nearby Grange "stone-circle" (Ó Ríordáin 1951, 48).

Another Beaker period association includes the "gold circular plates" found in a box (?wooden) bound with a gold band together with several jet beads of various shapes and two stone archers' wristbracers of Harbison's Type B1 (1976, 8, 25, Nos. 14, 16, Pl. 5) in a bog at Corran, Co. Armagh in 1883 (Wilde 1857, 89). Case (1977, 20. No. 3) wondered if at least one of the "plates" was a disc? The Ballyshannon discs accompanied an inhumation burial. Such burials are a feature of the British Beaker complexes but also the Irish Bowl Food vessel complex. In the absence of other grave-goods it is not possible to assign the Ballyshannon grave to a precise assemblage. In fact there is no other evidence for the use of discs in Ireland as grave-goods.

Regarding other associations, the Ballyvourney disc is claimed to have been found with a gold nail-headed pin but such pins are difficult to date precisely. The Ballydehob example was found in a cleft in a rock together with two or three similar pieces, portions of what have been described as bronze ring money, and a large bronze armlet 7.6 cm in diameter. On at least seven occasions discs were found in pairs but no other objects were present. The Corran objects appear to have been a hoard, one cannot be certain if the objects from Ballyvourney and Ballydehob were associated. If they were they would have constituted a small group of personal objects. There is also a dearth of information about the find circumstances, data being only available on five find places and each one is different – possibly a grave, a bog, a rock cleft, between tree roots and a habitation site. It therefore appears, as was the case in England, that discs were current during the primary Beaker phase. It can be assumed that discs closely resembling their supposed English forerunners, such as those from Kilmuckridge in the coastal lands of Co. Wexford, should be amongst the earliest.

None of this information helps much with interpretation of use. The relative thinness of the gold plus the presence of a pair of perforations indicates that discs were attached to a backing, possibly to a garment. As has already been pointed out the presence of V-perforated buttons indicates a change in costume fastening. As two discs have frequently been found together perhaps they were worn in pairs. However, the Mere (Wiltshire) grave which had two discs also contained two skeletons. This has prompted Case (1977, 19) to suggest that the discs were worn singly and that the finds of pairs in Ireland should be taken as small hoards. At least decoratively they could have served a similar purpose to pins, and if the English evidence from the Mere and Farleigh Wick graves is relevant for broader interpretation they would have been worn by males.

ASSESSMENT

Precisely how metallurgy commenced in Ireland is not known. There may indeed have been direct influences from the continent, Brittany for instance. This could have led to the introduction into Munster of items such as thick-butted copper axes like those found in the Castletown Roche, Co. Cork, hoard (Burgess 1980, 72–3; Case 1966) and the subsequent exploitation of the natural copper deposits that principally occurred in the southern peninsulas. There is also the problem of the role, if any, of the builders of the megalithic tombs of the wedge-shaped variety (*cf.* Herity & Eogan 1977, 117–19) and their relationship to the Beaker complex and early metallurgy especially in the south and west. The evidence is more straightforward in the east of the country. In that region a vigorous Beaker complex emerged with its background across the Irish Sea. A key area of settlement was in County Meath including the area of the former passage-tomb cemetery of Brugh na Bóinne where there is ample evidence for domestic activity at Knowth and Newgrange and also for the use of earthen and other forms of enclosures (*cf.* Eogan 1986, 221,

Fig. 90; Stout 1991). As yet associated gold or other metal objects have not turned up on any of these sites, the thin-butted bronze axe-head from Newgrange being on the perimeter of the area of Beaker settlement (O'Kelly and Shell 1979). In the south of the country the Knockadoon disc was found in a Beaker context (p. 19). There is also a variety of Beaker associated objects from other parts of the country, notably tanged copper daggers and archers' stone wristbracers (Harbison 1969a, 7–8; 1976, 3–13).

Despite the lack of association in the east of Ireland between metal objects and Beaker pottery, it may be suggested that incoming Beaker people from Britain introduced metal objects and the knowledge of metal-working. Amongst these could have been gold ornaments, or the idea of making and wearing them, as well as an event of greater importance, the discovery of native gold.

Chapter III

Gold-Working in an Age of Industrial Expansion and Wealth Consolidation: Insular Complexes in the Bell Beaker Tradition

Profound economic growth, agricultural and industrial, began over large parts of Europe about 2000 BC. Rich complexes emerged, generally on Beaker foundations, such as the Unĕtice (Aunjetitz) in central Europe or the Rhône in south-central France (Coles and Harding 1979, 27). In some areas richly-furnished burials reflect a newly assumed hierarchical pattern. Britain and Ireland also witnessed change around that time. By and large this involved alterations to the existing Beaker complexes, amongst these were industrial changes, particularly technological development (the alloying of copper and tin to produce bronze) but also ritual changes such as the placing of food vessels in burials, (initially bowl-shaped food vessels in Ireland, vase-shaped in north Britain). In addition there was a more broadly-based cultural enrichment, this was brought about by continental influence that were achieved through trade and commercial activities, especially from the middle German region.

BRITAIN

A characteristic feature of the whole of Britain is greater industrialisation leading to the increased production of more sophisticated bronze tools and weapons, such as flat axes and daggers with triangular-shaped blades. Single-grave burials usually in or under a round mound were a feature. In the south of England developed Beaker pottery was in use (Clarke 1970, 210–33) but northwards a distinctive pottery form emerged, the vase-shaped food vessel. In all areas 'ritual' enclosures were still being built and used and in areas such as Yorkshire and western Scotland rock-art was a feature (Simpson and Thawley 1972). In Scotland the industrial aspect is known as the Migdale-Marnoch stage (Britton 1963, 263–81), characterised by the use of open stone moulds which were used almost exclusively for casting thin-butted flat axes with a production area in the north-east. Hoards of bronze objects and personal ornaments became more common. Ornaments in metal are mainly confined to Scotland and consist of different types of bronze bracelets. Forms represented are those with solid body of rounded cross-section and closely-set unexpanded ends, similar bracelets but with broadish body decorated externally by parallel ridges, annular sheet-bronze bracelets that are usually decorated with low, parallel ridges and bosses, and the flat-bodied (band) penannular bracelet that is formed from a ribbon of bronze. Some examples of the latter class were decorated with incised lines forming herringbone patterns (Coles 1968–9, 50–2).

A feature of Scotland and the Yorkshire-Derbyshire area is the presence of necklaces with beads made from jet. In some examples only a small number of beads were used but other examples have up to seventy beads (Morrison 1979). The necklaces may be single-stranded with fusiform-shaped beads, or more elaborate examples with large flat beads which function as spacers between smaller beads (Fig. 10).

The Gold Objects

Apart from the Knowes of Trotty discs (Orkney), a small number of lunulae and a few miscellaneous items, gold was not widely used in Wales, northern England and Scotland. In the south of England, south of the Severn-Wash line, about twenty sites produced gold ornaments, mainly in the Wessex area where there are about fifteen find-places (Taylor 1980, 45–50, see also p. 28; Fig. 9, for distribution). Weight-wise, however, the amount of gold was limited. Gold-working was previously practised in the Wessex region during the Beaker period (p. 13–18) but now there was an expansion. This Early Bronze Age gold-work has features in common with that of the Beaker phase. It is found, mainly in Wessex, in graves and therefore forms part of a burial assemblage. A number of the burials were secondary intrusions into Beaker barrows and the objects were fashioned from sheet gold. Some graves contained more than one gold object; amongst these are the well-known assemblages such as those from the Bush Barrow, Wilsford G8, Manton, Upton Lovell (on the Salisbury Plain), Hengistbury Head, Hampshire, the Ridgeway and Clandon barrows in Dorset and Hammeldon in Devon. Outside Wessex an important find came from Little Cressingham, Norfolk (Piggott 1938, Fig. 22).

As was the case during the Beaker period the graves were again under round-barrows but the bowl-barrow was replaced by other forms – bell, disc and saucer-shaped barrows. These often occur in cemeteries, some of which accumulated due to the continued building of barrows close to a primary one. The burial rite was predominantly inhumation, often the body was placed in a crouched position. In the Bush Barrow burial and possibly in others the grave-goods were laid out in the positions that they had during use (Fig. 6). All the objects were personal items but very few consist solely of gold. A new feature is the emergence of a composite object where gold was used in combination with other exotic materials, such as amber, jet or shale. It was common to use gold foil as covering for buttons, usually jet. Among these are conical buttons, some with V-shaped perforations but there are also biconical and cylindrical forms. On some the entire surface is covered but on others the gold is confined to bands. Pendants also occur and for these gold may also be associated with other materials such as bronze as is the case with the halberd pendants. Gold discs and discs of amber bound with gold also occur.

Another interesting object is the shale mace-head from Clandon, into which four gold bosses were inserted (Clarke *et al.*, 1985, 211). Small 'boxes' and cones were also used. The most outstanding and striking pieces are the two lozenge-shaped plaques and the belt hook from the Bush Barrow (Taylor 1980, Pl. 25 a-c; Kinnes *et al.*, 1988; see Pl. II; Figs. 6–7). As the gold is paper thin, great care must have been taken in its manufacture, so as not to damage it in the final stage of production; wood or leather was probably used as a cushion, as would have been the case with the earlier Beaker gold objects (p. 13–18). The large plaque, 185.5 mm by 175 mm was probably attached to an organic backing as its edges were slightly folded back. It is decorated with finely incised or grooved lines that are concentrated in four bands and carry inwards the shape of the outline. Between the outer and the next band there is a zig-zag while in the centre there is a chess-board pattern. The small plaque is decorated with four concentric bands of lines. The belt-hook cover is in two parts – body and hook. As Coles and Taylor (1971, 11) demonstrated, these objects possess similarities in techniques of manufacture and ornamentation. The tooling on each is similar, as is the method used in working the objects into shape and the choice of ornamental motifs. As a result they can be compared to the sheet-gold button covers from Upton Lovell and Wilsford G8, the lozenge-shaped plaque from Clandon and the gold-bound amber disc also from Wilsford G8. In Coles and Taylor's view the Bush Barrow pieces and the other related objects were all made by a single master craftsman. The Little Cressingham plaque was made by a different craftsman, his work was less delicate than that of the Wessex master.

Beads, pendants and other items that were made from materials other than gold were also in use, sometimes in the same grave. A material that must have ranked high due to its colour and lustre was amber (Beck and Shennan 1991, 74–98). Visually it can be compared to gold and it

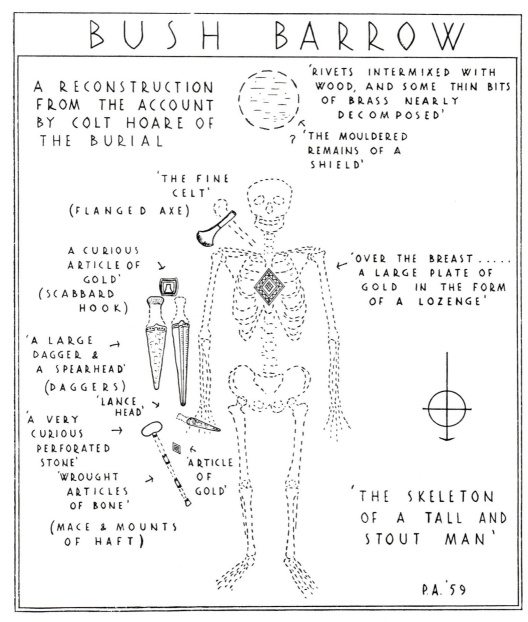

Figure 6. The Bush Barrow (Wiltshire) burial. (After Ashbee, The Bronze Age Round Barrow in Britain, *1960)*

was also an item that signified social prestige as can be gauged from the fact that nearly every Wessex female grave contains items of amber. As already mentioned amber objects were on occasions embellished with gold but many were not, these include the complex bored spacer-beads from necklaces such as that from Upton Lovell (Gerloff 1975, 199; see Fig. 8).

Apart from ornaments the graves contain various other objects, some of them items of prestige, the most famous being the stone cushion-shaped mace-head from the Bush Barrow, which had a wooden shaft decorated with indented bone mounts. Other forms of mace-head or battle-axe were in use but there were also mundane pieces such as metal tools (axes with cast flanges, awls) and weapons (triangular-shaped daggers). The graves provide evidence for ritual since on many occasions a variety of objects were added as grave goods and they also provide evidence for the wide range of objects in use. Yet graves were not the only ritual monuments,

George Eogan

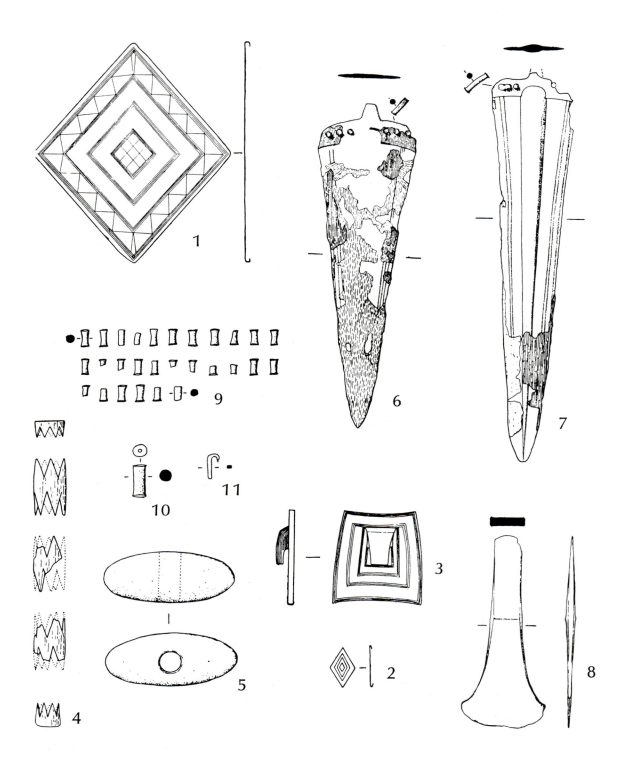

Figure 7. Objects from Bush Barrow burial, Wiltshire. Nos. 9–11 shown at 2/3 size; the remainder at 1/3. (After Annable and Simpson, 1964).

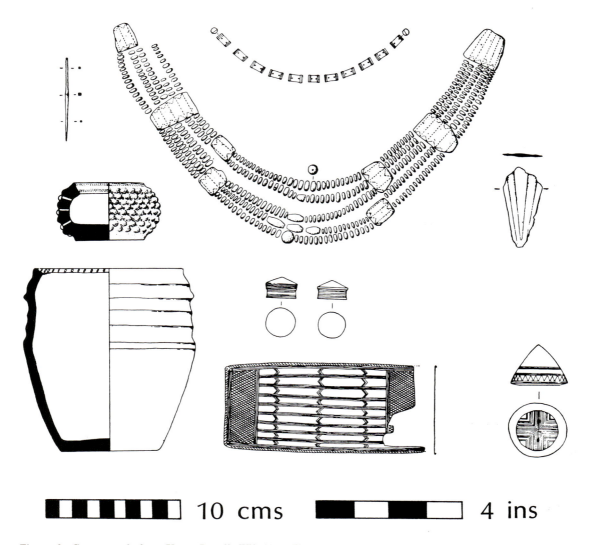

Figure 8. *Grave goods from Upton Lovell, Wiltshire. The collared urn may not have been part of the group.*
(After Annable and Simpson, 1964).

the enclosure was still being used. The most notable was Stonehenge now in its developed (third) phase with its impressive lintelled stone circle.

Assessment

The south of England had a long history of intensive settlement as is clear from the remains of both the Neolithic and the Beaker period. This was a leading agricultural area and that was its major source of wealth. It, therefore, need not come as a surprise that during the Early Bronze Age a wealthy society continued to flourish and increase its riches. Wessex I clearly demonstrated that there was an increase in productivity by an agrarian society but not in isolation. Wessex had contacts with Brittany, further afield to the Unĕtice region as well as eastwards to the Mediterranean world (Piggott 1938, 95–6). These wide-ranging contacts, possibly two-way, were important but more important would have been the absorption of the area into a wider socio-economic system which apparently took place at this time. Economic success could lead to the emergence of a stratified society. In particular the Salisbury Plain with its heart around Stonehenge formed a core, a centre of a ritually sophisticated but also politically developed society. In fact it is an example of what Jørgen Jensen (1967, 1981) defined as a wealth-centre. Such a centre was usually quite small in area but due to economic development became rich. A classic wealth centre is focussed on a prominent feature which can be natural or artificial. For the Wessex "culture", Stonehenge with its lintelled stone circle is a typical prominent feature. In addition there is a concentration of other features such as rich graves and a range of gold and bronze objects, some of which are not only unusual but also elegant and splendid in appearance. In view of the well-preserved nature of this delicate gold-work Coles and Taylor (1971, 13) have argued that the period during which it was in use was rather short and that the objects were specially manufactured for deposition in graves. However, if the gold pieces were only used on special occasions their life could have been relatively long (Megaw and Simpson 1979, 227). While the Stonehenge area was one of great significance it was not the only rich area as the Ridgeway finds in Dorset and Little Cressingham in Norfolk show. Obviously Wessex society was wealthy and this highlights the importance of gold, it was a scarce commodity – as Coles and Taylor have pointed out, all the Wessex gold only equals a few lunulae in weight.

Although having distant contacts eastwards towards middle Europe and southwards towards Greece and Crete, there is very little evidence for northward contact, either British or continental. The Knowes of Trotty spacer-plate amber necklace is one but, as noted, the associated discs may be of Irish origin. Building on Beaker foundations Wessex became an important Early Bronze Age centre, as barrow construction, the use of daggers and gold shows. However, to the north, other parts of Britain also had flourishing early Bronze Age communities. Amongst the artefacts personal ornaments, notably jet necklaces featured but items made from gold were exceedingly rare in those areas.

IRELAND

In Ireland the new complex, termed the Frankford-Ballyvalley/Bowl food vessel complex (*cf.* Herity and Eogan 1977, 133–47), is characterised by a distinctive type of pottery vessel and other grave-goods, as well as by individual finds and sometimes hoards of metal objects. These include objects made from gold but also bronze, such as round-butted riveted daggers, Type Corkey (Harbison 1969a, 8–10, 23) and awls. Thin-butted bronze axes of Ballyvalley-Killaha types and halberds were also in use (Harbison 1969a, 24–55; 1969b, 35–55). Some axe types, especially the Killaha type, were cast in open stone moulds. Burials provide the best evidence for ritual, the remains being that of one person either inhumed or cremated in a cist. Grave goods, such as a bowl-shaped food vessel and a dagger, were often present. Sometimes a special mound was built to cover the burials but they have also been found in flat cemeteries. The erection and use of other ritual monuments, such as stone circles and individual standing stones probably continued. From the point of view of gold-working a characteristic of this Frankford-Ballyvalley/ Bowl food vessel stage is a continuity in technology with sheet-gold as the principal medium. The complicated technique of cladding the surface of a bronze object with gold sheet was also practised as the flat axehead of Ballyvalley type from Scariff river, Co. Clare shows (Armstrong 1922, 135; Harbison 1969b, 39, No. 997).

The Gold Objects

Discs. As has been previously discussed the disc was introduced from Britain during early Beaker times. Thereafter, developments led to the emergence of larger specimens but also to variation in decoration such as the Maltese cross on the pair from Co. Roscommon or the more elaborate design on the pair from "Co. Wexford" and more particularly on the two from Tedavnet, Co. Monaghan (Pl. VII, top). A further progression could have occasioned the elimination of the

Figure 9. Distribution of Early Bronze Age ("Wessex I") graves containing gold objects. (After Taylor, 1980).

cruciform motif, hence the Cloyne and Ballyvourney designs. This hypothetical internal development receives some support from the resemblance between the non-cruciform decoration on the two latter discs and those from the Knowes of Trotty, Orkney which are considered to be late, as the associated amber necklace with spacer-plates is poorly preserved and therefore had a long life (Pl. III). There is also some resemblance between the Irish discs with elaborate cruciform design and the conical bead covers from the Wessex I burial at Upton Lovell in Wiltshire (Fig. 8) which also had a spacer-plate amber necklace. A similar design occurs on the jet buttons from Harehope, Pebbleshire (Clarke et. al.1985, 273–4: Pl. 5: 46). One could visualise an ordered typological and chronological development from the pristine Beaker period into the Frankford-Ballyvalley/Bowl food vessel period. But before accepting that view another factor has to be taken into account. As Clarke (1970, 95, Figs. 140–2) and Taylor (1980, 23) have pointed out there is a close resemblance between some discs with cruciform design and the decoration on the bronze racquet-headed pins of the Unětician (Aunjetitz) culture, especially in Bohemia and Slovakia. The Unětician culture influenced Early Bronze Age complexes as far west as Ireland but the intermediate areas did not have racquet-headed pins. However, the similarities between some Irish cruciform-decorated discs and the racquet-head pins is undeniable, yet could this resemblance be fortuitous as is the resemblance between the pestle-shaped pendants from Irish passage tombs of a much earlier date and the similarly-shaped pendants from Wessex I contexts, such as Little Cressingham?

The *lunula* (Pls. IV–VI; 2–3; Figs. 11–12) is a crescentic-shaped flat plate with a subrectangular expansion at each end constituting the terminals which were used for fastening. These are usually turned at right angles to the plane of the body. From a maximum width in the centre the body tapers towards both ends. Lunulae were manufactured by beating out an ingot or rod into the required shape. This involved very considerable skill especially with large examples such as that from Athlone the body of which is 13 cm. in maximum width. Most are well-preserved with a fresh appearance but on some examples the surface is uneven. There is, however, evidence for wear, apparently during use, on the Glengall, Co. Tipperary specimen while the example from Coolaghmore, Co. Kilkenny was repaired in antiquity.

Details are available for forty-seven Irish examples and sixteen from outside the country. There are five definite undecorated examples from Ireland and one from Germany. In all decorated examples the art is confined to one face and is concentrated at each end on approximately a quarter of the body. Here there is all-over decoration with negative areas contributing motifs in their own right. Decoration extends on to the body in the form of a band, or border, parallel to the inner and outer edges. The motifs are geometric, either angular or linear, concentric designs do not occur. The principal motifs are bands of criss-cross hatching, parallel lines, zig-zags, squares, triangles and lozenges. In general the designs were carefully and intricately applied, showing precision and accuracy and were obviously the work of skilled craftsmen. The impressed decoration was applied by incision and by hammering or punch-work. For incision a small sharp tool was needed but to create a groove a chisel was hammered along the sheet. Sometimes the designs were in faint repoussé work and again a chisel was used for line work and a small punch with a fine point for the dots.

Taylor (1970, 1980, 25–41) has distinguished three groups, mainly on decoration but also on shape and distribution.

1. Classical. (Pls. IV–V; 2:2,3; Figs. 11:1–3, 12) This group contains the largest and most elegant lunulae of all. They are distinguished by having the widest and thinnest sheet and as a result some individual examples contain more gold than any example of the other two groups. The small terminals sometimes lie on the same plane as the body. The decoration is more lavish than in the other groups being of high quality and skill, incised with a finely-pointed tool. The combination and positioning of the various motifs may vary and often a horn panel can be divided into simple motifs, complex motifs (which sometimes can be

PLATE I

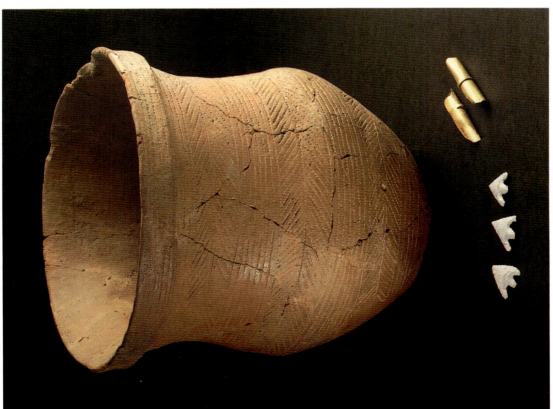

Left: Grave-goods from Beaker burial, Radley, Berkshire. *Photo: Ashmolean Museum, Oxford and National Museum of Scotland.*
Right: Grave-goods from Beaker burial, Culduthel Mains, Inverness-shire. *Photo: National Museum of Scotland.*

PLATE II

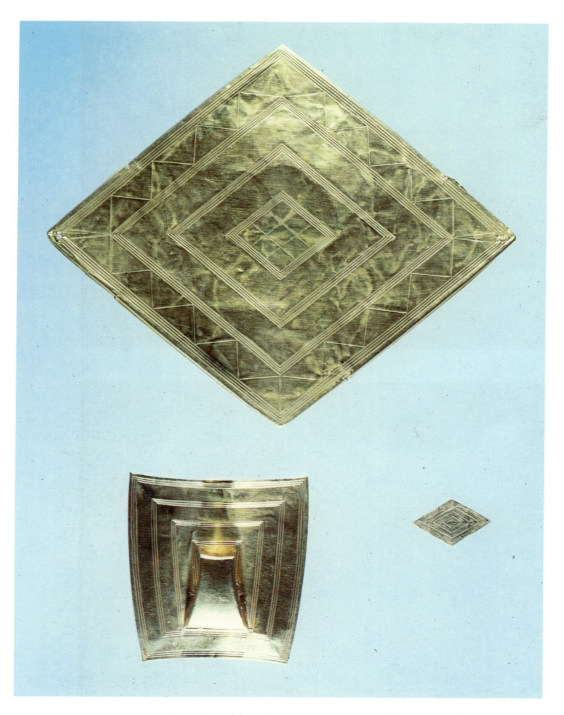

Gold objects from burial, Bush Barrow, Wiltshire.
Photo: British Museum.

PLATE III

Left: Gold discs from burial, Knowes of Trotty, Orkney. Right: Amber beads from burial, Knowes of Trotty, Orkney.

PLATE IV

Top: Full view of Classical lunula, Rossmore Park, Co. Monaghan.
Bottom: Detail of one horn of Rossmore Park lunula.
Photos: National Museum of Ireland.

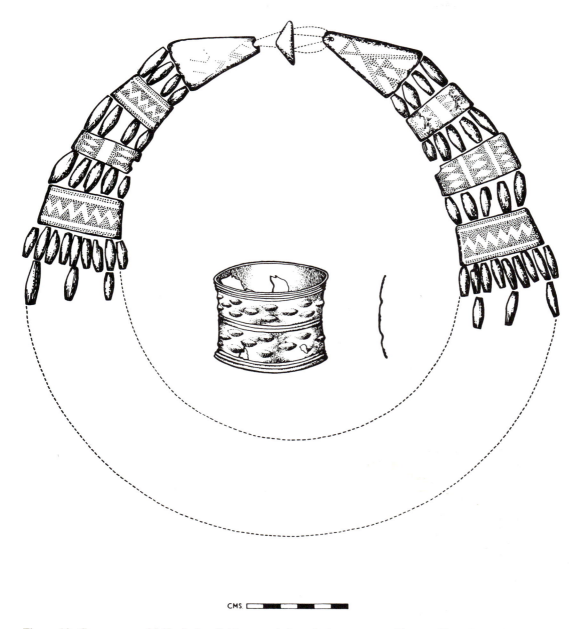

CMS ▭▬▭▬▭

Figure 10. Grave group, Melford, Argyllshire, consisting of a jet spacer necklace and broad annular bracelet. The grave contained a second similar bracelet but this does not survive. (After Inventaria Archaeologia *G.B. 25).*

divided into two halves each of which is a mirror image of the other), voids, and a narrow border edging panel. Sometimes both horns have precisely similar decoration. The centre part of the body also has a border which consists of varying motifs. There are at least thirty-six examples but there are only three definite find-places outside Ireland, all in Cornwall.

2. Unaccomplished. (Pl. 2:1; Fig. 11:4) Taylor relates these to the Classical group but they are narrower, thicker, and the decoration is inferior and sometimes irregular. On the whole the workmanship is less careful and while the motifs and arrangement tend to follow Classical lines, departures such as central vertical decoration on the horns, do occur. Taylor (1970, 55) places the undecorated lunulae in this group on physical grounds, although in this connection the possibility of the former being unfinished pieces must be borne in mind. At

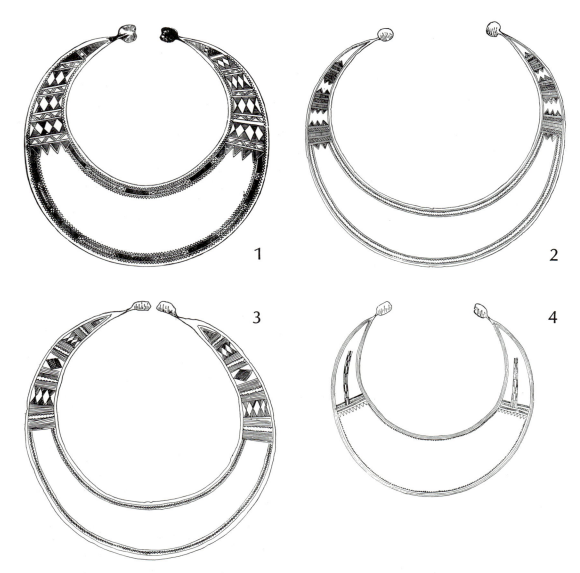

*Figure 11. Gold lunulae, Killarney, Co. Kerry (1), no location, Co. Galway (2), no location, Ireland (3).
All Classical. [1–3 shown at about 1/3]. Dunfierth, Co. Kildare (4). Unaccomplished. [4 shown at about 1/4].
(After Coffey, 1909).*

least thirty-eight Unaccomplished lunulae are known, occurring more frequently in the
northern part of the country and they have not been found outside Ireland. Within the lunula
family their sequential position is difficult to establish. They could represent a developed
stage but they could also be considered as plainer and poorer examples but generally
contemporary with Classical lunulae. Taylor has shown however that at least one example,
Ballinagroun, Co. Kerry may be a modified Classical piece. Its width and thickness is similar
to the Classical lunulae and furthermore the decoration may also have originally been
Classical but was added to.

3. Provincial. (Pl. V, top) As lunulae in this group are made from a thick sheet they are more
    rigid than those of the other forms. The terminals are crescentic in shape with barbs, the
    decoration is sparse but in comparison with the other groups the motifs are similar. Lines,
    usually deeply incised, and dots are common. At least twelve examples are known. Apart
    from one specimen, Cooltran, Co. Fermanagh, all examples come from the highland zones

of Britain and the western continental area, especially western Brittany and less so in Belgium, Luxembourg and Germany.

Chronology and Origins. As Taylor has pointed out lunula decoration can be compared to that found on Beaker pottery (1970, 56–62; 1980, 41). However, she drew her parallels from British beakers, especially the indigenous Northern and Southern groups but this is not necessarily relevant as Classical lunulae are an Irish type. There is of course equivalent Beaker pottery from Ireland, such as Dalkey Island, Co. Dublin (Liversage 1968, 156) and from the point of view of the motifs, bowl food vessel decoration is also relevant. It may also be noted that somewhat similar decoration is found on flat and flanged axes principally of the Ballyvalley and the later Derryniggin types (Harbison 1969b, 32–63). The Irish associations, which are with other lunulae, are not helpful and neither is the Kerivoa, Brittany hoard (Pl. 3) despite its more varied content of three Provincial type lunulae, a rod with lunula-type terminals and pieces of sheet gold. This deficiency is compensated for by the hoard from Harlyn, Cornwall with its Classical and Provincial type lunulae and thin-butted flat axe (Pl. VI). As has been noted since the days of Craw (1928–29; Clark 1932) both the motifs and their positioning recall the spacer-plate jet necklaces of Scotland (Morrison, 1979) and northern England, mainly east Yorkshire and Derbyshire (Sheppard 1929, 106, No. 1017; Howarth 1899, 57–64) where the burial rite was inhumation and the remains those of females. Jet necklaces with spacer plates are frequently found associated with food vessels of the Vase variety. There are also other associations such as that from Melford in Argyll where the other objects were two broad decorated annular bronze bracelets (Fig. 10). These are usually assigned to the period of the Migdale hoard which can be equated with Phase A1 of Reinecke in Central Europe and parts of similar bracelets were found in a dagger grave at Masterton, Fifeshire (Henshall 1968, 189–90). Daggers of the Masterton type are mainly contemporary with the Wessex I stage of the southern English Early Bronze Age but continuing into a period contemporary with Wessex II (Gerloff 1975, 58–63). Of further interest is the fact that the Wessex "culture" also had crescentic necklaces with spacer-plates made from amber rather than jet. Gerloff (1975, 199) considers that such necklaces were confined to female graves. They were a feature of Wessex I as grave associations such as Upton Lovel, G2e (Annable and Simpson 1964, 48, Nos. 225–33) and Hengistbury Head, 3 indicate (Longworth 1984, 183, No. 375) but it seems that they remained in use into Wessex II (Gerloff 1975, 199).

Taking the British evidence it appears that there could have been an overlap in the use of spacer-plate necklaces whether of jet in the north and midlands or amber in the south. Both post-date the preceding Bell Beaker stage as there are no associations with such vessels. In form and decoration the necklaces and lunulae are close and they have a complementary distribution. Therefore, it seems that they represent a fashion for wearing different forms of crescentic ornament in three different insular regions and in view of their general similarity apparently at the same time, that is, during the Frankford-Ballyvalley, Migdale-Marnoch and Wessex I stages.

Taylor sees the lunulae of her Classical type as the earliest, even as forerunners of the jet and amber necklaces but does not attempt to explain developments. On the other hand, Butler (1963, 185) would see lunulae originating in the Bell-beaker cultures of Portugal from whence they spread to Brittany and then to Cornwall, Scotland and Ireland. He would consider the Classical lunulae decoration as embellishment derived from the spacer-plate decoration of the Scottish necklaces but of course, that raises another unsolved problem, namely the origin of those necklaces.

In addition to Britain and Ireland crescentic neck ornaments were also favoured in other parts of Europe, three different types being represented in the Kerivoa hoard, but the question is did the lunula mode originate in Ireland? This is unlikely; as is the case with the basket earrings and discs it appears that the idea was externally inspired, and in its formation various items may have been a source of stimulation and inspiration. From early in the metal age in different parts of Europe crescentic metal ornaments were worn. Amongst these are the German sheet bronze collars (Butler 1963, 180–85; Sprockhoff 1939; Hachmann 1954), oar-ended ornaments from

Denmark and other forms of sheet gold ornaments from the west Baltic area and Iberia. There are also neckrings with flat terminals in both gold and bronze from Britain, Brittany and the Low Countries (Taylor 1968). Another gold type has a flat body with elongated slots in its centre, the terminals are usually unexpanded but an example from a mound at Cicere (Santa Comba, near Coruña, north-western Spain) has terminals that are rounded externally and barbed at the sides, rather like those on Provincial lunulae. The Cicere neck ornament came from a hoard that may be assigned to the Beaker horizon (Monteagudo 1953, 293, Fig. 32; Hardmeyer 1976, Pl. 4). The type has an Atlantic distribution, examples being known from Brittany. One occurred in a dolmen at Saint Père-en-Retz, Loire Atlantique and may have been associated with what appears to have been a neckring with flat terminals of the type already mentioned and at least two flat axes made from copper (Briard 1965, 71, Fig. 19:2[1]; Eluère 1982, 266, Fig. 145). The flat piece in the Kerivoa en Bourbriac hoard, Côtes-du-Nord, may have come from a similar or related ornament (Pl. 3). It is therefore clear that a range of crescentic neck ornaments made from copper/bronze and gold were worn in western continental Europe during the Beaker-Early Bronze Ages and that innovations and developments were taking place. As a result a *milieu* existed within which ongoing developments could have been a feature. However, the lack of finds from stratigraphically secure contexts and the scarcity of wide-ranging associated finds allows typology to function in a somewhat uncontrolled manner. In such circumstance one could speculate that the gold lunula developed on the continent despite the small number found there. This involved regional expressions; a group in north-western Iberia, (the lunula from Cabeceiras de Basto, Braga, Portugal associated with gold sun discs), another group in South Scandinavia (Taylor 1980, Pls. 21, 22, 23b), and in between a central group consisting of Provincial lunulae. In addition the practice of wearing crescentic neck ornaments could now have spread to Britain and Ireland. In Britain possibly due to the scarcity of native gold, other materials were used, amber in the south and jet in the north. As a result a virtually new type of neck ornament, the spacer plate necklace emerged. While the angular decoration of the spacer plates could have its background in the decoration found on Beaker pottery, the composite construction is new and its development involved considerable ingenuity. The lunulae also involved manufacturing and decorating skills but these were within the established techniques of sheet gold working. In Ireland, possibly due to the availability of native gold, it was the lunula mode that was adopted, the prototype being the continental Provincial lunula, a form that was used in small numbers in Britain. This basic form was elaborated on in Ireland, the ensuing manifestation was the lunula of the Classical form. This event must have taken place in conjunction with the British developments, as the art motifs and their disposition are similar to that on the spacer plate necklaces, as has already been noted.

Use. Some of the lunulae are in excellent condition indicating that they were well cared for both in and out of use. They must have had some form of protection like the case made of wood for the Newtown, Crossdoney, Co. Cavan lunula (Fig. 12). They were probably in use for a long time as some have been repaired while secondary art was applied on others (Taylor 1980, Pl. 13). It has often been suggested that they were worn as neck ornaments with the terminals hooked behind the neck. If used this way most of the ornament would be obscured. They would also have been tight-fitting, at least for adults, as the interior opening is rarely over 15 cm. It is also possible that they could have been worn with the body upright on the forehead. In view of the pristine condition of some Taylor (1980, 36) wondered if they could have been placed on statues during ceremonial occasions. It is, however, likely that lunulae were worn on the person but it is not possible to say if they were the property of an individual. Perhaps they served as a symbol of rank or power, in other words a badge of office of a leader, belonging not to an individual but the common property of the tribe for use at times of tribal gatherings. There is also the possibility of lunulae being used as part of the paraphernalia of religious ritual, part of the trappings of priests or priestesses. Could the spread of gravel on which it is claimed four lunulae were discovered at Dunfierth, Co. Kildare represent a ritual feature?

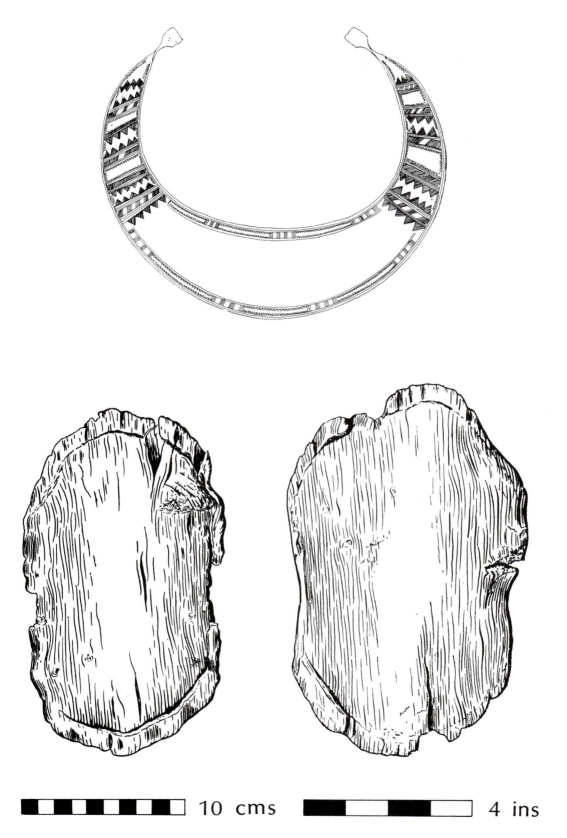

10 cms   4 ins

Figure 12. Gold lunula, Classical, and wooden container, Newtown, Crossdoney, Co. Cavan. (After Coffey, 1909).

George Eogan

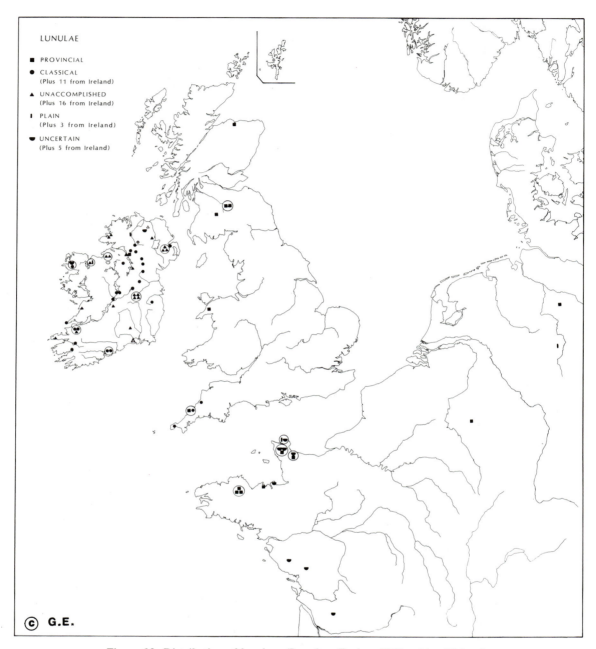

Figure 13. Distribution of lunulae. (Based on Taylor, 1970, with additions).

Distribution (Fig. 13). Details of the place of discovery of forty-four *Irish* lunulae have been recorded. Twenty-two were found on dry land or agricultural land. Of these thirteen were placed close to prominent landmarks such as large standing-stones. There are three pairs, two with three examples and one of four, all of the same Unaccomplished group. Lunulae of this group occur in all six hoards and are exclusively represented in three hoards. Perhaps these were hidden for safe-keeping with the intention of recovery but they could also have been ritual deposits. A lunula was discovered at a megalithic tomb, now destroyed, at Highwood, Co. Sligo (Wood-Martin 1888, 180–1) but it cannot be established that it served as a contemporary grave offering. In fact there is no definite evidence that lunulae served such a function and this contrasts with the jet and amber spacer plate necklaces. The lunulae distribution is in the northern two-thirds of the country but the find place of as many as thirty-five have not been recorded. The distribution in Britain is restricted to west Cornwall, north-west Wales and south-west Scotland. The continental distribution is confined to the coastal areas of northern Brittany and Normandy. Northwards there is a single example from Luxembourg and another near Hannover in Germany. The most distant specimen from Ireland was found at Butzebach in Hessen (Herrmann and Jockenhövel 1990, 335, Abb. 104).

Bracelets. Only one, possibly two, gold annular bracelets can be assigned to the Early Bronze Age. One, made from sheet gold "2 5/8 inches in length and 3 inches in diameter", has an outward expansion along each end, and the body is decorated with fine, evenly-spaced ridges formed by the repoussé technique. At regular intervals each ridge expands outwards to form a series of lenticular-shaped bosses. At the end, on both sides and on the inside of the edge ridge, there are rows of tiny dots. This object was found at Whitfield (Lisnakill), Co. Waterford, in a cist within a burial mound associated with a pottery vessel "shaped like an inverted cone" and inhumed and cremated bone. As Herity pointed out, the description of the vessel suggests a vase food vessel (Herity 1969b, 10–11). Another annular gold bracelet, the find place of which has not been recorded, has three prominent but plain ridges on the body apparently repoussé-formed and a ridge along each edge, this has ornament, possibly incised, in the form of zig-zags (Herity 1969b, 10–11). Herity noted that both bracelets have parallels in bronze examples from Melford and Masterton in Scotland (*I.A.* [G.B.], 26; Fig. 10:2; Henshall and Wallace, 1962–3, 50). The unprovenanced bracelet has a counterpart in the bracelets from the Migdale hoard (Coles 1968–69, 51, Fig. 39:2–3).

These Scottish armlets may have an ultimate background in the *Manchette* armlets of the central European Unětice (Aunjetitz) complex (*cf.* Coles 1968–69, 51). It is also possible that the pair of bronze bracelets with tapering ends found with a bowl food vessel at Luggacurren, Co. Laoghais (Lalor, 1879) have a Scottish background.

Assessment

Ireland, mainly due to its natural resources, had a rich Early Bronze Age industry (Frankford-Ballyvalley stage) as is clear from the large number of flat axes (over 1300), halberds (*c*. 350) and round-butted riveted daggers (over 80). A major gold industry also emerged as is obvious from the presence of ninety or so lunulae and close to twenty discs. As already noted this abundance of gold is highlighted when one takes into account that all the Wessex gold objects could have been manufactured from the equivalent of a couple of lunulae. Some of the products of this industry were welcomed abroad, or influenced external developments, not only in Britain but further afield, in south Scandinavia and middle Germany. Assuming that Classical lunulae are Irish in origin and manufacture, then those examples that have been found abroad should have been exported. But there are only three definite examples, all from Cornwall. Two other examples have been given a Scottish provenance. The 'Monzie' example is almost certainly a modern import (Eogan 1969, 119, f.n.4) and that may also be the case with the 'Ayr or Lanark' example (Wallace 1986). As Taylor (1985, 190) has pointed out the latter lunulae and an example from Co. Galway are so similar that they "might have come from the same Classical workshop". There are four other Scottish finds but all belong to the Provincial variety as does the single Welsh lunula, which comes from Caernarvonshire in the north-west, opposite Co. Wicklow.

The Irish Sea was now an active transport waterway, providing a transit route in and out of Ireland and also facilitating wider trade that extended from the south of Ireland to Orkney in the far north. Despite their association with a spacer-plate amber necklace the Knowes of Trotty discs can, due to their size, be best paralleled in Ireland. There was also influence from Scotland on Ireland. This is shown by a decorated spacer-plate jet necklace with disc-shaped beads from Rasharkin, Co. Antrim (Jope 1951) and also the necklace of fusiform beads found with a bowl food vessel at Oldbridge, Co. Meath (Coffey 1895), only a short distance upstream from the mouth of the river Boyne. On the other side of the Irish Sea there is a jet spacer-plate necklace from Pen y Bonc, Anglesey (Lynch, 1970, 121). The presence of fusiform beads suggest a Scottish rather than a Peak District-Yorkshire background. The grave contained other objects including two bronze armlets but these have not survived (Lynch 1970, 121–22). Scottish influence is carried further south as the Whitfield (Lisnakill), Co. Waterford, bracelet shows (p. 37). Equally significant from the distributional point of view are the Cornish lunulae finds. Cornwall would have had a special commercial relationship with Ireland in view of its natural deposits of tin, a material that was vital to the Irish bronze industry. But Cornwall may have been of further significance, it could have been a stage on a route from Ireland to the continent or vice-versa, hence the lunulae finds from the Breton and Cherbourg peninsulas.

As far as can be determined, all Continental lunulae are 'Provincial'. The possibility that they might be the primary form has already been raised. On the other hand if their background is in Ireland their external distribution would indicate influence from Ireland. Regardless of their place of origin they provide evidence for cross-channel connections due to the fact that one of the Harlyn Bay (Cornwall) lunulae is identical to one from Kerivoa (Brittany) suggesting either the export from one area to the other or that the craftsman was mobile and worked in different lands (Taylor 1980, Pl. 15). Their distribution indicates wide connections as they occur north-wards in Luxembourg and Hannover. From Luxembourg eastwards are the valleys of the rivers Mosel and Lahn taking one into central Germany. That area also has the headwaters of the river Unstrut which joins the Saale to the south of Halle. While this region was part of the wider Unětice (Aunjetitz) cultural province it was also an area where a most powerful sub-province arose. It was a district that had rich natural supplies of copper and tin and this was a factor in the emergence of a complex characterised by rich graves such as Leubingen and Helmsdorf and the bulky metal hoards from Diskau and Halle-Kanena (Von Brunn 1959, 55–6; 59). As Helle Vandkilde (1988, 133) stated these finds suggest the presence of prosperous, stratified and specialist societies which owed their economic success to the control of metal resources, production and the distribution of metals and metal objects. This development was directly connected with the metal demands of the peripheries such as south Scandinavia. It could have been this Unstrut-Saale complex that contributed also to the insular Early Bronze Age by providing prototypes for flanged axeheads, halberds and some ornaments such as solid and sheet penannular bracelets (p. 23). In turn the west, especially Ireland, contributed, for long it had been considered that one of the axes in the Diskau No. 3 hoard was insular, possibly an Irish Ballyvalley type. The Butzbach (Hessen) lunula adds to this supposition, for although undecorated it has the proportions of a Classical lunula and as such might even be an export from Ireland.

Conclusions

Gold reflects ostentation in society, a society that had divisions along rank. For the Early Bronze Age that society had a network of foreign contacts, those from Wessex going as far as the east Mediterranean, in addition to Brittany, while Irish contacts reached the rich Early Bronze Age cultures of central Germany and the west Baltic region. In both Britain and Ireland during the Wessex I/Migdale-Marnoch/Frankford-Ballyvalley stages rich societies flourished in different parts but how were they organised and can gold help our understanding of this period? Industrially and ritually these societies represent a continuation of Beaker traditions but in regions such as Yorkshire and Argyll, gold objects were not used. This can be attributed to the fact that gold had to be acquired from outside, and apart from Wessex, communities living elsewhere only rarely had the wealth to acquire it. In England the plaques from the graves at Bush Barrow (Wiltshire), Clandon, Dorset, (all lozenge-shaped), Upton Lovell (Wiltshire) and Little Cressingham, Norfolk (both rectangular) could have continued the Beaker tradition of placing discs in male graves. Discs as such were also used, those from Manton and Wilsford were made from amber but bound with gold. While there is evidence for male chiefs in Wessex, females were also given considerable status after death as the amber necklaces show. This may be due to the fact that they were the spouses of wealthy men or they may have been wealthy in their own right. The wide distribution of burials with jet necklaces and other items of personal adornment in female graves in other parts of Britain, and also male graves with daggers, suggest that in Britain during the Early Bronze Age members of both sexes fulfilled key roles.

A parallel situation may have existed in Ireland. Discs may have been worn by males (the equivalent of the Wessex lozenge-shaped plaques) and lunulae by females. Furthermore, in contrast to amber and jet necklaces, it was not the practice to place lunulae in graves nor, apart from a couple of instances all outside Ireland, do they occur in hoards in association with other types. Perhaps this was due to the fact that their (?female) wearers held public office; with death the lunula reverted to the community for use by a successor, eventually being deposited, sometimes in pairs or in small groups, when the community felt that the time had come to do so. Lunulae may have served as indicators of female authority but the extraordinary thing is that they were not granted the privilege of being buried with the symbol of such authority. In that regard greater privilege was granted to the male who was often formally interred in a well-constructed stone-lined grave and accompanied by grave-goods, the most prominent of which was a bowl-shaped food vessel. This could represent a continuing but now different role for the male in afterlife.

GOLD-WORKING AT THE END OF THE EARLY BRONZE AGE

After the period of the Irish (Frankford-Ballyvalley/Bowl food vessel) stage and the Wessex I stage in England, the use of gold diminished. This is difficult to explain in view of the fact that active cultural complexes flourished in various regions. However, these complexes reflect changes and these were more wide-ranging than an alteration in the nature of personal ornaments. They affected metal production and ritual.

Britain

For this stage the south of England provides the best evidence for gold-working. In Wessex and adjoining areas cremation burials associated with cinerary urns and Aldbourne type cups became standard in burial. Industrially, triangular daggers were replaced by ogival daggers and cast-flanged axes became standard. It was at this time that the earliest spearheads emerged, firstly tanged but soon having an incipient socket which led to the true socket. Daggers, axes and spearheads are frequently found in hoards (Arreton complex), although hoards were not a feature of the core Wessex area (Britton 1963, 284–97). Stone hones, often well-fashioned, were common, while symbols of ritual or authority were represented by stone battle-axes but in a new form, the Snowshill type (Roe 1966, 212). Personal items are represented by bone tweezers, bronze pins with ring-shaped or bulbous beads and the continued use of some amber spacer-plate necklaces but a new type of bead with an east Mediterranean background came into use. This was the segmented faience bead, also found in star and quoit-shaped forms. The introduction of the razor (Class 1, C. M. Piggott 1946, 122–6) indicates beardless males and facial embellishment, perhaps an alternative to the wearing of ornaments. In addition to pottery, there was a small number of cups in other materials – shale, amber and one, or possibly two, in gold. An object from Cuxwold, Lincolnshire, only known from an old illustration, may be part of a gold cup but the unequivocal example is that from a cremation burial at Rillaton, Cornwall (Gerloff 1975, 107, No 195), a splendid piece with corrugated body and flat base, which is also decorated with concentric ridges (Pl. VIII).

Another grave with gold objects that dates from that late stage, despite the fact that the burial appears to have been an inhumation, was found at Lake, Wiltshire. In addition to the four plain gold discs which constituted a double set it contained an incense cup, bone and stone beads, parts of a spacer-plate amber necklace, amber pendants, an awl, a flat riveted knife dagger and faience beads (Piggott 1938, 105, No. 67, Pl. 10 top). The discs lack parallels, in size they fall into two pairs, one pair being 2.5 cm, the other about 8 mm in diameter. Despite the fact that gold ornaments were rarely placed in graves, this does not indicate a wholesale impoverishment of society. There were a number of well-furnished graves, such as Wilsford G23, which had a well-finished whetstone, bronze crutch-headed pin and two daggers. The Wessex II-Arreton stage was, therefore, a time of continued prosperity. It received types from afar but also contributed to adjoining regions as is demonstrated, for instance, by the earliest socketed spearheads and ogival daggers (Britton 1963, 284–97). Industrially it was a time of considerable innovation as the emergence of the earliest spearheads show. Collared and other urns predominate throughout Britain, as well as in Wessex, and so also did some further relevant types such as battle-axes of the Snowshill variety. Outside the south of England, contemporary gold objects were rare and in the main Wessex gold-working did not influence regions to the north. A fragment of sheet-gold with two incised lines parallel to the edge was found with a collared urn of Longworth's secondary series and a centrally perforated lozenge-shaped bone button, in a cremation grave at Pendleton, West Riding of Yorkshire (Longworth 1984, 220, No 835). In Scotland, the two discs from Broughty Ferry, Angus have a band of decoration close to the edges consisting of dots, grooves/ridges and notches. They were found in a cist associated with a flat riveted knife-dagger (Gerloff 1975, 165 No. 285). The latter closely resembles that from Lake and the discs also share some resemblance to the Lake discs. Apparently of contemporary date were the gold dagger pommel mounts which were found in graves on Collesie (Fife), Skateraw (East Lothian), Blackwaterfoot (Arran) (Henshall 1968, Nos. 6, 8, and 5, Fig 42) and Monkie, Angus (Taylor 1980, 49, Pl. 28 a–f). The two former were associated with daggers that were related to, or connected with, daggers of the Masterton type, which in the main appears to have been contemporary with Wessex I. The Blackwater piece was with an ogival dagger (Gerloff 1975, Nos. 84, 83 and 227) and the Monkie piece accompanied a cremation in a pottery vessel of uncertain type, either a cinerary urn or a food vessel.

Ireland

Parallel developments were taking place in Ireland. A changed industry emerged – the Omagh Phase, named after a hoard of double-piece stone moulds (Herity and Eogan 1977, 153, Figs. 57–8). This was based on casting bronze objects in double-piece stone moulds and amongst the objects were spearheads (tanged and the early socketed forms), Class 1 razors, ogival daggers and flanged axes (Derryniggin type). The working of flint continued as the well-fashioned plano-convex knives show, while in stone the battle-axes of the "Bann" type display a refinement in workmanship and skill in the art of fashioning and polishing. In dress the buttoned garment was replaced by the pinned cloak and the use of a belt. In this connection it should be recalled that a bone belt ring with plain shaft and a bone pin with perforated head was found with a vase-shaped food vessel in a cremation grave containing the remains of an adult male, a female and a child at Labbamolaga, Co. Cork (O'Kelly 1950). A change in burial ritual also took place with urns usually inverted over the cremation deposit, thereby becoming containers. The number of varieties of pottery vessels increased considerably – amongst these were urns of the collared, cordoned and encrusted classes but also vase-shaped food vessels, enlarged food vessels and pygmy cups. During this time there was a change in the use of ornaments, those in gold went out of use but the prestige that they would have conveyed could, at least to some extent, have been replaced by necklaces of segmented faience beads and by bone pins of the ring and T-headed varieties but more especially by stone battle-axes, in particular those of the "Bann" type, and by the transference or continuation of angular art designs to the axes which were now flanged. Mundane objects from graves, like stone hones and Class 1 razors (Kavanagh 1991) may also have had a symbolic role. The large number of burials clearly show that ritual remained a prominent feature, furthermore, some indicate that the graves were those of prominent persons. For instance, Burial XVI at Mound of the Hostages, Tara, Co. Meath contained a collared urn, a vase-type food vessel, a bronze dagger, triangular in shape, with a riveted butt, a battle-axe of Bann type and a small ferrule of bone (Kavanagh 1976, 350, No 36). There was an enlarged food vessel alongside which was also inverted. The same site produced another rich burial, the inhumed remains of an adolescent male 14–15 years of age about 1.50m in height and of sturdy build. This youth wore a necklace consisting of one large biconical-shaped jet bead, five amber beads (one disc-shaped piece being larger than the rest), eight tubular bronze beads and four segmented faience beads. Near the foot there was a simple bronze knife and a piece of bronze that might be part of an awl (Ó Ríordáin 1955).

The multiple necklace may provide a parallel for the necklace from Cruttenclough, Co Kilkenny. This consists of various gold beads, three tubular, four which tend to be barrel-shaped but longitudinally perforated for stringing, seven biconical which are decorated with cross-hatching and have holes for longitudinal suspension and thirteen or fourteen amber beads (Armstrong 1933, 41, 90, Pl. 14: 242). However, it is not possible to date the Cruttenclough piece accurately as it has elements that can be paralleled in the later Beerhackett-Taunton phase (biconical gold beads), while tubular beads are known from Late Urnfield contexts such as those forming part of a composite necklace from Blanot, Côte d'Or, France (Thevenot 1991, 60–4). Returning to gold, a cist grave on Topped Mountain, Co. Fermanagh contained the remains of a male. This was accompanied by a vase-shaped food vessel and triangular-shaped dagger, the pommel of which had a ridged mount made from gold like the Scottish pieces already described. Like those, it also had a high tin content (Hartmann 1970, 30) while the presence of the earlier form of dagger in association with a later vase-shaped food vessel suggest a similar stage to that represented by the Collesie and Skateraw burials.

Despite the virtual absence of gold objects, the Omagh phase was important as it constitutes a new stage of the Bronze Age. It borrowed from both Wessex and Scotland and during this phase an active and novel metal industry emerged. Prestige objects still featured, principally the stone battle-axes of the Bann variety and some rich burials showing the presence of wealthy individuals in society.

Chapter IV

Gold-Working in an Age of Cultural Transformation: *c.* Thirteenth-Twelfth Centuries

CONTINENTAL BACKGROUND

These centuries are being taken as a central date but it should not be assumed that all the gold types discussed in this chapter were exclusively used during a single century or so. This stage of the Bronze Age is termed Late Tumulus–Bronze Age D in west-central Europe while in the north of Europe the term used for the corresponding stage is Late Period II–Period III. However, as cohesion existed between the complexes of those two areas a term that would reflect is more appropriate. Accordingly the term Milavče-Trundholm stage is proposed. This was a time of major changes not only in the centre and north but throughout most of Europe. From the industrial and metallurgical points of view this period was characterised by a major expansion in production, by greater efficiency in distribution, by the emergence of novel types and techniques (including sheet-gold and bronze work often highly decorated by new motifs such as concentric circles) and by prestige goods and wealth objects. In particular in central and northern Europe the use of the four-spoked wheel for vehicles, both two-wheeled and four-wheeled, and the greater use of the harnessed horse revolutionised transport, thereby facilitating long distance communication and the dissemination of objects. It was probably these improved methods in transport that were the most revolutionary of all but horses and vehicles could also have had a role as status symbols. While local inventiveness was a feature, nonetheless, both central and northern Europe were enriched from the Mycenaean world. This included body armour, the technique of sheet-bronze working and probably improvements in transport vehicles. On the other hand, items such as Class IIa flange-hilted swords, flame-shaped spearheads and vase-headed pins indicate "barbarian" contributions to the Mycenaean and east Mediterranean area. The central European region was in the forefront of developments (principally Bohemia, Slovakia, Austria, Bavaria). This is reflected not only in changed and new types of metal objects but by ritual changes also. To quote Christopher Hawkes (1981, 123) there was a change to a "more supernatural conception". Cremation now became the predominant burial rite, while in some areas, in particular Slovakia, large and elaborate burial mounds were constructed. Not only were such burials as those of Čaka and Očkov impressive, the graves contained a rich array of goods (Točík and Paulík 1960). The Čaka grave in particular clearly indicates the presence of a warrior element. These burials were only part of wide-ranging changes that affected different parts of continental Europe. An important new element was sheet-bronze working, a technique that led to the production of a range of new types – buckets, cauldrons, cups and other bronze vessels and also body armour, helmets and shields (Von Merhart 1969, 280–379, 111–47; Schauer 1978, 1982; Hencken 1971). Art styles were also changing, the boss and multiple concentric circles replacing the running spiral. Most relevant from the point of view of the present study is the fact that an expansion in gold-working also took place. Grandiose items, especially those made from sheet-gold, appeared and most were embellished with decoration.

For Britain and Ireland two areas are relevant – west central Europe (in particular the region embracing the adjoining parts of Austria, Bavaria, Bohemia, Slovakia and Hungary) and the west

Baltic region. In both of these areas there is a long history of gold-working going back to the beginning of the metal age but it is difficult to cite the immediate background to its rise, which took place at a time that is traditionally called the end of the Middle and the beginning of the Late Bronze Age. In neither of the areas can one isolate clear-cut prototypes, however, these can be cited from outside their respective regions but at an earlier date. Back around the middle of the millennium, centred in Transylvania, was the rich and brilliant Otomani culture, especially its Hajdúsámson Horizon (Gimbutas 1965, 200–18; Mozsolics 1965). This culture was characterised by defended settlements, large-scale metal production (including gold, scarce before but now in abundance), pottery vessels, four-wheeled wagons and harnessed horses. A principal feature is the elegance of its artifacts, whether in pottery or metal and their lavish decoration which probably owes something to Mycenaean Greece during the Shaft-grave stage. In gold-working both bar and sheet was used and there was a variety of objects including pendants, bracelets, discs and apparently vessels. This complex has all the background components for the west-central and north European thirteenth century gold schools but there is a problem about the chronology. From around the middle of the millennium, coinciding with the rise of the Tumulus cultures to the west, the Otomani weakened and that leaves a gap of more than a century at least. However, it does appear as Gimbutas has pointed out that in some areas, notably north-east Hungary and north-west Romania, the Otomani lingered on as the Felsöszöcs–Suciu-de-Sus group. Corroborative evidence comes from the cemetery of Strede nad Bodrogom in Slovakia (Chropovský, Dušek and Polla 1960, 299–350). These groups were poor descendants of the classical phase but yet could they have been strong enough to enrich the late Tumulus culture to the west? Chronologically this seems impossible, unless there was sufficient strength within the late Otomani to sustain elements such as gold working and transport including horse-drawn wagons. For unexplained reasons the Czech and Slovak region was becoming a focal place. This is suggested by the elaborate burials at Čaka and Očkov and by new items such as sheet-bronze objects. Although only known from models, wagons with four-spoked wheels were in use, that from Milavče, Bohemia with its miniature sheet-bronze cauldron is most relevant.

Coupled with all of this was a rise in gold working. What seems to be the earliest evidence is provided by finds from burials, dating to the late Tumulus period (Bronze Age C2) from the Pilsen area of Bohemia (Čujanová-Jílková 1975; 1970, 52–3, 62–3, 85–6, 123–4). These include decorated gold discs, either domed or flat and averaging 10 cm in diameter, from inhumation graves and one cremation (Nová Hůt), all were probably male burials. The Sedlec Hůrka disc has bosses surrounded by running spirals, on the Milínov-Javor and the Nová Hůt' discs the bosses are surrounded by triple concentric circles with a meandering line curving around them. The ornament on the Zelené disc is the most elaborate of all. In addition to concentric circles, rows of bosses and ridges occur on all discs. The ornamentation recalls the decoration on discs and other gold objects of the Hajdúsámson horizon as well as on objects of bronze, bone and pottery. In form and decoration the disc from the Early Bronze Age hoard from Orolik, in the Zagreb region of Croatia (Majnaric-Pandzic 1974) provides a close parallel. The meandering decoration on the Milínov-Javor and Nová Hůt discs and the running spirals on the Sedlec Hůrka piece stand closest to their presumed Carparthian prototypes but with Zelené assuming the style of the later Bronze Age, that soon became common in west-central Europe as on the disc from Mühlau in the Austrian Tyrol and also in the west Baltic lands of northern Europe (Fig. 14). Other items, however, need not have had their origin in the east-central region, for instance, the diadems recall Mycenaean pieces but of an earlier Shaft-grave date. Local development also created rectangular-shaped plaques and bands but the most striking innovation of all was the cone, three examples of which are known (Schauer 1985; 1986; see Pl. IX). These and the other gold objects clearly demonstrate new features both in manufacture and in decoration. The most easterly cone from Ezelsdorf near Nürnberg is 88.5 cm in height; it has one hundred and fifty five zones of ornament and in applying its repoussé decoration up to twenty different types of punch could have been used (Schauer 1986, 27–9). The cones, which must have served as cult objects, represent the pinnacle of gold working, not only due to the difficulty of manufacture

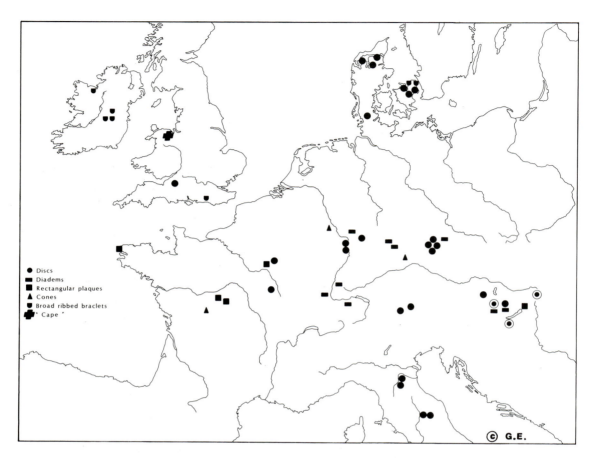

Figure 14. Distribution of gold discs, diadems, cones, plaques, cape and broad-ribbed bracelets mainly of Late Tumulus-Early Urnfield (late Period II-early Period IV) date. (Discs after Eogan, 1981a, with additions).

as a result of their shape but also to the lavish repoussé decoration and in particular the height of the Ezelsdorf piece. It is, therefore, clear that from a little before 1300 or so a revitalised gold industry emerged in central Europe and to the west of it. Objects in sheet-gold are the most spectacular but bar-gold was used for bracelets.

Gold ornaments were not particularly favoured by Early Tumulus culture people, or even by the inhabitants of the previously rich areas of the Carpathians, now represented by the Forró-Ópályi horizon (Mozsolics 1973). Its leading types, bracelets with broad body and double spiral terminals and penannular bracelets with body of lozenge-shaped cross-section tapering to the ends, are much less refined than those which went before but they are much more international in distribution. Gone were the splendid and elegant objects of the Hajdúsámson horizon of the Otomani culture, including not only objects in gold but also in bronze, pottery, and bone/antler (Mozsolics 1965, 1967). However, as has been pointed out, within the late Tumulus cultures of Bohemia prestige grave-goods were becoming a feature. The discs of the Pilsen area could represent the end of an old tradition or the beginning of a new one (Eogan 1981a, 154); they may have stimulated new developments in gold-working. The Mühlau disc in the Tyrol could be an early descendant with others immediately following (Eogan 1981a, 153–4). Further types, such as diadems, rectangular plaques and cones also emerged (Fig. 14).

Sheet gold-working had now reached a high level of excellence due to technological advances and that applies also to the method of decoration which was generally placed all-over in bands or zones. This was applied by the repoussé technique and for the creation of circles, a die or at least a form of punch was used, such as that from the Stockheim hoard, Bavaria (Torbrügge and Uenze 1968, 248, fig 217; Müller-Karpe 1959, 288, No 52, Taf. 156, also pp 147–9) or Génelard, Saône-et-Loire (Abbaye de Daoulas *Exhibition Catalogue* 1988, p. 37, Pl. 4.01, 20–49). The sheet would have been beaten from one side into the depressions on the die and this would have produced a very regular motif. In other cases an individual tool was hammered along the surface to create motifs in relief on the opposite face. On some objects the decoration consisted of only one motif such as a concentric circle which was placed in a band but the combination of several motifs is more common; these include circular bosses, lenticular-shaped bosses, plain ridges, decorated ridges (transversely notched), zig-zags, lines or zones of punch marks and above all concentric circles, which replaced the running spiral. The skilful manufacture of sheet-gold and its decoration led to the creation of a series of remarkable objects. Some, the Mühlau disc for instance, are small but gold was also used expansively as is demonstrated by the diadem from the Velem-Szentvid hoard in western Hungary (Mozsolics 1950, 7–8, Taf 1) which is over 30 cm long or the previously mentioned Ezelsdorf-Buch cone, Franconia, which is almost 1 m in height. This newly-emerging craftsmanship in sheet-gold and its ornamentation is what has been termed the "diadem-vessel" style (Eogan 1981b, 361–3). In the broad sense of the term it is a west European style, west of a line from the river Oder to Budapest. In west-central Europe it emerged at the end of the Tumulus period (Bronze Age C2) or the beginning of the Later Bronze Age (Bronze Age D). The production and use of flashy golden pieces during this innovative age were just part of far-reaching developments that affected central, northern and western European society as a whole. These changes included an increase in metal produc-

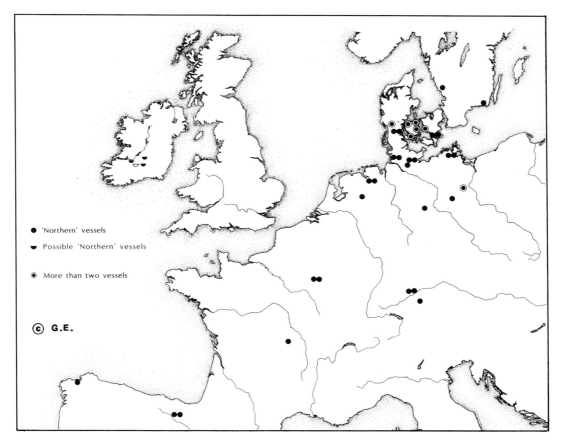

Figure 15. Distribution of 'Northern' gold vessels of the Later Bronze Age.
(After Eogan, 1981b, with modifications).

tion and its associated crafts and also in ritual, as the alteration in burial practices testify. As already mentioned, the use of the traction horse and the four-wheeled wagon (possibly also the two-wheeled cart) revolutionised transport and facilitated trade, exchange and the spread of goods. It is clear that west-central Europe had now become a focal point for gold-working but this was only part of wider changes that were taking place, amongst them was the emergence of a new cultural complex, Bronze Age D.

Although Period II, in the north of Europe, had a number of well-furnished burials, changes that took place at a time coinciding with its end and with the emergence of Period III initiated even greater richness. In view of the similarities in types and in gold-working techniques, the changes can be attributed to direct influence from the centre of Europe. This is shown by the presence of model wagons similar to that from Milavče (p. 43). Such wagons carrying a miniature sheet-bronze cauldron have been found at Peckatel in Mecklenburg and Skallerup in Zealand (*cf.* Piggott 1983, 114–15). But the most famous of all is the bronze vehicle model from Trundholm, Zealand. This consists of a harnessed draft horse mounted on a four-wheeled frame and drawing a highly decorated gold foil-covered bronze disc that is mounted on a two-wheeled frame. Although precise dating is difficult a remarkable cist burial found under a cairn 70 m in diameter at Kivik in Scania, southern Sweden, can be considered as an equivalent in the south of Sweden of the late Mycenaean chariot krater or in the words of Henrik Thrane (1990, 169) a "northern equivalent of the Hagia Triada sarcophagus". The grave was a slab-built cist with decoration on the inner faces of the slabs. Amongst the scenes represented is a cart with four-spoked wheels and a driver, drawn by two horses. Rock-art, such as that from Frännarp, Sweden (*cf.* Thrane 1990, Fig. 8) provides further evidence for land vehicles (carts) while water travel is demonstrated by the engraving of boats or barges. All emphasise the importance of transport.

The Trundholm disc has parallels in half a dozen discs from Denmark (Eogan 1981a). It is possible that in origin the discs represent a development from the earlier circular bronze belt-plate which involved a modification in form and decoration, plus the application of an overlying gold sheet. However, this does not appear to be so as there are differences. For instance, discs lack the prominent central projection; and belt-plates were only placed in female graves whereas discs occur in male graves. Such graves are amongst the richest of their class; in the Danish area most are coffin burials, indicating pomp and ceremony at burial (Eogan 1981a, 155–6). Discs do not occur in isolation; in the two core regions, the Danish area and west-central Europe, they are found in graves but on the southern and western fringes (except for Lansdown, England) they occur in hoards. At least in the Danish area the burials suggest wealthy and powerful males with the discs, which have a much larger diameter than those of central Europe, having a wider function as symbols of a new ritual, as is demonstrated by the Trundholm example.

Other emerging gold types were bowls and ladles but in contrast to the discs these are rarely found in graves or as single finds, the general practice was to deposit the bowls as hoards in pits on dry land, usually associated with other bowls or gold personal ornaments. Therefore, the discs can be considered as personal objects but the bowls could have had a communal function. For the manufacture of the bowls and ladles the gold-working technique must have had its background in central Europe but in view of the concentration in south Scandinavia–northern Germany with over sixty examples spread through the Late Bronze Age, the North must have been a manufacturing centre. Each is a splendid example of sheet-gold craftsmanship in the "diadem-vessel style". Other gold objects current were bar bracelets, especially the penannular forms with either plain or twisted body.

This was also the time of expansion of gold-working in the Danish area. Out of 426 grave finds of Period II studied by Randsborg (1974) 34 contained gold but in Period III the number had risen to 93. Therefore, gold-working as such is not new in the Danish area but what is new is the appearance of novel types lavishly decorated and using a greater quantity of metal. The leading types are discs, bowls and broad bracelets. The technique of gold production and decoration as well as the motifs are similar to those occurring in west-central Europe. Furthermore, some objects such as discs and model vehicles with four-spoked wheels and cauldrons are shared by both areas. While it is difficult to give chronological priority to central Europe yet, despite the fact that Denmark had lavishly decorated bronze objects during Period II such as the belt-plates, other items notably wagons with multiple-spoked wheels, the use of the horse for traction and the gold bowls indicate outside influence. This may have come from central Europe but did the North of Europe receive independent influence from the Carpathian area? Direct influence from that area is nothing new for Denmark, it was strong during the earlier Hajdúsámson horizon and gave rise to the Mosbaek group (Hachmann 1957, 147–50), contacts may have been revived which explain the beginning of gold bowl manufacture in the north of Europe. Mozsolics (1964, 1965–66, 48 Taf 12 (Biia), 56–7 Taf 4–10 (Bihar)) has assigned the Bihar and Biia cups to the Hajdúsámson horizon. Comparing the range of types in the North with that in the Centre it does appear that it was the latter, rather than the Carpathian region, that influenced the former.

INSULAR GOLD OBJECTS

Ireland and Britain received influences from types that originated in both the centre and north of Europe. These include bronze objects, principally ornaments and tools, which form part of the southern English Beerhackett ('ornament horizon'/Taunton) phase but objects in gold also occur. The closest part of the continent is north-western France and in that region, especially in Brittany, there are numerous finds of both individual gold objects and also associated finds in hoards. Amongst these are penannular bracelets with solid body of round or lozenge-shaped cross-section and unexpanded terminals, plain or decorated bar-neckrings, bar-torcs and composite rings. In Britain and Ireland the number and variety of gold objects increased considerably over those in use during the Early Bronze Age. There were now up to twelve main types. Neck ornaments, as such, and earrings were again in use but prominent types such as discs are only represented by one specimen, Lansdown. There are now four different forms of neck ornament and within the groups there are varieties. Bracelets are represented by six varieties, while there are two main varieties of earrings. Less prominent items are 'tress rings', ribbed rings, 'finger rings' and composite rings.

Technology and Decoration

In Ireland it appears that there was a change in the composition of the gold used (Hartmann 1970, 22–31; 1979, 221; Raftery 1971b, 102–3). According to Hartmann, gold of his group M was current. This had a silver content of about 10%, copper 1.1% and about 0.16% of tin. This composition differs from the Wicklow gold. Other objects, notably bar-torcs were made from Hartmann's Group OC. The average content of this group is tin 0.28%, silver 16%, copper 6–7% and tin 0.4%. Although Group OC was common during the Dowris Phase, the deliberate alloying of gold with copper probably commenced during the Bishopsland Phase. This point is confirmed by the analytical results of the Moulsford bar torc, Berkshire (Hawkes 1962) which had a high copper content. As has already been commented on, the gold used in the manufacture of those ribbon torcs that have been analysed by Hartmann has been assigned to his PC group, which has a small amount of platinum, averaging around 0.012% but up to 30% silver, 5% copper and 0.03% tin. PC gold with its platinum is typical of the gold used during the La Tène period especially in the Rhineland. This could imply that ribbon torcs date to the La Tène period. Brian Scott (1976) has questioned such an interpretation on the grounds that only a small number of samples were analysed and that it is possible that platinum could occur naturally in Wicklow gold.

Two principal techniques were used in manufacture, sheet-gold and bar-gold but there were also distinctive details of manufacture and decoration, as will become clear from the following outline descriptions of the various types. Sheet-gold was formed by hammering an ingot, as has been the case during the Early Bronze Age. All the objects in this medium were decorated and for this repoussé or incision was used. Distinctive repoussé work is a feature as is clearly

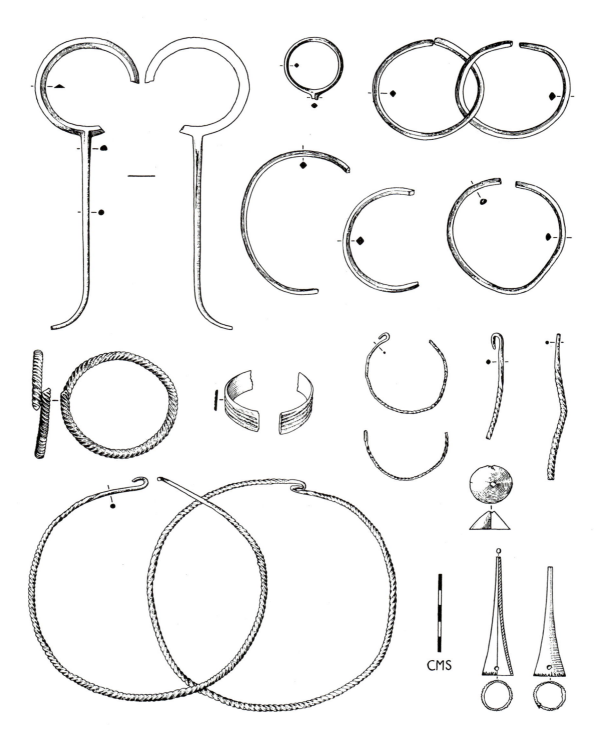

Figure 16. Part of a hoard of bronze objects, Monkswood, Bath, Somerset (Avon)
(After Inventaria Archaeologia G.B. 42 2[1]).

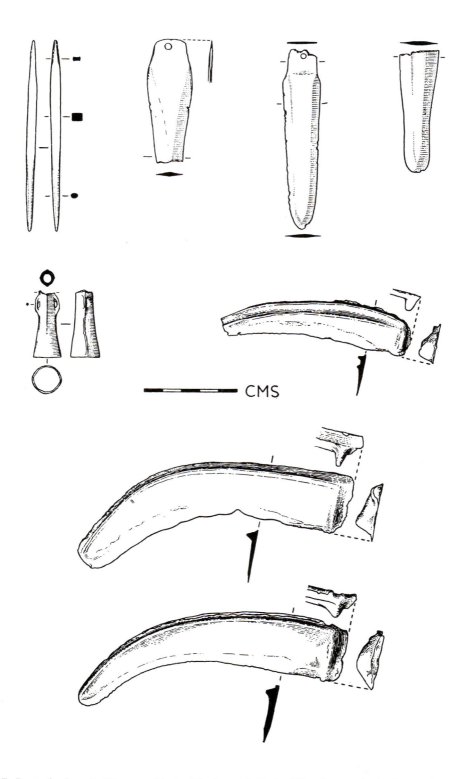

CMS

Figure 17. Part of a hoard of bronze objects, Monkswood, Bath. (After Inventaria Archaeologia *G.B. 2[2]).*

demonstrated on the broad ribbed bracelets, especially those from Derrinboy where, in addition to a hammer, different forms of punches were used to produce elaborate ornamentation, which in the main consists of plain and notched ridges placed vertically or horizontally. To create the plain ridges a blunt punch would have been needed but for the transverse notches a chisel-ended punch was used. For the ornament parallel to the edge, a punch with a finer point came into use. In addition to hammer and punch work, engraving was used. This technique was not widely practised and is mainly found on objects of bar-gold.

In bar-gold work, the object was manufactured by hammering the bar into the required shape. Unfinished bracelets occur in the Towednack (Cornwall), Beerhackett (Dorset), Mountfield (Sussex), Cappeen (Cork) and Derrinboy (Offaly) (in copper) hoards (*cf.* Pls. X, XI; Fig. 27:A,3). Bar-gold objects were also decorated. Twisting the body was the most common method; motifs are rare and when they occur they are formed by incision or engraving. On bracelet No 9 from the Downpatrick hoard No.1, the decoration is confined to the terminals and consists of three incised lines surrounding the outer part of the terminal; on the inside there are three incised triangles, with concentric ornament on the outer face. Excluding the latter design an unprovenanced bracelet from Ireland (Armstrong 1933, 93, No. 411, Pl. 18, 373) has similar decoration. Amongst the bar pieces, the most highly decorated is the Downpatrick neckring with its three main bands of incised ornament, consisting of transverse lines, herringbone shapes and zig-zags (Fig. 29). But the objects with the most delicately formed lines are the 'tress-rings' and the similarly formed bracelets. These have parallel lines which may have been formed by chasing. One of the Tremblestown bracelets has all-over dot ornamentation (Fig. 28:C). The bodies of most torcs (both bar and ribbon), earrings and some bracelets were embellished by twisting. The simplest form is achieved by hammering a bar, usually to produce a square cross-section, and then twisting. The Enniscorthy, Co. Wexford, torc is an excellent example of an untwisted body of square cross-section, while the bracelet from Cappeen, Co Cork is incompletely twisted (Figs. 24:G, 27:A,3). A more complex system was also used involving the beating up of flanges on a bar, usually four, to give a cruciform cross-section and then twisting. This was used on one variety of the bar torc and one variety of earring. In manufacture sophisticated workmanship was used. Some flanged torcs were made in two parts, firstly the body to which the terminal was then attached by inserting it over the end of the body in cap-like fashion and then hammering to secure it (*cf.* Taylor 1980, Pl. 40b). According to Maryon (1938, 208) some of the torcs show evidence for the use of solder.

On the continent twisting has a history going back to the Early Bronze Age (*cf.* Piggott 1965, Pl. 16b). There twisted neckrings of bronze became common during the later Middle and the beginning of the Late Bronze Ages in the north (Kersten 1935, 36–8) but also in the centre and in France (Hawkes 1942, 36, fig 6). In Britain the technique makes its appearance in Beerhackett ('ornament-horizon'/Taunton) contexts (Smith 1959, 149; Butler 1963, 136–144).

The Gold Objects

1. Bracelets: These were the most common type and were made from both bar (i-v) and sheet-gold (vi).

> *Bar bracelets* (i-v) all are penannular and the terminals are unexpanded except for the looped variety (*cf.* Pls. X, XII; 7:2, 4, 5, 9–10). Decoration is rare and when it is present it consists of incised lines or engraved lines as already noted.
>
> i   Plain body of rounded cross-section (*cf.* Pl. 7:2; Fig. 26:A,1–10).
> ii   Same as (i) but the body cross-section is lozenge-shaped (*cf.* Pl. 7:1).
> iii Twisted body of square cross-section (*cf.* Fig. 27:B,2–3).
> iv Plain double body of rounded cross-section, loop at both ends (Fig. 20:2).
> v   Same as (iv) except that the body is twisted (Fig. 20:3).

From published sources, it is not possible to determine the number of gold penannular bracelets with body of rounded cross-section and unexpanded terminals (i) from Britain but they are known from the south of England where they occur in about five hoards with bar-torcs (e.g. Towednack, Cornwall) but also from Scotland, as grave goods at Duff House, Banffshire and single finds from Briglands, Kinross and Bonnyside, Stirling (Pl. 7:1,2,4,5,9,10). In Ireland twenty examples are distributed amongst six hoards with the majority coming from the Downpatrick hoards. According to Armstrong's *Catalogue* there are at least half a dozen other bracelets that are typologically similar and may be contemporary, however, the type was occasionally used during the final stage of the Bronze Age. Bracelets with body of lozenge-shaped cross-section (ii) are rarer, with Downpatrick Hoard I again providing the best evidence. The form with twisted body (iii) is less common, all were made from a square-sectioned bar. The double stranded bracelets both plain and twisted (iv and v) are only known from the Beerhackett hoard, Dorset (Fig. 20:2–3) but related examples in bronze occur in the contemporary hoard from Barton Bendish, Norfolk (Smith 1959, Fig. 3:8).

Sheet Bracelets. These are broad and ribbed bracelets (Pl. XI, bottom, XII, bottom; Fig. 24F) with four examples in gold known from Ireland and one from England. The most elegant is the pair from Derrinboy, Co Offaly. Both are quite similar in form, method of manufacture, decoration and size. The basic form is a rectangle of sheet-gold curved into a cylinder with the ends touching. A flange is provided all around by bending back the edges. In applying the ornament two main techniques were used, repoussé and punching. On the body the area between the flanges is decorated with a series of parallel repoussé ridges. Five are plain and six are embellished with vertical bosses which extend across the ridge. This body decoration is continued within a frame that consists of plain ridges. Between this and the end there is a panel which is formed of three rows of punched dots alternating with plain ridges. The bracelets average 7 cm in height. The other two bracelets are less elaborate. The example from Dysart, Co. Westmeath has recurved ends which form flanges. The ornament consists of seven plain ridges with dots in the hollows in between. The fourth example from Skrene, Co. Sligo is similar in form and ornament except that it has five ribs. The English piece from Mountfield, Sussex is incomplete and consists of part of the body decorated with six ridges. The base of each channel has a row of punched dots (Fig. 21:2). This hoard also contained what appears to have been a fragment of another similar bracelet. Broad ribbed bracelets also occur in bronze in Beerhackett-Taunton contexts, a close parallel is that from Ramsgate, Kent (C. M. Piggott 1949, 120; see Fig. 18). A related bracelet forms part of the Thirsk hoard, Yorkshire (Needham 1990, 257).

Another form of bracelet also has a broad but undecorated body but it has a hook and eye terminal. A hoard of four was found at Capel Isaf, Carmarthen (Savory 1977), a fifth specimen comes from Maesmelan, Radnorshire (Green *et al.* 1983). The Thirsk and Maesmelan hoards each has a penannular bracelet with flat body and unexpanded terminals.

2. Armlets
i.   Plain with solid body of rounded cross-section and unexpanded terminals (Fig. 24:G2).
ii. Twisted body (Fig. 24:E). As it is larger than the twisted bracelets the object from Skelly, Co. Tyrone is being referred to as an armlet. It is loosely twisted from a rod of triangular cross-section but the ends which are plain and straight have a circular cross-section. Another armlet forms part of the Cappeen (Co. Cork) hoard, the surviving terminal is straight and plain. This piece was also fashioned from a rod of triangular cross-section.

3. Neckrings
i.   An elaborate ring but unfortunately incomplete due to damage, comes from the Downpatrick hoard No. 1 (Fig. 29). The body has an oval cross-section, it is thickest

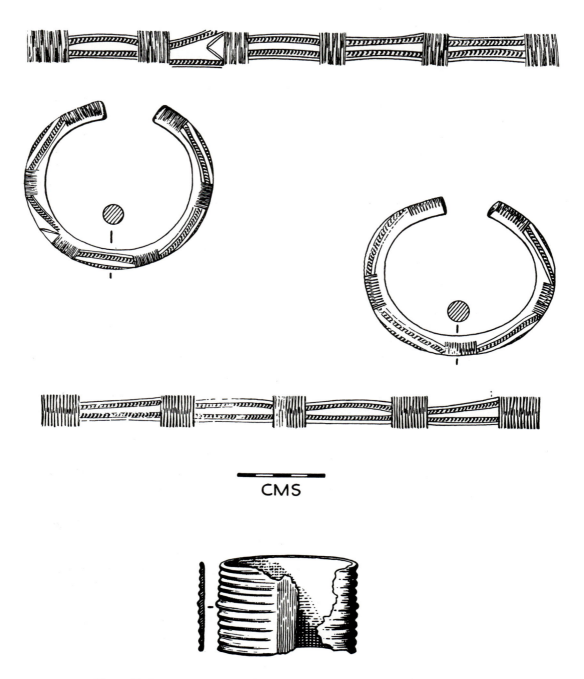

Figure 18. Bronze grave goods from an inhumation burial nr. Ramsgate, Kent.
(After Inventaria Archaeologia *G.B. 48).*

at the middle and tapers to both ends, each of which has a small, solid and evenly
expanded terminal. There are three encircling lines at the base of the terminal and a
short distance in a further three lines. Due to damage one cannot be certain about the
art but from Proudfoot's (1955, Fig. 2) suggested reconstruction it appears that there
was a large central panel with two side panels. The large panel is divided into two
sections of equal length with a very narrow undecorated area in the middle. Apparently
each panel had similar decoration, which was delineated on the inside and outside by

zigzags and on the inside there were four incised lines. The area in between has three roughly equal-sized bands of chevrons separated from each other by two groups of four or five incised lines. Approximately mid-way between this central panel and the terminals there are two further panels each of which is fairly similar to one of the central panels except that it has two areas of chevrons.

A plain unprovenanced Irish neckring which tapers from the centre of the body to the ends, where it expands into small knobs may be related (Armstrong 1933, 61, No 75, Pl. 12: 93).

Two neckrings which are fairly similar to Downpatrick are known from Britain. One, a recent find, came from the other side of the Irish Sea to Downpatrick at Greysouthern, near Cockermouth, Cumbria (information from Dr Ian Longworth). The second piece was found at Ickleton, Cambridgeshire (Longworth 1972). These neckrings may be related to continental decorated neckrings of the Berzocana type, like the gold examples from the Breton hoard of Hinguet, Vieux-Bourg-Quintin, Brittany (Briard 1965, Fig. 46) which date to about the 13th century BC.

ii.   An unusual piece, a composite neckring, forms part of the Derrinboy hoard (Pl. XI, bottom). This object, 94 cm long, consists of a cylindrical leather core, 4 mm in external diameter formed by folding over a strip and then sewing with gut with zigzag stitches. Closely coiled around this was a gold wire of D-shaped cross-section 1 mm wide and 15.25 m in length, it was formed by joining a number of pieces together. Both ends were fitted into a cylindrical-shaped clasp 1.6 cm long and 7 mm in external diameter. Its outer end was closed and externally was surrounded by a low flange. Two opposing holes near the open end probably held a pin which would have secured the ends of the body. The necklet is of special interest technologically providing evidence for the use of leather but in addition as Raftery (1961, 57) already pointed out the manufacture of the wire, altogether 15.25 m long, was an impressive achievement. This neckring is without parallels in Ireland. Its cylindrical fastening clasp, however, resembles the pair of sheet-gold terminals into which were inserted the four body strands of the Moulsford (Berkshire, England) gold bar-torc (Hawkes 1961b, 240–2, Pl. 31a). The two multi-stranded collars from Blanot, France (already mentioned) consist of cylindrical gold beads threaded over a leather core but these are of a later date, Hallstatt B (Thevenot 1991, 60–64).

iii. Ribbon torcs (Figs. 23:B2, 25). These were manufactured by hammering an ingot into a flat band. In general the body is well-twisted but some examples have a loose twist. The width of the body tends to remain constant but the diameter of the torcs can vary from large examples over 21 cm to small examples about 8 cm in diameter. The latter could only have functioned as bracelets. The terminals are bent-back to form hooks at the end. In a minority of cases these are simple but most expand at the end into rounded or truncated knobs. In rarer cases, more elaborate terminals occur, such as four knobbed or disc-shaped as in examples from the Inishowen hoard Nos. 14 and 9 respectively (Eogan 1983a, No 12). Approximately one hundred and twenty-two ribbon torcs are known from Britain and Ireland, the latter has the largest number, sixty-four, from about forty find places. Scotland is not far behind with up to fifty or more, if some old but uncertain finds were ribbon torcs. There, the normal type had a thicker and more rigid body and the simple hooked terminals are more standard than in Ireland. Wales has only one find, a hoard of three from Heyope but there are three finds from Somerset in western England – Eddington Burtle, Wedmore and Winterhay Green – all Taunton Phase/'ornament horizon' hoards. Two were bronze but the Winterhay torc was of gold (Eogan 1983b, 124–26).

iv.   Bar torcs (Pls. VII bottom, X, XI top; Figs. 23–24:G, 28:A). As the name implies, these are made from a bar and consists of a body and bent-back terminals. The body is usually of square cross-section, although bodies of triangular and round cross-section also

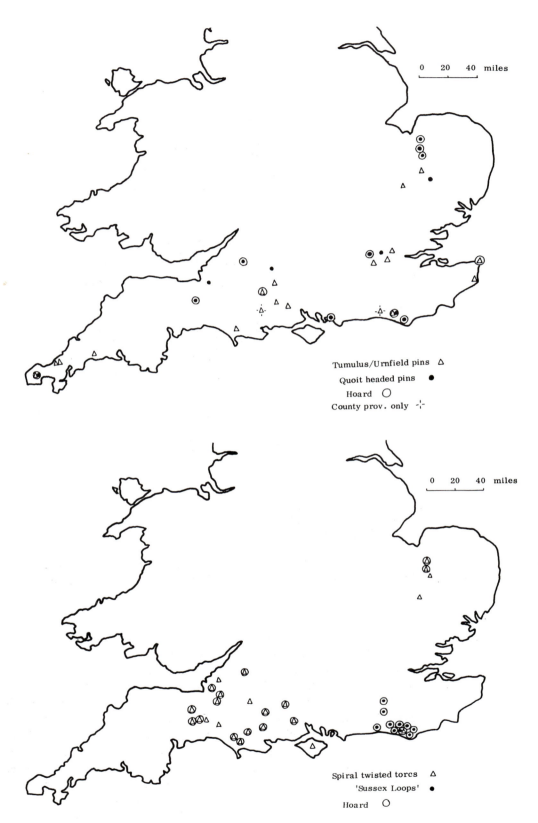

Figure 19. Distribution of Tumulus/Urnfield pins and quoit-headed pins (top).
Distribution of bronze torcs and Sussex loops (bottom). (After Rowlands, 1976, Maps 21–22).

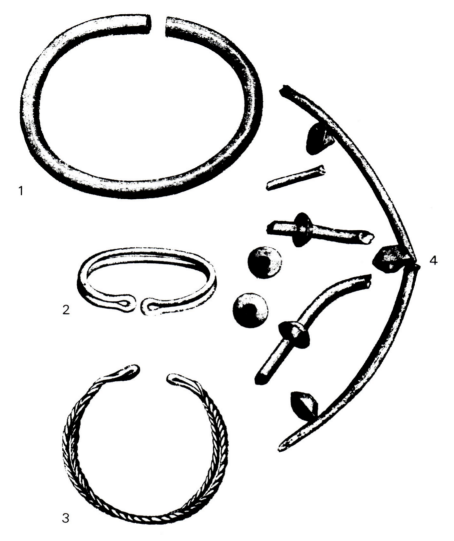

Figure 20. Part of a hoard of gold objects from Beerhackett, Dorset. 3 and 4 are shown at full size. This may also be the case with 1 and 2 but it cannot be conclusively established. (Reproduced from Archaeological Journal, 7 (1850), Figs. A–D).

occur. There are four torcs from Ireland (Aughrim, Co. Galway, Priestland, Co. Antrim and unrecorded localities in both counties Armagh (Fig. 23:A) and Kilkenny, three from England (Aylesford, Chatham and Dartford in Kent and Hill Top Farm near Grantham, Lincolnshire) and three from Wales (Llanwrthwl and two from Tiers Cross), which have bodies of round cross-section. As round bodies could not be effectively twisted they were left plain, except for the two Kent pieces which have apparently transverse or oblique groove decoration. The circular body of the Aughrim torc has a series of longitudinal grooves cut into the surface of the body which was subsequently twisted. The Enniscorthy torc with its body of square cross-section could have been twisted effectively but it too was left plain. This torc gives a good idea of the mode of manufacture, which involved the beating into shape of a bar of gold, the body was then squared off but the ends were rounded and bent back (Fig. 24:G,1). From the junction with the body the terminals thicken outwards. On some examples there is a ridge between the terminal and the body. There are, however, two torcs (Athlone and

Ireland), with terminals consisting of simple hooks. The next stage was twisting the body; in general this was twisted to the right in a clockwise manner. As well as torcs of this bar-twisted variety, there is another but much more elaborate form, the flange-twisted variety. To produce such a torc it was first necessary to provide a plain body preferably of square cross-section. From this flanges were hammered up and to facilitate hammering an elongated groove could have been firstly formed on each face with a chisel. The more splendid examples have four flanges and thus a cruciform cross-section, a smaller number have three flanges. Untwisted flanged torcs – Coolmanagh, Co. Carlow and Co. Down (Fig. 23:B,1) – show the condition before twisting. The terminals have a circular cross-section and reach their greatest diameter at the extremities; they rarely have decoration and when present it is confined to an overall incised

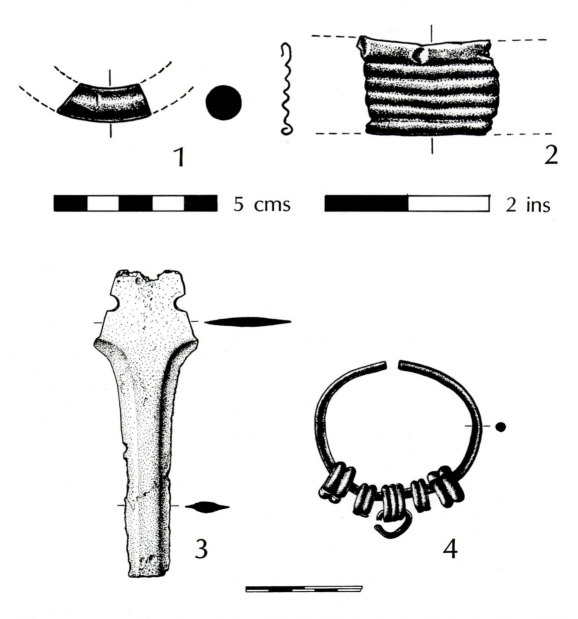

Figure 21. Part of a hoard from Mountfield, Sussex (1–2). Part of the Stretham hoard (3–4). (After Eogan, 1967).

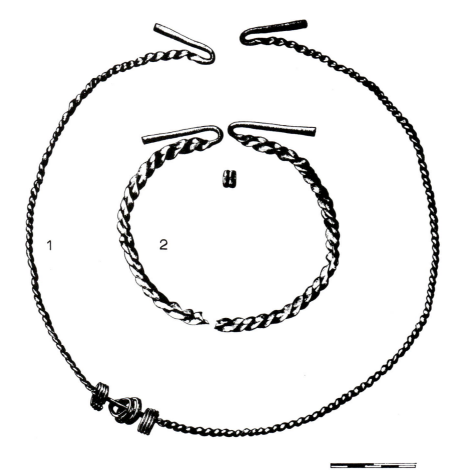

Figure 22. Flange-twisted gold torcs and composite rings from Haxey, Lincolnshire (1), and Boyton, Suffolk (2). (After Eogan, 1967).

herringbone pattern, for example on the terminals of the Co. Mayo torc, or hatched triangles as on a terminal of one of the Armagh torcs (Fig. 23:A).

Thirty-eight bar torcs are known from Ireland and like the ribbon torcs the distribution is concentrated in Leinster and east Ulster. The main area of distribution is a roughly triangular-shaped area of Leinster with its widest part in the coastal region and its apex across the river Shannon in east Galway. The other concentration is smaller numerically, also coastal and extends from Co. Down to north-west Donegal, with a couple of finds from north Connaught. Britain has almost fifty specimens; these are concentrated south of a line from north Wales to the Humber, with only five finds north of this line. The principal continental distribution is in northern France – up the Seine valley to the Paris region, Normandy and Brittany. From central France there is a scatter southwards towards the Mediterranean but the most distant find is down in west-central Spain at Bodonal de la Sierra (Almagro 1974a; Distribution Fig. 32). In the main, bar-torcs would have served as neck ornaments but the torcs found at Tara are so large that they could have been worn as belts around the waist.

v. An unusual gold neck-ring was found in 1857 in the district of Duhallow, Co. Cork (Megaw, 1964). It consists of nine slender rods of triangular cross-section, fused at certain points by a film of gold. At each end they join on to a circular terminal, each consisting of two members similar to the body strands. Megaw discussed the piece in detail but could not cite parallels.

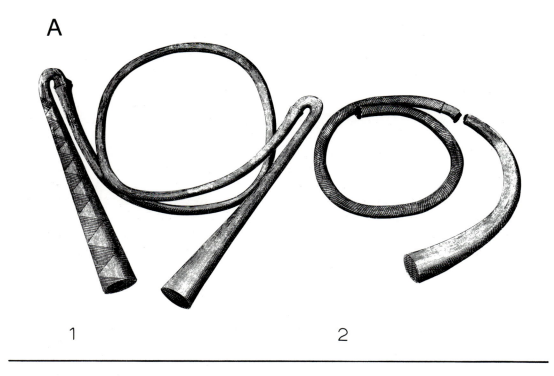

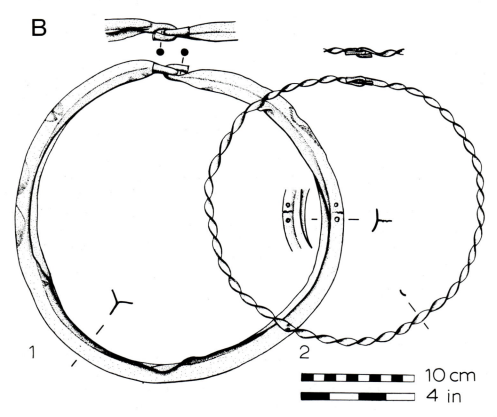

Figure 23. **A.** *Gold bar torcs, Co. Armagh (1–2).* **B.** *Flanged bar torc (1) and ribbon torc (2) from Coolmanagh, Co. Carlow. (After Eogan, 1983a).*

4. Rings

i.   *Composite Rings* (Figs. 21,4; 22) These ribbed rings are common in both England and France (Taylor 1980, 56–7; Eluère 1982, Pl. 172). In England at Haxey (Lincolnshire) and Boyton (Suffolk) they were threaded on to flange-twisted gold bar torcs (Fig. 22), while in the Stretham hoard (Cambridgeshire), which also contained a flange-twisted bar torc, six were threaded on to the associated penannular bracelet with unexpanded ends (Eogan 1967, 149–51, 142–43; Fig. 21:4). Composite rings are rarer in Ireland. An example is threaded on the previously mentioned armlet from Skelly, Co. Tyrone, and there is a single find from Rathfarnham, Co. Dublin (*Archaeological Journal* 14 (1857), 356) and an unprovenanced piece (Sotheby 1990, 55).

The Largatreany and Cappeen hoards have (ii) *small plain rings* with body of rectangular cross-section (Eogan 1983a, Fig 8, A:7 and Fig. 27, A:5). These appear to be unfinished but may have been intended as finger-rings, as were apparently the two interlocking bronze rings in the Bishopsland hoard (Eogan 1983a, Fig 10:13). Spiral or coiled rings resembling Cappeen No. 2 have a wide geographical and chronological spread in Europe (*cf.* Kersten 1935, 55–6; Torbrügge 1959, 78; Catling 1964, 73, 232–34; Jope and Wilson 1957, 79–8).

5. Earrings (Fig. 24:A & B)

These are formed by twisting except for two moulded examples which have a disc in the middle that surmounts a biconical "bead"; each bead decreases in diameter towards the ends (Hawkes 1961a, 472). As Hawkes pointed out earrings of this variety imitate in solid form threaded beads with central disc. Like the bar torcs there are two varieties of the twisted earring, bar-twisted and flanged twisted. Hawkes has drawn attention to the presence of a variety of earrings in the Levantine region, especially Palestine and Cyprus (add Hennessy 1966, 161 to references) amongst which are bar-twisted and strip-twisted varieties. In the latter two strips of gold were bent to a V-shape, each were placed side by-side at the apex, soldered and then twisted. Hawkes put forward the view that these two forms are ancestral to the Irish series but as the west European goldsmiths did not master the complex strip-twist technique they devised a method of imitating it, that was the flange technique. While bar-twisted earrings occur in western Asia, examples are also known from late Middle Bronze Age/Bronze Age D contexts in the Carpathian region (Mozsolics 1973, Taf. 92).

Ireland has about fifteen examples, England a couple, but the greatest number, about twenty, is known from France (Eluère 1982), where there were also good associations in the Lanrivoaré and Carcassonne hoards. The question of origin is further complicated by the presence of bar and flange-twisted earrings in west Africa, notably Senegal, where a gold-working tradition existed from early to fairly recent times (Eluère 1980). As Senegal was part of the French Empire, perhaps some of its gold products could have found their way to Europe as modern collection items, as already remarked (Eogan 1990, 158). It is remarkable how close in form some pieces are, as is clear if one compares the Irish piece from Castlereagh, Co. Roscommon (Fig. 24:B) with that from Senegal (Eluère 1980, Fig 2, f & g).

6. 'Tress'-rings (cf. Fig. 24:D)

While several of these objects could have served as hair ornaments, the Saintjohns pair are large enough (8 cm in diameter) to be bracelets and probably should be considered under that category. They are also made from a rectangular sheet of gold and the bodies were decorated externally by fine lines (p. 50). The Derrinboy, Co. Offaly pair, 3.7 cm in diameter is the more elaborate as the edges have been thickened by hammering (Pl. XI bottom). They are an Irish type without external forerunners unless the Saintjohns, Co. Kildare pair are refined examples of the broad ribbed bracelets (Fig. 27:B,4–5)

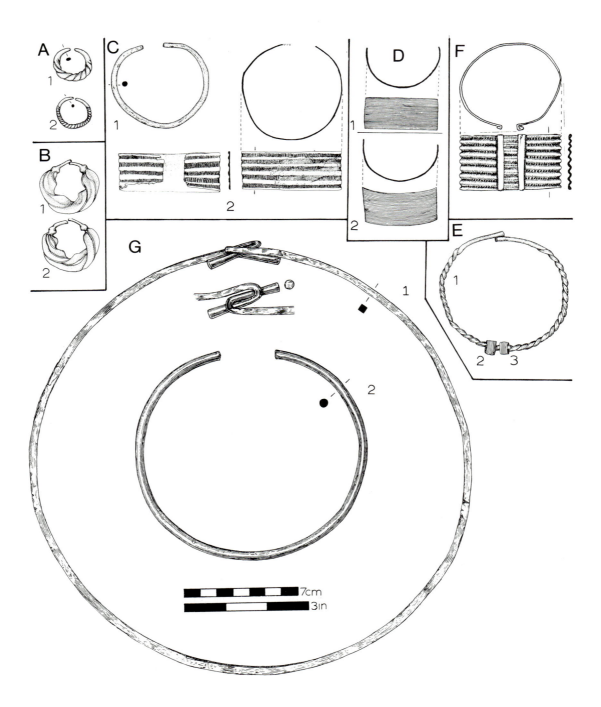

Figure 24. **A.** Bar-twisted earrings from Tara, Co. Meath (1–2). **B.** Flanged-twisted earrings from Castlereagh, Co. Roscommon (1–2). **C.** Penannular bracelet with unexpanded terminals (1) and ribbed bracelet (2) from Clooneenbaun, Co. Roscommon [Both bronze]. **D.** 'Tress-rings' from Co. Tipperary (1–2). **E.** Twisted penannular armlet with two small ribbed rings from Skelly, Co. Tyrone (1–3). **F.** Broad ribbed bracelet from Dysart, Co. Westmeath. **G.** Bar torc (1) and penannular neckring with unexpanded terminals (2) from nr. Enniscorthy, Co. Wexford. (After Eogan, 1983a).

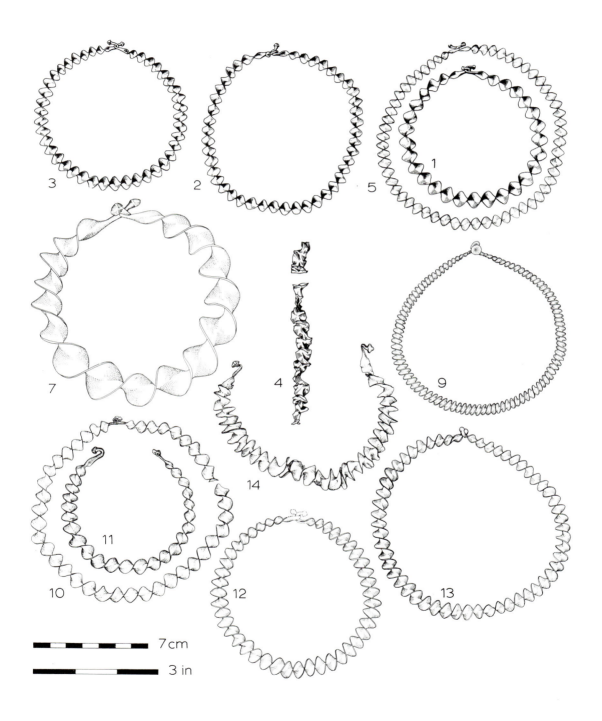

Figure 25. Gold ribbon torcs from Inishowen, Co. Donegal (1–14). (After Eogan, 1983a).

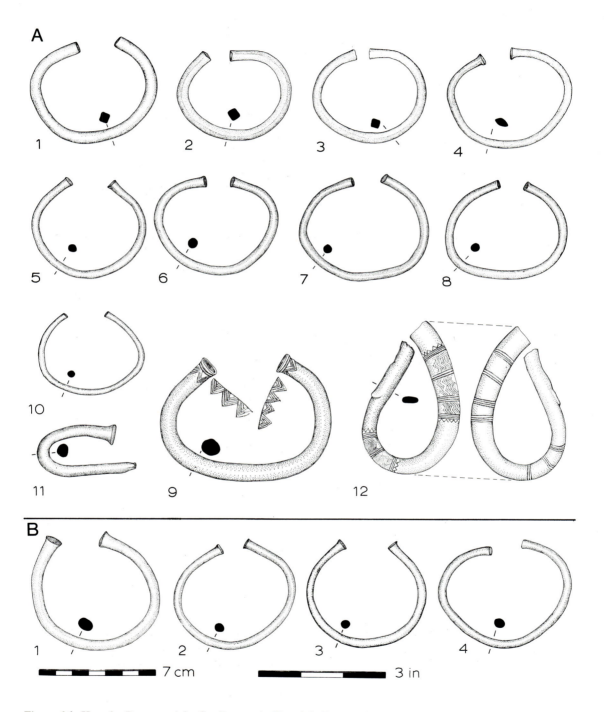

*Figure 26. Hoards. Downpatrick, Co. Down. **A.** Hoard 1. Penannular bracelets with unexpanded and slightly expanded terminals (1–11) and decorated penannular neckring (12). **B.** Hoard 2. Penannular bracelets with solid terminals that are slightly but evenly expanded (1–3) and penannular bracelet with terminals that expand inwards slightly (4). (After Eogan, 1983a).*

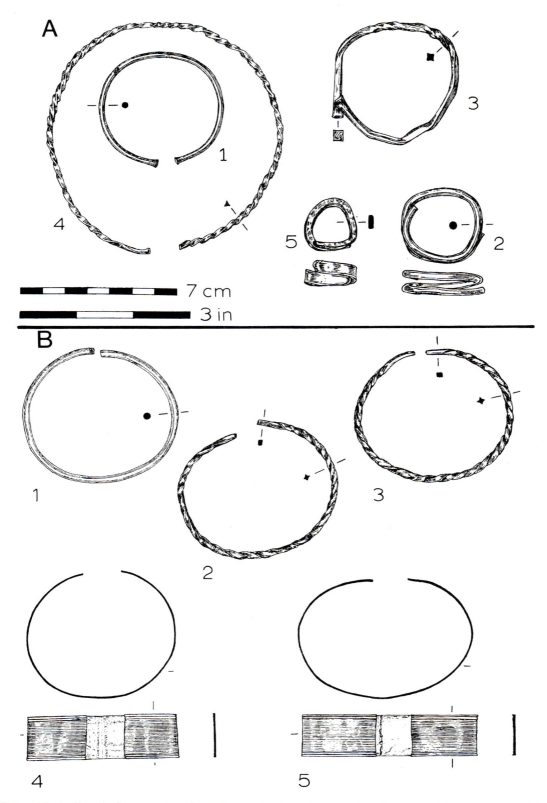

*Figure 27. **A**. Hoard. Cappeen, Co. Cork. Penannular bracelets with slightly expanded terminals (1, 3, latter may be an unfinished twisted penannular bracelet), solid rod (2), twisted penannular armlet (4) and small plain ring (5). **B**. Hoard. Saintjohns, Co. Kildare. Penannular bracelet with unexpanded terminals (1), twisted penannular bracelets or armlets (2–3) and 'tress-rings' (4–5). (After Eogan, 1983a).*

64 George Eogan

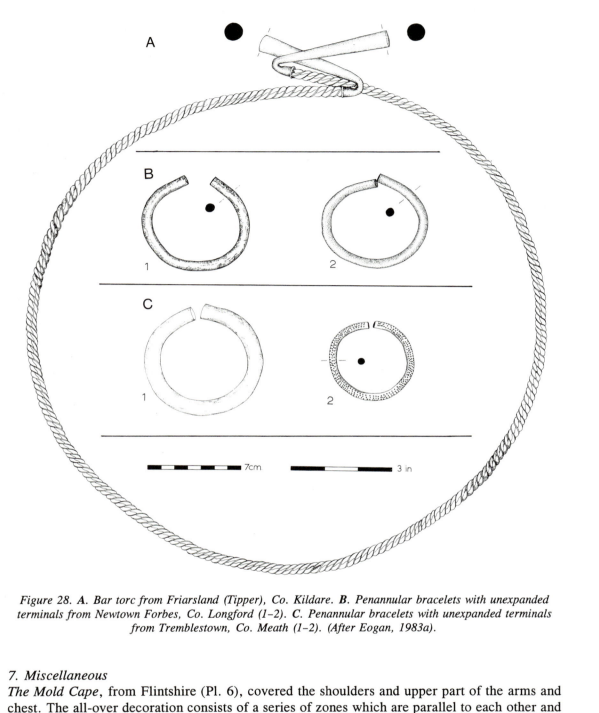

Figure 28. A. Bar torc from Friarsland (Tipper), Co. Kildare. B. Penannular bracelets with unexpanded terminals from Newtown Forbes, Co. Longford (1-2). C. Penannular bracelets with unexpanded terminals from Tremblestown, Co. Meath (1-2). (After Eogan, 1983a).

7. Miscellaneous

The Mold Cape, from Flintshire (Pl. 6), covered the shoulders and upper part of the arms and chest. The all-over decoration consists of a series of zones which are parallel to each other and also to the inner and outer edges. The motifs are confined to plain ridges or rows of bosses; the plain ridges are single except for the neck zone where there are four. The bosses vary in shape between lenticular forms, which are less common, round forms, which occur frequently and square forms which are confined to two rows. The lenticular-shaped bosses do not vary in size from row to row but the round bosses do and relatively speaking there are two sizes, large which always occur in single rows and small where usually there are three rows to a zone. Due to the curvature of the object and to preserve harmony in the overall design, decoration in the lower shoulder area was placed in a D-shaped panel. The cape was attached, internally, to a bronze frame which gave rigidity with the whole mounted on a backing of leather and cloth. The seamless nature of this piece shows that it was beaten from a single ingot – an extraordinary accomplishment (Powell 1954).

Disc (Pl. 5). There is only one example, from Lansdown, Bath (Hawkes 1980). This was made from thin sheet that was mounted on a bronze backing. Unfortunately the object, which was approximately 17.25 cm in diameter, is in an exceedingly poor state of preservation, so much so that the accompanying illustration, originally published in the British Museum *Bronze Age Guide* (1920), Fig. 91, should only be considered as a possibility. The technique of ornamentation is repoussé with all-over decoration. In the centre there is a boss surrounded by a plain ridge with a row of small bosses concentric to it. This motif occupies a mid position within a star-shaped pattern, the outer voids of which are filled with small bosses. The central motif is bounded by a band which consists of a ladder pattern that is flanked on each side by a plain ridge, a similar band is parallel to the edge. The band in between is wider and has boss and circle motifs with bosses in the intervening spaces.

Origin and Dating

As has already been discussed gold-working continued in southern England during the Wessex II stage but much reduced in quantity, elsewhere in Britain and Ireland its use was limited at that time. By the succeeding Acton Park–Killymaddy Phases gold-working, indeed the use of personal ornaments in any media, ceased to exist. This leaves a gap of some centuries, accordingly it is not possible to derive the Beerhackett-Taunton/Bishopsland gold production, despite the presence of such factors as sheet-gold manufacture, either morphologically, technologically, typologically or decoratively from the Early Bronze Age tradition of gold working. It must, therefore, be

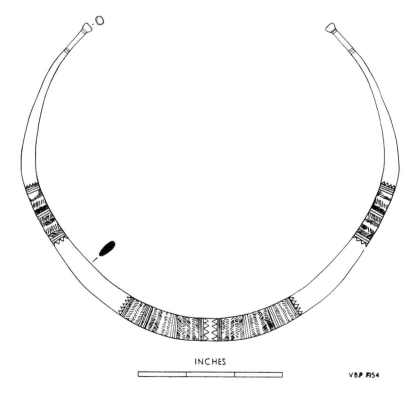

INCHES

VBP R54

Figure 29. Drawing showing possible original form of gold neckring from Downpatrick Hoard no. 1.
See Fig. 26:A,12 (After Proudfoot, 1955).

assumed that thirteenth century gold-working was not the result of native revival but on the contrary the result of external inspiration. To understand it more fully, one has to consider the wider context of late second millennium BC gold-working and also the more widespread use of personal ornaments in continental Europe and the augmentation of techniques (p. 43–7).

In the western parts of the continental mainland, especially Brittany and Normandy, from the middle of the 2nd millennium, there was an active Middle Bronze Age industry. This Tréboul stage was characterised by rapiers, some of which were large and impressive weapons, palstaves, and leaf-shaped, but also some looped, spearheads (Briard 1965, 79–108). In Britain at the end of Wessex II (or its equivalent) a new industry likewise emerged, the Acton Park stage (Burgess 1980, 126–29). In content it is equivalent to the cross-channel Tréboul stage and so is the contemporary Irish industry, the Killymaddy stage (Herity and Eogan 1977, 159–64). As has already been pointed out the 12–13th centuries represent a period of considerable and wide-ranging change that affected most facets of continental society. This involved long-distance and international contacts but above all there were major industrial developments including gold-working. Bronze types and hoards from eastern France such as Porcieu-Amblagniu, Isère (Déchelette 1924, Fig 49, App. i, 63) and Malassis, Cher (Briard, Cordier and Gauchet, 1969) but also graves as at Barbuise-Courtavant (Aube) and Magny Lambert (Côte d'Or) (Eluère 1982, Pls. 138, 149) show that west-central European influences were penetrating westwards, as they had also penetrated northwards, and France too had some remarkable gold finds such as the hoard from Rongères (Allier) close to the upper reaches of the river Loire, with its gold bowl, bracelet with double spiral ends, finger ring and two spiral ornaments of double wire (Eogan 1981b, 374; Eluère 1982, Pl. 157). Further north in the Marne at Villeneuve-Saint-Vistre, there is an equivalent gold hoard with its two vases, two broad undecorated sheet bracelets, three finger-rings, one spiral of double wire and sixteen pieces of round-sectioned wires (Eogan 1981b, 374; Eluère 1982, Pl. 158). Closer to the coast in the Dept. of Vienne at Avanton not far from Poitiers, is the find-place of one of the cones (Eluère 1982, Pl. 128; Schauer 1986, Taf. 10–18). In the west, Brittany became the main area of gold-working. An interesting hoard was found at Lanrivoaré in Finistère close to the Atlantic coast which contained two penannular bracelets with body of lozenge-shaped cross-section and unexpanded terminals, a D-shaped bracelet with body tapering to the closely-set ends, six bar-twisted earrings, a plain 'hair-ring', three pieces of gold bar and two pieces of sheet gold, at least one of which may have been part of a central European rectangular plaque. The other may be part of a ribbed bracelet (Eluère 1982, 259–60, Pl. 171; see Pl. 4, bottom left). Bracelets with solid body of lozenge-shaped cross-section have parallels to the east in the Carpathian region (Mozsolics 1973, 90–101, Taf. 78, 85–8).

A feature of the continental west, especially in the coastal lands of Brittany and western France, is a heavy gold industry characterised by the use of solid bar gold. The gold industry should be considered in relation to wider and intensified developments in Atlantic Europe, not only western France but Iberia likewise. Although the chronology of the Later Bronze Age in western Iberia is not clear-cut, it may be noted that the sheet-bronze vessel in the Berzocana hoard is considered by Schauer (1983, 179–83 Fig. 2 for distribution) to be an eastern Mediterranean type dating to the latter half of the second millennium. It is therefore possible that from before 1,000 BC an increase in industrial activities took place leading to greater metal production including gold. The latter could even have commenced earlier with such objects as those constituting the Caldes de Reyes hoard, Pontevedra (Ruis-Gálvez 1978) being an early manifestation. Hill-top settlement, especially in the north-west, may have been a feature while cultural contacts to the south leading to the Mediterranean existed (Silva 1986). Regarding gold objects the principal types, often found in hoards, are neckrings with body of round cross-section thinning from the centre to the ends (Berzocana-Hinguet type, Kalb 1991; Coffyn 1985, 60, 235–7, Maps 15, 46; see Figs. 30–31) and penannular bracelets with body of round or lozenge-shaped cross-section and unexpanded terminals. Related to the neckrings is another form characterised by the presence of one or two catch-plates (Sagrajas type). Incised decoration consisting of bands of transverse lines, cross-hatching and zigzags occurs (Almagro 1974b; 1977, 17–35). Such decoration resembles that on the bronze bracelets from Brittany and northern France, the Bingen type (Briard 1965, 123–35), which may have a background in the North German Ilmenau complex (Rowlands 1971a, 192–3). Both forms of neckring lack clear forerunners but the Berzocana type may represent the emergence of a distinctive west Iberian neckring but under external stimulus, especially with regard to its art, while the neckring with catch-plates (Sagrajas type) is a more exclusive Iberian form. In addition to the incised art, penannular bracelets may also reflect influence from areas

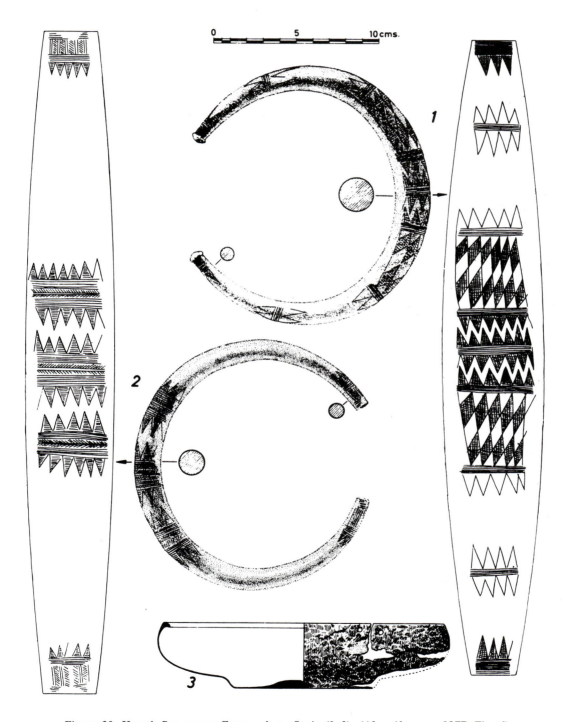

Figure 30. Hoard. Berzocana, Extremadura, Spain (1–3). (After Almagro, 1977, Fig. 6)

Figure 31. Distribution of incised decorated gold neckrings of the Berzocana and related types.
(Based on Coffyn, 1985 and Kalb, 1991, with additions).

to the north, such as Brittany where relevant finds occur in the hoards from Saint-Jean-Trolimon, Saint-Marc-le-Blanc and Roudouallec (Briard 1965, 144–6; Eluère 1982, Pl. 155).

Apparently at this time in different parts of western Europe, in the broadest sense of the term, the wearing of heavy neckrings was becomming fashionable. In the northern zone, Denmark and adjoining regions (also the south of England notably Somerset), bronze torcs became common (Kersten 1935, 36–8) while in the central zone, Ireland, Britain and the north-western France, it was the gold bar torc. While in western Iberia the incised decorated neckring (Berzocana type) was worn. Interchange between the central and southern zones was limited. In Brittany the Hinguet, Vieux-Bourg-Quintin hoard contained neckrings of the Berzocana and related types while the most distant example comes from Downpatrick in north-east Ireland (Fig. 29; see p. 51–53). Likewise, the influence from the north-west on Iberia was also limited, the best evidence is provided by the bar torcs in the hoard from Bodonal de la Sierra, Extremadura (p. 57). Thus, a heavy gold industry became a feature of western Europe but this was in tandem with a heavy bronze industry that also included ornaments, notably bracelets and neckrings.

In the south of England the existing metal industry characterised by palstaves, looped spearheads and Class II rapiers, altered but more importantly it was augmented from the continent by specialist tools and ornaments mainly in bronze, the Taunton Phase or 'ornament horizon' of Butler (1963) and Smith (1959), but also in gold. Amongst those in bronze were twisted neckrings (torcs), ribbed bracelets, penannular bracelets with unexpanded terminals and having either a plain or a twisted body, armrings with incised decoration, ribbed and coiled finger-rings, and stick pins. A new form of razor, tanged with bifid-shaped blade (Jockenhövel 1980, 58–64; C. M. Piggott 1946, 126–8) was also introduced, indicating once again the importance of facial care and grooming. Amongst the new tools, socketed axes indicate improved methods of wood-working and so likewise do the non-socketed sickles for farming. Soon local development took place. The quoit-headed pins were an adaption of the ring-headed pins of the Tumulus Culture, while the "Sussex loop" was a local rendering of the double and hooked bracelet. In addition to objects, new technological innovations such as twisting, were mastered. Hoard deposition was another aspect, old (i.e. palstaves) and new (i.e. socketed axeheads) types are found together and well-preserved objects occur with worn and incomplete pieces. The novel bronzes are mainly found in the coastal counties of southern England (*cf.* Fig. 19) but there are concentrations such as the preponderance of non-socketed sickles, torcs, armrings and hoards in Somerset (Rowlands 1976, Maps 13, 22, 23, 26; see Figs. 16, 17). The continental background varies, for some (Picardy pins and armrings with incised decoration) this is close-by across the channel in north-west France but with an ultimate background further afield to the centre (pins) or north (armrings) of the continent. It is difficult to be precise regarding place of origin of some objects as at this time central and northern Europe shared many types.

There has been a tendency to look on the Beerhackett-Taunton ('ornament horizon') Phase as an autonomous industry, but concentrating on bronzes and not including the gold objects has led to spatial restrictions and to only partial evaluation of what appears to be a unified industry despite the fact that gold and bronze ornaments do not normally occur in association. Even so, both media were utilised, therefore it would seem more appropriate to use a name that reflects this, accordingly the term *Beerhackett-Taunton* industry is proposed. During this stage the greater industrialisation of the south of England which took place was in keeping with the industrialisation of Europe at the time. As already noted the bronze and gold objects have a wide-ranging background – Denmark and northern Germany, west-central Europe, north-western France. In particular, the latter area was indebted to central Europe but it should not be assumed that it showed a peripheral reflection of central European culture. The twisted penannular bracelet is common in the north of Europe but it is also known in France (Eluère 1982, Pl. 112). The broad ribbed bracelet from the Mountfield, Sussex hoard has, as has previously been mentioned, its counterpart in bronze which was found with an inhumation burial in a chalk-cut grave between Ramsgate and Dumpton, Kent, with three (one lost) incised-decorated armlets (Fig. 18). Bronze ribbed bracelets are a fairly common continental type of Tumulus culture ornament (*cf.* Torbrügge

1959, 76) but the background to the Ramsgate grave-goods may be to the north (*cf.* female grave dating to Period III from Deutsch-Evern, Lüneburg, northern Germany, Jacob-Friesen 1963, 275, Abb. 267). As already inferred the double bracelets from the Beerhackett hoard, Dorset seem to be modified versions of the doubled and hooked bronze bracelet as is known from the Barton Bendish hoard, Norfolk (Smith 1959, Fig. 3.8 with pp. 156–8). As Smith pointed out double bracelets are known in Montelius III contexts in northern Europe but they have a wider continental distribution and also a wide chronological span on both the continent and in Britain, for instance an example occurs in the Llangyllog hoard in Anglesey, dating to the end of the Bronze Age (Lynch 1970, 206, Fig. 68,3). Spiral rings could also be due to Nordic inspiration. While the Beerhackett-Taunton industry contains items of north European origin, there was also a strong western French contribution. The contents of the Sporle hoard, Norfolk, two heavy plain penannular bracelets, one of which has a round-sectioned body, the other with body of lozenge-shaped cross-section and part of a twisted object, have parallels across the channel (Pl. 7:1–3). The composite rings also have a French background, as have the bracelets with broad plain body and hook and eye terminals from Capel Isaf, Carmarthen and Maesmelan, (see p. 51; *cf.* bracelets from Belz, Morbihan; Eluère 1982, 90). North-western France also provides the immediate background to the bulk of the incised decoration bronze bracelets (Rowlands 1971a) and the Picardy pins (Hawkes 1942). In the south of England a type common to gold and bronze workmanship is the penannular bracelet with solid body, of rounded or lozenge-shaped cross-section and unexpanded terminals (Rowlands 1976, Map 23, for distribution of bronze examples). This type, as such, has a widespread continental distribution, including the west Baltic area. There are also good associations in Breton hoards, such as that from Saint-Jean-Trolimon, already mentioned, or Lanrivoaré.

For Ireland, the Berzocana type neckring from Hoard I, Downpatrick and possibly the penannular bracelets, especially the heavy piece, could possibly be imports from western France (Briard 1965, Fig. 46). For England the bar neckrings from Ickleton, Cambridgeshire and Greysouthern, Cumbria are in the same continental tradition, the geometric-decorated neckring with small hook terminals from the Isle of Wight may also be related (Rowlands 1976, 240, No. 61, Pl. 17). The multi-stranded, twisted, torc from Moulsford, Berkshire (Hawkes 1961b) is based on other forms of neck ornament which also form part of the Hinguet hoard as Briard (1965, Fig. 47) has shown. As noted, in Britain, Ireland and north-western France a heavy gold industry emerged in its own distinctive way, the most outstanding item being the neck ornament that was embellished by twisting, the bar torc. The distribution pattern indicates that their origin may be insular but it is difficult to pinpoint the precise place. Ireland had natural gold and skilled and inventive craftsmen to work it but southern Britain was closer to the Continent. In form the torc from Carrowdore, Co. Down (Taylor 1980, Pl. 37b) with single hook terminals could, if genuine, be a rendering in gold of the bronze torcs and in addition Ireland has typologically simple torcs with hooked terminals and three flanges that are in form close to bronze torcs. In view of this and of the greater simplicity in manufacture and in form, perhaps they represent initial renderings. As Northover (1989, 120) has pointed out torcs of this form are a "specific Irish type". Perhaps the gold bar torc emerged in Ireland as a copy of the bronze torc, a type, however, that is rare in Ireland but with more elaborate flange-twisted forms developing and having a wider area of use and manufacture that encompassed England and Wales, as well as Ireland, and to a lesser extent France, especially the north-western part (Fig. 32). As this suggestion cannot be conclusively proven a more generalised judgement on the place of origin should be considered, that is that bar torcs came into existence so as to satisfy the need for a stylish neck ornament by wealthy people who were living on both sides of the English Channel and in eastern and north-eastern Ireland. This regional fashion was part of a wider fashion that expressed itself in different ways and in different media in other parts of Europe at about the same time, such as the previously mentioned western Iberian gold neckrings of the Berzocana type and the widespread use of bronze torcs in northern Europe (p. 66–9). It is more difficult to establish the place of origin and chronology of ribbon torcs. The only well-dated examples are those in

PLATE V

Top: Provincial lunula, Auchentaggert, Dumfriesshire. Bottom: Classical lunula, Blessington, Co. Wicklow. Photos: National Museum of Scotland.

PLATE VI

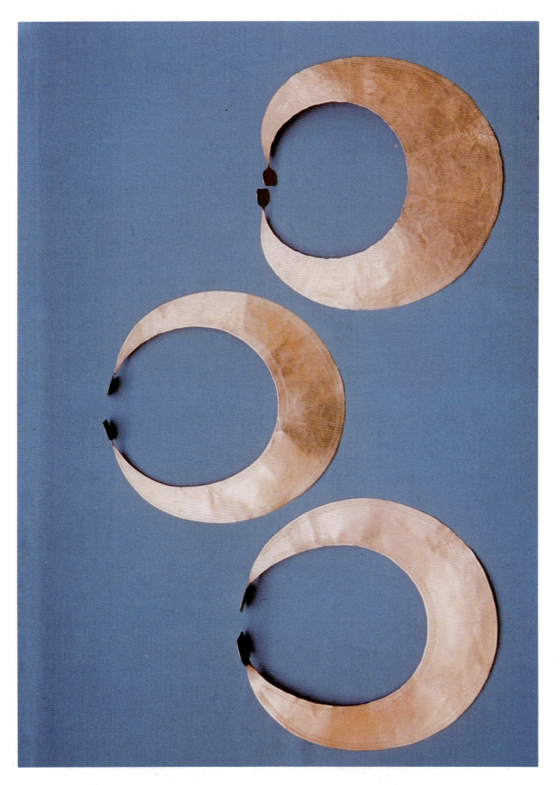

Hoard of lunulae, Harlyn Bay, Cornwall. Photo: Truro Museum.

PLATE VII

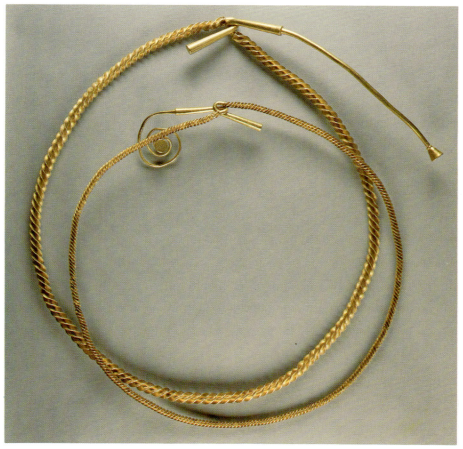

Top: Disc, Tedavnet, Co. Monaghan. Bottom: Bar torcs, Tara, Co. Meath.
Photos: National Museum of Ireland.

PLATE VIII

Gold cup, Rillaton, Cornwall. Photo: British Museum.

PLATE IX

*Cones: Avanton, France (left), Etzelsdorf (middle) and Schifferstadt (right), Germany.
Photo: Römisch-Germanische Zentralmuseum, Mainz.*

PLATE X

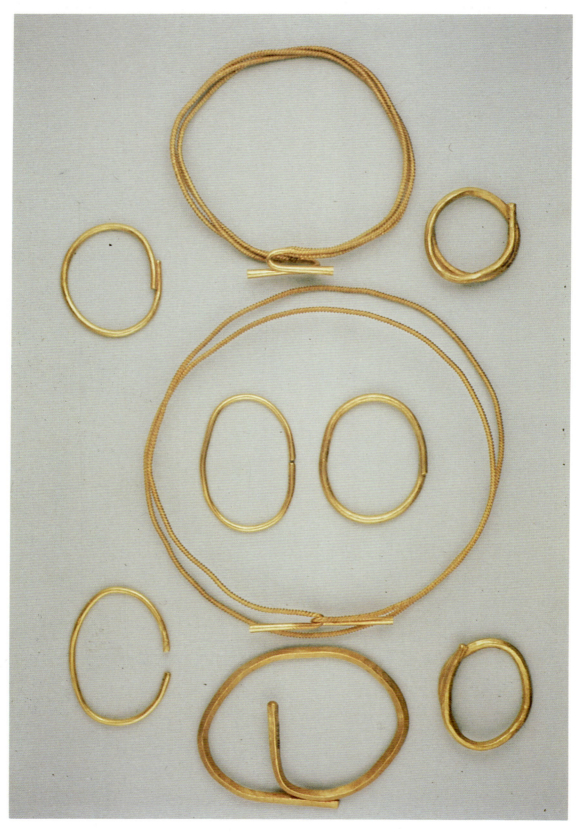

Hoard, Towednack, Cornwall. Photo: British Museum.

PLATE XI

Details of terminals of bar torcs (top) and broad sheet bracelets from Derrinboy hoard, Co. Offaly (bottom).
Photo: National Museum of Ireland.

PLATE XII

Hoards from Saintjohns, Co. Kildare (top) and Derrinboy, Co. Offaly (bottom).
Photos: National Museum of Ireland.

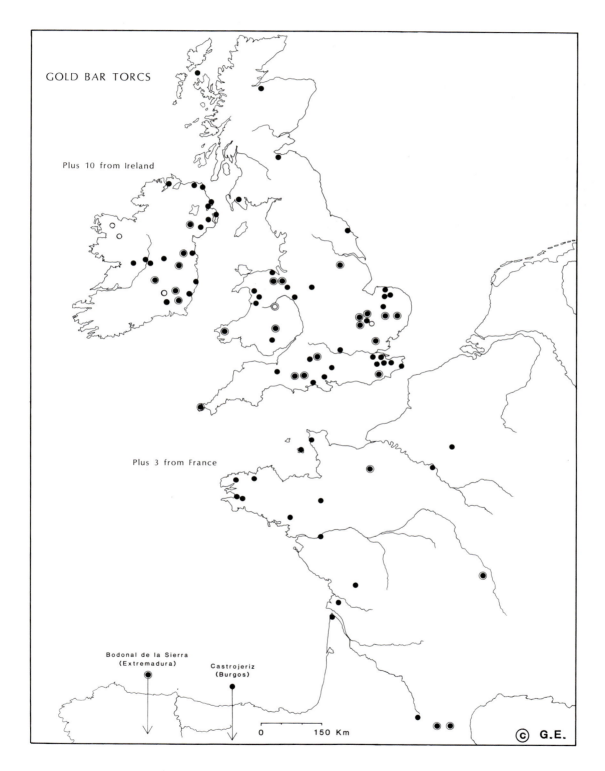

GOLD BAR TORCS

Plus 10 from Ireland

Plus 3 from France

Bodonal de la Sierra
(Extremadura)

Castrojeriz
(Burgos)

0   150 Km

Ⓒ G.E.

Figure 32. Distribution of gold bar torcs. (Based on Eogan 1967, with additions).
(Symbols encircled indicate a hoard; open symbols indicate that only county of origin is known)

hoards of the Beerhackett-Taunton industry in Somerset (shire) England and the Tully, Co. Roscommon (incorrectly attributed to Clonmacnois (Ireland 1992) and Somerset (townland), Co. Galway hoards in Ireland. It is also taken that the Coolmanagh, Co Carlow example was found with the flanged bar torc (Manning and Eogan 1979). The crude ring in the Largatreany, Co. Donegal hoard resembles that in the Cappeen hoard, Co. Cork (Fig. 27:A5) but due to the simple nature of these pieces not much reliance can be placed on them for dating purposes. The fragment of sheet-gold from Largatreany, due to its small size, cannot be assigned to a particular object. It should also be noted that on one of the Heyope torcs, the recurved terminals have a round cross-section that in form resembles terminals on the bar torcs but much smaller. The Tully (Roscommon) and Somerset (Galway) hoards date to the Iron Age but it should be noted that both torcs from these finds have terminals that differ in form from all other examples.

There are only two finds of ribbon-torcs of apparent Bronze Age date from the continent. One comes from near Quimper, the other from Saint-Marc-le-Blanc, both in Brittany (Eluère 1982, 72–3, pls. 87–88). Due to its continental rarity, the type must be considered as an insular contribution. In view of connections between the Beerhackett-Taunton Phase ('ornament horizon') and the Bishopsland Phase, it is tempting to suggest that south-western England was the place of initial development but that is difficult to prove in view of the overwhelming strength of the distribution in Ireland and Scotland (Fig. 33). Perhaps one should look for the origins to those regions, possibly Ireland where gold-working was developing rapidly and other twisted ornaments were being manufactured.

The Mountfield hoard, Sussex, with part of a broad ribbed sheet bracelet, a bar bracelet and possibly a bar torc (Eogan 1967, 151–2, Fig. 6; see Fig. 21:1–2) links the bar with sheet gold work. The two repoussé decorated strips from Geldeston, Norfolk (Taylor 1980, 84), a local invention, are probably of similar date. The most outstanding piece in any part of Europe at this time is the Mold cape (Pl. 6). This piece demonstrates the expansive use of sheet but also lavish decoration very much in keeping with the art and craft of the cones which predate it, as there is no clear evidence for insular forerunners. Powell (1953, 173; Pl. 27 top) correctly dated the cape to within the bracket 1350–1250 BC but he also drew attention to the similarly-shaped lenticular bosses on the broad bracelet from the Migdale hoard, which are also present on a more recent Scottish find, from Masterton, Fife (Henshall 1968, 189–190, Fig. 44:10), therefore, Joan Taylor (1980, 51–2) preferred an Early Bronze Age date. Lenticular motifs frequently occur as decoration during the continental Tumulus culture (Torbrügge 1959, 105, Taf. 3:20–3) and further north in Germany, for instance in the already-mentioned Period III grave from Deutsch-Evern, in the Ilmenau-Kreis (Jacob-Friesen 1963, 275, Abb. 267). They occur on the Avanton, Schifferstadt and Ezelsdorf cones (Pl. IX) and in Britain on the Picardy pins (Hawkes 1942, Fig. 2:2–5) and incised-decorated bronze bracelets (Rowlands 1971a, 188, Fig. 5, motifs I, J and M). Ornamentally and technologically the Mold cape fits into a date centred around the 13th century BC. Its background and milieu is the continental "diadem-vessel" style of the bowls and cones in particular but more especially the cones in view of their size. The extraordinary thing is that it seems more likely that the Mold cape was manufactured in England or Wales as it lacks concentric circles, which are such a feature of continental sheet-gold work at this time. If imported, or made by an immigrant continental craftsman, one would expect that circles would be part of the art repertoire. However, the craftsman must have had a continental training, the location being some place in west-central Europe. It, and possibly the Geldeston pieces, reflect influences from the centre to the west, influences otherwise demonstrated by the presence of some bronze pieces such as the pins of the Picardy type.

Although absent from the Mold and Geldeston objects, concentric circles make their appearance at this time, on a disc also from a burial associated with cinerary urns at Lansdown near Bath, Somerset (Avon) (Hawkes 1981). Its star-shaped central motif suggests a Danish (*cf.* gold disc from Jaegersborg (Menghin and Schauer 1977)) or possibly north German background and so does the broad-ribbed bracelet from Mountfield, Sussex. This north European area was also the place of origin of some bronze ornaments and also tools (Smith 1959).

Regarding earrings, the bar-twisting technique could be central-western European but flange-twisting is not. Hawkes (1961a) argued that this technique originated in western Asia, especially the Palestine-Cypriot region; the dagger from Pelynt, Cornwall (Childe, 1951) indicates eastern Mediterranean contacts with the west of Europe at this time. It should also be noted, however, that gold rings with transverse ribbing on the body, rather like an example in the Lanrivoaré hoard, also occur in the Carpathian region during the Forró-Ópályi hoard horizon (Mozsolics 1973, Taf. 92) and that industry also had other items that may be relevant to the western gold industry, such as plain bar bracelets with body of lozenge-shaped cross section. Lanrivoaré also contained portions of sheet-gold plaques, a west-central type (Eogan 1981b, 367; see Fig. 14).

Concerning chronology both Smith and Butler equated the Beerhackett-Taunton Phase with Period III of the north European Bronze Age. Subsequently Burgess (1980, 153) has argued that

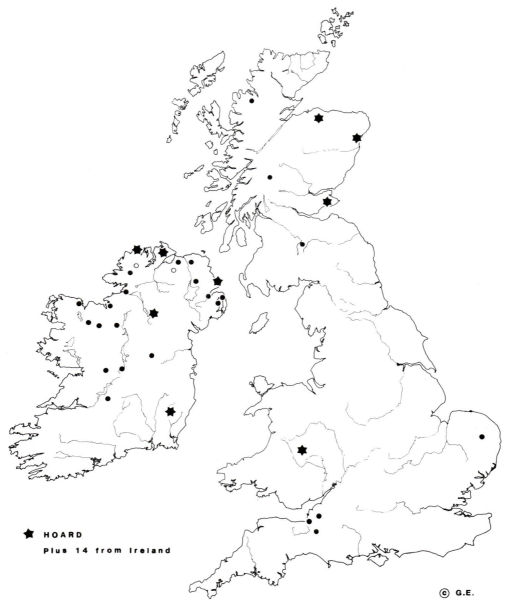

★ **HOARD**

Plus 14 from Ireland

© **G.E.**

Figure 33. Distribution of ribbon torcs. (After Eogan, 1983b).
(Open symbols indicate that only county of origin is known).

the correlations are with Tumulus C–Montelius II B/C. It is true to say that some types, such as the non-socketed sickle or ribbed bracelets were in existance during Tumulus C–Montelius II but it is also true that many types were current during the succeeding stage in their respective areas (Br.D-Montelius III). In absolute terms it is therefore likely that the Taunton Phase was established about or just before the late 14th century and continued into the 12th. In view of the restricted distribution in the south of England perhaps the novel bronze types were the first to come into use but this cannot be confirmed. Relevant gold work has a similar date range. The local context of the gold discs from the Pilsen region is late Tumulus and the Schifferstadt cone with its associated palstaves may be close to them in date, while in the north of Europe the Jaegersborg disc could have appeared during late Period II. In the main, where dates can be assigned to other objects – the cones from Schifferstadt, the Gönnebek bowl and the Mühlau disc – they are Bronze Age D or Period III.

In southern England the Beerhackett-Taunton Phase was succeeded by the Penard Phase during early Urnfield times, about the 12th century. It may be remarked that the gold flange-twisted bar torc from Stretham, Cambridgeshire was found near a rapier of Burgess and Gerloff's (1981) Group IV. The Grunty Fen (Eogan 1967, 140–1) and Monkton Deverell (unpublished) torcs were found with transitional palstaves while the Croxton, Norfolk torc was also associated with a transitional palstave, a spearhead with protected openings in the blade and a penannular bronze bracelet with body of D-shaped cross-section (Needham 1990b). These finds suggest a continuation of at least some objects into the Penard Phase. Otherwise, that phase is not distinguished by gold-working while typologically it was looking eastwards to the continental mainland. The evidence, however, is hardly sufficient to allow us to say unequivocally that gold torcs with hook terminals date to the Beerhackett-Taunton Phase and that the flange-twisted torcs date to the Penard Phase (Northover 1989, 123).

Under stimulation from the Beerhackett-Taunton Phase a parallel industry, the Bishopsland Phase emerged in Ireland (Eogan 1964, 272–88; Herity and Eogan 1977, 167–82). During this period, the "diadem-vessel" style, and consequently sheet gold, had a limited role in Ireland and instead heavier solid goldwork predominated, notably bracelets (both plain and twisted), earrings and bar-torcs. Decoration, when present, largely consisted of twisting the body and there is limited evidence for engraving. The origin of the torcs has already been discussed and penannular bracelets (both plain and twisted) in both gold and bronze are a feature of the Beerhackett-Taunton Phase; earrings however could have had a more distant background. Bar-twisting of gold at this time became very much a feature of Irish and British gold work. While gold-working was initially stimulated from southern England, very soon Ireland became a leading producing and manufacturing centre. Its sheet gold work almost exclusively reflects the continental diadem-vessel style, both Central and Northern Continental, but the 'tress-rings' proclaim native innovation. Objects made from bar gold appear less refined but some of the items, such as the torcs from Tara, can stand side by side with the elegant Schifferstadt cone. It is difficult to determine a final date but the use of gold ornaments does not appear to have continued during the Roscommon Phase.

Assessment

Fundamental changes took place on the continent around the late 14th–13th centuries. These involved an acceleration in the production of goods and greater specialisation in their manufacture. In central and northern Europe an altered society emerged, a feature of which was the use of prestige goods, status symbols and other changes such as improvements in transport and, therefore, greater mobility which would have facilitated communication, trade diffusion and movement of goods and people. The islands of Britain and Ireland also witnessed change as is shown by the importation and acceptance of new metal types and skills, and ensuing native development. An important contributing factor to this was the westward march of Middle

European prosperity but other parts especially the Nordic area also contributed. The initial insular area of change was the south of England where there were active farming families as the Deverel-Rimbury and contemporary complexes testify. The vigour of the continental complexes led to the spread of external types of artifacts to southern England, this brought about the emergence of materially enriched farming families which in turn gave rise to a desire for personal aggrandizement and exaltation as ornaments and improved facial care (Class II razors) show.

How did change come about? If it can be explained as an intensification of existing trading contacts this would have involved people, and it is reasonable to ask could some of them have settled? Evidence provided by a small group of burials suggests the presence of continental immigrants (Fig. 34). In these burials the rite of inhumanation in a cist or pit under a round barrow was a feature; the remains seem to have been those of males and the accompanying grave goods were rich, consisting of personnal ornaments with gold items prominent. One such burial in a chalk-cut pit between Ramsgate and Dumpton close to the Kentish coast of Thanet, may have been that of an immigrant from northern Europe as is suggested by the grave goods, one broad ribbed and three incised decorated bronze bracelets (C. M. Piggott 1949, 118–21; see p. 51, also Fig. 18). While there is no evidence that the nearby finds from the grounds of St. Lawrence College, Ramsgate – a pottery urn, possibly belonging to the Dutch "Drakenstein" series, and its contents of three bronze pins of Picardy variety – accompanied a body in a grave, nevertheless their owner must have been a continental (Hawkes 1942, 26–29). The person or his/her immediate ancestors buried at Lansdown may have originated in the Nordic area as the decoration of the gold disc, especially the star-shaped motif suggests (p. 65). Due to the uniqueness of the gold cape it is difficult to know if the individual buried at Mold was a foreigner but this was possibly so, at least the gold-work was continentally inspired. The bronze objects from the grave in a barrow at Hanley Cross, Sussex consisting of a large pin with a disc-shaped head and a diamond-shaped protrusion covering the perforation on the stem, a quoit-headed pin and two Sussex "loops" (Curwen 1954, 201–2) were of insular forms so the person buried in that grave would, at best, represent a first generation inhabitant and that may also have been the status of the Duff House, Banffshire person who was accorded a traditional cremation burial with the bones and the grave-goods (two gold penannular bracelets with unexpanded terminals, three gold rings related to the composite variety and fragments of a bronze razor) placed within an inverted urn of uncertain type (Coles 1963–4, 150; see Pl. 7:4–8).

Metal production increased and a change or a reorganisation of the metal industry took place. Bronze was in plentiful supply and gold was also available as is clear from the number of individual objects as well as hoards. For ornaments, bronze was used more commonly than gold and hoards of bronzes are more numerous and varied in content. In contrast gold objects are rarely found with bronzes and when they are, they consist of the later 'transitional' palstave and Group IV rapiers. Exclusive hoards of bronze ornaments are less frequent and very often bronze ornaments are associated with tools and on some occasions weapons. For Rowlands (1976, 164) hoards of bronze objects, which have been found both in dry- and in wet-land, "represent a stock of implements in the process of being distributed". This could be interpreted as the coming into being of a sales network of finished products but as some hoards contain broken pieces the collection of scrap for re-smelting also appears to have been a feature. Rowlands (p. 163) would see bronze-smithing "possibly as a dispersed occupation associated with small settlement units or aggregates". Production would have been seasonal and in the hands of "part-time specialists". It need not, however, be assumed that all hoards represent secular activities, ritual deposition was certainly an important feature. In this connection it should be recalled that items occurring as grave-goods in the two (already mentioned) richly-furnished inhumation graves from Ramsgate, Kent and Hanley Cross, Sussex could, if unassociated with a grave, constitute hoards. Nevertheless, taking the bronzes as a whole, it is not necessary to visualise sweeping social changes or marked social stratification as part of the new developments. On the other hand gold suggests a different interpretation both socially and spatially for, in contrast to bronze, ornaments made from it have a wider distribution in southern Britain.

Figure 34. Location of 'Rich' graves of c. 13th century BC in Britain.

Taking the combined distribution of bronze and gold ornaments it may be suggested that initially the novelties consisted of bronzes in the use of coastal or near coastal southern English communities (*cf*. Fig. 19). Consequent to new and improved methods of production, prosperity now spread northwards outside the coastal southern counties to a line from the mouth of the Mersey in the west to the Humber in the east and this involved much greater use of gold. Evidence for this is provided by the hoards, for instance the objects in the Mountfield hoard, Sussex may have weighed about 12 or 13 1bs (Eogan 1967, 151), while the presence of over thirty bar torcs, a number of bracelets and some other items indicate the existence of persons who controlled sufficient wealth to enable them to support skilled craftsmen who, in the first instance, had to acquire the raw gold and then to manufacture grandiose pieces mainly from bar but some from sheet. A number of these items form parts of hoards and sometimes as at Towednack, the objects are well preserved but in other cases they are incomplete or damaged. Depending on the geographical location, deposition took place in either dry- or wet-land. The distribution is not evenly dispersed, the pieces tend to occur in a circular band (Fig. 32). This contrasts with the distribution of the bronze ornaments which as already noted are to a large extent confined to the coastal counties of the south and less so in Norfolk (Fig. 19). The gold objects spatially extend the area of ornament wearing and it is interesting to note that geographically this area consists of a variety of landscapes – rich agricultural land in the south and east but poorer land in the west but also having other contrasts such as fenlands, chalk downs and mountains. Within the overall area a puzzling feature is the void in central England (Fig. 32). This is not confined to gold ornaments as there is a somewhat similar gap in the distribution of Middle Bronze Age hoards (Rowlands 1976, Map 26). At that time perhaps it was not a favoured agricultural area, due to natural causes such as unsuitable agricultural land or heavy forest, woodlands such as Charnwood Forest, south of Nottingham and the Forest of Arden, south of Birmingham survived to modern times.

Communities living in northern England and Scotland only participated in a limited way in the wearing of gold ornaments. Scotland has a small number of isolated finds of penannular bracelets with unexpanded terminals, examples being Briglands, Kinross and Bonnyside, Sterling (Nat. Mus. Nos. FE 62 and 8, see Pl. 7:9–10). Ribbon torcs are more common with at least half a dozen finds and amongst those are the three large hoards from Belhelvie, Lower Largo and Law Farm all of which came from the east between the Firths of Forth and Moray (Eogan 1983b, 122–4, see Fig. 33). Apart from these items and the grave goods from Duff House (Banffshire) burial (p. 75) ornaments of any sort are rare in Scotland (Coles 1963–64, 127–8) but it had a lively bronze industry.

For Ireland the gold ornaments have also to be considered as part of a wider industrial phase but taking them on their own they contribute to our knowledge and interpretation of the Bishopsland Phase. Bronze ornaments are rare, there is only one exclusive hoard, Clooneenbaun, Co. Roscommon (Fig. 24:C) but ornaments occur with tools in the Annesborough and Bishopsland hoards (Eogan 1983a, Nos 26, 7 and 16). A technological transformation is attested by the fact that there were so many gold ornaments, about one hundred and twenty are recorded with the two Tara bar torcs alone weighing about 40 ounces, while many spectacular pieces show that master craftsmen were at work. This can be attributed to an increase in industrialisation but it also indicates the emergence of a wealthier society. Hoards of ornaments and bar torcs are distributed mainly in the eastern part of the province of Leinster but in addition the bar torcs occur sporadically to the west of the River Shannon with a thicker spread in the coastal lands of east and north-east Ulster (Fig. 32). This might be explained on geographical grounds, since Leinster is closest to the area of the Beerhackett-Taunton industry and Wicklow had both gold and copper, such natural resources and their exploitation could have led to the emergence of wealthy families. Ireland might also have been exporting raw material and in this regard it should be noted that the south of England did not have native supplies of copper or gold. In other words a similar situation may have arisen in Ireland, as was visualised for Wales and southern England, wealthy families arose and these could afford prestigious personal ornaments made from exotic material which also indicated craft specialisation. Such types in both Britain and Ireland have a striking appearance and their manufacture consumed considerable quantities of rare metal; they were luxury goods and as such could indicate rank. These ornaments can be termed sumptuary goods while the wealth of the area was regulated by sumptuary rules, such as the limitation of individual wealth in the interest of a higher order (Levy 1982, 69–84). By its nature this could lead to an unequal social distribution of objects of prestige. In her study of Danish material Levy (1982, 23) considered superb pieces, equivalent of the Mold cape or the Tara torcs, as special sumptuary items and as indicators of the presence of individuals that occupied a unique social or political position. Hoards can also be included in this category and can be referred to as sumptuary sets. They are a novel feature of the Bishopsland Phase and at least two dozen are known (Eogan 1983a, 6–7, 26–46). Apart from three hoards the ornaments in the others are made from gold and only one (Co. Westmeath) does not contain ornaments. An important point is that the contents of all, are "new", it is, therefore, clear that the hoards consist of sets of objects selectively chosen and consciously deposited. Within these sets levels can be detected depending on the variety and number of the objects present. Hoards consisting of two pieces of straight-forward craftsmanship, like the contents of those from Newtown Forbes or Tremblestown, might be placed in the lower strata while the Derrinboy or Saintjohns hoards represent a higher level. Levy postulated that the presence of a wider range of items in a hoard may be interpreted as reflecting the acquisition of additional social characteristics by the owner, leading to an increase in rank and influence. If a sumptuary system existed it could indicate that during the Bishopsland and Beerhackett-Taunton phases, society was wealthy and stratified with leaders, or at least persons of rank, possibly the wearing of ornaments was confined to special occasions such as quasi-political gatherings.

Perhaps this secular view is too limited as it does not explain the reason for deposition. In Ireland the find places of sixteen of the twenty five hoards are known, five were found in wetland, and eleven on dry land. The Downpatrick, Co. Down, hoards were carefully deposited in small pits with flat stones over the mouth of each. The Largatreany-Inishowen (Co. Donegal) hoards appear to have been concealed in a crevice between natural stones. Dysart was in a pit at the base of a standing stone and the Ballylumford material, probably more than one hoard, was close to a passage tomb of much earlier, Neolithic, date. Apart from the large ribbon torc hoards of Largatreany, Inishowen and Derravona, and possibly also the Downpatrick 1 hoard, none could be described as founders or traders hoards. Perhaps some were hidden when not in use but the formal deposition of the Downpatrick hoards and possibly that from Dysart, Co. Westmeath, may suggest another reason, thereby, raising the question of ritual change, a question that has been discussed previously (*cf.* Eogan 1964, 310–14; 1983a, 3–4). It is possible that there was a discontinuance in burial practices and that in some way the deposition of hoards and even individual pieces, at least the more elegant ones, might have been a substitute. In other words the emphasis shifted from formal burial of the remains to the burial of a possession or possessions of the individual. In order to possess a sumptuary item the individual must have been a person of rank but that could be religious as well as secular. Other interpretations can be put forward, for instance the object or objects need not have been a personal possession but the possession of the community or tribe and it was only when the leader died that deposition was carried out. Or it may be that deposition was not a funerary event at all but part of some other ceremonial affair such as seasonal gathering where various activities took place amongst which could have been (on occasions at least) hoard or object deposition at a particular site in the neighbourhood.

As has been argued it is likely that the presence of gold ornaments reflects the wealth of a society as a whole but also the significance of individuals within it. In particular there are two finds that help to make the individual visible or at least suggest high status; these are the previously mentioned graves of individuals (p. 75). The gold disc from the Lansdown cremation burial indicates a person of power (p. 65) but evidence for possibly greater power still is provided by the golden cape and multi-stranded necklace of amber beads from Mold. Were these people immigrants, as has been previously suggested, who became agrarian chieftains deriving wealth, influence and status from farming activity, or were they leading merchants or industrialists of their regions? To some extent the Mold cape can be compared to sheet bronze body armour found on the continent which, when clean, would have a gold-like appearance. This was part of the regalia of warriors (Schauer 1978) as is clearly shown by the contents from a grave of that class at Čaka. In addition to body armour the Čaka warrior was arrayed with weapons (sword and spears). No such equipment was present in the Lansdown or Mold graves, therefore, the role of those individuals was civilian. Both could have acquired status through descent, or by rising to prominence through personal endeavour, such as controlling land. There may have been other factors. For instance, not far from Mold in the Llandudno area, on Great Orme Head, are copper deposits, but it has not been established that they were worked at this time (*Current Archaeology* No. 130, Vol. XI No. 10 (1992), 403–9). Furthermore, the location of Mold, up the valley of the river Alun from the Dee estuary, may suggest trade. If so, trade could have been more than local, it could have extended further afield, to and from Ireland. The grandest gold object, the Mold cape, does not stand alone as there are finds of bar torcs close by, the isolated find from Bryn Siôn Bach and the pairs from Tan-y-Ilwyn and Hampton (Eogan 1967, Nos. 62, 60–1, 35–6). These emphasise the possible importance of the Dee estuary as a trading area. A commercial explanation may also be offered for the Lansdown chieftain. The location of the grave was somewhat similar, in this case up the Avon valley from the Severn estuary. The Towednack, Cornwall hoard (Pl. X) was probably the regalia of a tin merchant who achieved wealth due to the exploitation of that material not only for the British but also for the Irish market. In addition to the possible longer sea routes, a land route may have led westward from the area of the Beerhackett-Taunton industry across south Wales to a port on the Irish Sea, as is suggested by the contents of the Monkton hoard in Pembrokeshire (Savory 1980, 117, No. 265).

It may be noted that the large hoards of gold torcs, both bar and ribbon, from England and Wales as well as the heaviest bar torcs are confined to the western area. The grouping of torcs in the Mold area has already been discussed. To its south in central Wales there are three hoards – Llanwrthwl (four bar torcs), Heyope (three ribbon torcs) and Capel Isaf (four bracelets with broad body and hook-and-eye terminals, piece of gold). In the south-west at Tiers Cross, Pembrokeshire there is another hoard of three bar torcs (unpublished, National Museum of Wales). Furthermore, two other gold hoards, containing bar torcs, also came from the west, both in Dorset, the Hilton hoard and the large Beerhackett hoard, which was found close to the Somerset border, near Yeovil, a place that also produced a bar torc. Therefore, these western areas provide clear evidence for wealth which can be attributed to the rise of farming and possibly also merchant families that succeeded in attaining power. This could have given rise to pomp which was reflected in gold finery thereby leading to a demand for gold. As a result Ireland assumed a prominent role as a provider of metal and thereby initiating large-scale exploitation and manufacture a consequence of which could have been the emergence of industrial and merchant families.

THE END OF GOLD-WORKING

In England, as has been shown, bar torcs were being deposited during the Penard Phase, a phase that might have started as early as the 12th century and during which England witnessed industrial and possibly social realignments. There was also a change in fortunes of the Irish industry at about the same time. Ireland now lost its southern English market, and there was consequently a falling off in wealth and a possible change in ritual. Ireland only received limited influence from the south of England during the Penard Period and the succeeding Wilburton Phases with bronze swords amongst the novel items (Eogan 1965, 5–10, Classes 1, 2 and 3). Therefore, could the changes also involve intrusive and aggressive bands? There is no evidence for the continuation of gold-working during the Roscommon Phase and with its cessation one of the most creative and prosperous periods in Ireland's prehistory came to an end.

Chapter V

Gold-Working in an Age of Interaction and Diversification: Final Late Bronze Age Gold, Apogee and End

In central Europe around 1200 BC the initial stage of the Later Bronze Age, Bronze Age D, was succeeded by what is termed the Early Urnfield cultures or Hallstatt A (Müller-Karpe 1959). This period is characterised by an industrial revolution and widespread changes in metal types. An integral aspect was deep mining for copper in the Alps and the consequent abundance of copper which led to mass production of artifacts, and a greater variation in artifact form, particularly of bronze ornaments, but also of gold. Ritually, flat cremation cemeteries were standard. After 1000 BC, the early Urnfield cultures altered (Hallstatt B); from the artifactual point of view, this was to a large extent, typological. Towards 700 BC a new technology, iron-working, appeared from the south (Hallstatt C) and this and other changes ushered in the end of the Bronze Age.

In the north of Europe there is a somewhat equivalent sequence – Periods IV, V, VI. During Period IV burials decline in importance and consequently so does the display of wealth and social status from graves. In contrast the number of hoards and the volume of objects, such as ornaments, that were worn apparently by females increases. The succeeding Period V in Denmark is characterised by pronounced cultural growth due to an increase in productivity by an agrarian society. This was a peak industrial period in Denmark and adjoining lands. Imported goods, mainly from the Alpine region, increased enormously (Thrane 1975) and so must have supplies of bronze. As a result the number of metal objects being produced was greater than ever before. Hoards became more common while the volume of metal items of female personal adornment was larger than previously. But there was also an increase in metal objects that were part of the male paraphernalia; these included wind instruments (lurs), shields, helmets, sheet bronze vessels, horse-gear and other items. Another aspect is the presence of unusual items, such as miniature swords. In the Nordic area there are a small number of well-furnished graves, such as Seddin in Mark Brandenburg and Voltofte in Fünen (Kiekebusch 1928; Thrane 1984) as well as hoards of gold ornaments, including the huge hoard from Messingwerk, near Eberswalde, Brandenburg, north Germany (Pl. XX). A hierarchical pattern of settlement emerged with the well-off using gold to display their wealth and social status. There was a considerable increase in the volume of gold used, for instance in Zealand during Period IV (*c.* 1000 BC) graves and deposits yield about 1,450 grams but during Period V this increased to nearly 6,000 grams. Some of the items, such as bowls, represent continuity but penannular bracelets with hollowed evenly expanded terminals ("oath-rings") demonstrate innovation.

Important changes also took place in the west of Europe. There was an expansion of the metal industry in Atlantic lands, with particular developments in western Iberia where by the 9th–8th centuries large-scale and diversified production was under way. A greater variety of symbolic items appeared and the male warrior was well represented by swords and spears. Personal ornaments were also a feature (Ruiz-Gálvez 1991). Hill-tops were occupied in the north-west but it is not clear if large fortified settlements, *castros*, were occupied as early as this time (Silva 1986). In the south-west influences from the Mediterranean region brought about changes in the weapon types, in personal defence and in transport (Almagro 1966). The ship that sank in the harbour of Huelva may have been a merchant vessel whose cargo largely originated in 'carp's tongue' lands to the north (M. Almagro-Basch, *Invent. Archeo. España.* Fas. 6. Madrid, 1962, E.7 (1–2)). This assemblage indicates movement up and down the Atlantic coasts.

On both sides of the Channel, in north-western France and southern England, the previously established industrial province (Rösnoën-Penard stage) of the 12th–11th centuries expanded and consolidated. The succeeding industry, altogether more vigorous than its predecessor, is termed the Saint-Brieuc-des-Iffs/Wilburton Stage (*c.*11th–9th centuries). Emphasis on weapons continued; these included flange-hilted swords with leaf-shaped blades, plain spearheads with leaf-shaped blades and spearheads with lunate-shaped openings in the blade, long tongue-shaped chapes, tubular spear-ferrules. Socketed axeheads were becoming more common and harnessed horses appeared. A characteristic aspect was the simultaneous deposition of dozens of bronze objects, in some cases hundreds such as at Isleham, Cambridgeshire (Britton 1960). In these so-called founders' hoards most of the objects were in a broken and unusable condition (Briard 1965, 175–98). In contrast changes in the north of Britain were limited during the Poldar-Wallington stage. Basically the bronze artifacts in use had their background in the preceding traditions of the Glentrool and Auchterhouse stages (p. x).

The trans-channel Saint-Brieuc-des-Iffs/Wilburton industry was succeeded by a more developed stage, the 'carp's-tongue' sword complex/Ewart Park stage. Large founders' hoards with an emphasis on weapons remain but a wider range of tools, not only socketed axes but also chisels and gouges were current. Hoards of specialist tools occur with those consisting solely of socketed axes predominating (*cf.* Kalemouth, Roxburghshire; Schmidt and Burgess 1981, Pl. 145:C) but a wider range, including small tools, is sometimes found (*cf.* Westow, Yorkshire; Schmidt and Burgess 1981, 181, Pl. 145:B). Harnessed horses and wagons with four-spoked wheels were also characteristic. This industry represents development from existing types, some such as the swords of the Ewart Park type are direct modifications of the Wilburton type swords but the 'carp's-tongue' sword represents more distinctive developments. A feature of this stage is the re-emphasis on personal ornaments. Bronze penannular bracelets with terminals that usually expanded outwards were prominent. The body was normally solid but there were large examples with inward hollowed body, sometimes decorated as in the example from Shoebury, Essex (*Invent. Arch.* GB. 38, 1, 6th set, 1958) with geometric or linear motifs. Gold ornaments were also worn. These consist of two main groups; one is Late Urnfield/western continental inspired and predominates in the south and east; the other is Irish inspired and has a predominantly westerly distribution (Figs. 38–39)

The greatest number of novel and continental types are found in the old Wilburton complex area of southern England – 'carp's-tongue' swords, purse-shaped chapes, bugle-shaped objects, a variety of knives (hog-backed and triangular-shaped, tanged and socketed), gouges and chisels (both tanged and socketed), items of horse harness and personal ornaments, especially penannular bracelets. Founders' hoards remained a feature. In its pure form this industry is termed the ''carp's-tongue' sword complex'. Local, or indigenous development was also a feature, examples being native renderings of the flange-hilted swords of the Wilburton stage now termed swords of the Ewart Park type, and fully developed socketed sickles. These items (Ewart Park element) but also some of the introduced types – chisels, knives and gouges – were widely used throughout Britain. At this time there is also considerable evidence for settlement sites, farmsteads such as Thwing in Yorkshire (Manby 1980, 321–3) and riverside settlements as at Egham-Runnymede, Surrey (Longley 1980; O'Connell 1986; Needham 1990c; 1991).

As has already been suggested, during the preceding Bishopsland Phase, Ireland was considered an exporter of metal, notably to the area of the Beerhackett–Taunton industry (p. 69). But due to the emergence of changed conditions, part of which would have been the realignment of economic and trading relationships, Ireland's postulated export of metal came to an end and as a result a period of wealth and innovation diminished. That also included other aspects of activity such as hoard deposition and gold-working and if gold indicates either wealth or ritual activities, or both, then they also changed.

After the end of the Bishopsland Phase an insular and less productive industry emerged, at least with regard to exotic objects, the Roscommon Phase. It is characterised by the use of rapiers of Group IV, late palstaves and possibly wing-flanged axeheads, kite-shaped and base-looped spearheads may have continued in use. There was only limited contact with the Penard industry, Class 1 swords (Eogan 1965, 5–9) being the most prominent. But with the emergence of the Wilburton industry, new arrivals became more prominent. These include flange-hilted swords with leaf-shaped blades (Classes 2 and 3, Eogan 1965, 9–10), long tongue-shaped chapes, tubular ferrules for the base of spear shafts, spearheads with lunate-shaped openings in the wings and at least one founders' hoard (Eogan 1964, 288–93).

Soon a new and vigorous phase emerged, the Dowris Phase (Eogan 1964, 293–320). In many ways this new phase compares with the Bishopsland Phase but it was on a grander scale. Both phases showed similar techniques of gold object manufacture, a number of the earlier art motifs reemerged or were reintroduced but now there is even greater lavishness, the number of types increased and had a wider distribution than previously and above all, there was a massive increase in the amount of gold used. This is clear from the weight of individual pieces, as is demonstrated by such items as the lost 'dress-fastener' from Dunboyne, Co. Meath that weighed over 43 ounces (information from Ms Mary Cahill) but especially from the presence of large assemblages, such as that from Mooghaun, Co. Clare, that consisted of over one hundred individual objects (Eogan 1983a, 69–72; see Pl. XV).

The Dowris Phase was a time of major economic expansion that affected agricultural as well as metallurgical production. A mixed farming economy existed, this was characterised by individual farmsteads such as Ballinderry 2, Co. Offaly (Hencken 1942, 6–27) but there may also have been larger centres of settlement. Bronze smiths worked from fixed locations, there was an increase in the tool-kit but also greater variety in the form of tools used such as hammers, anvils and chisels. Of course, none of these items need be considered as tools exclusive to the metal-worker, they could likewise be used by the carpenter who was also very active at this time as for instance the presence of seven hoards of specialist wood-working tools and about fourteen hundred recorded socketed axeheads shows. During this phase there is greater evidence than before for the working of non-metal materials into artifacts – stone, jet/lignite, amber, and for other activities such as weaving wool and manufacturing leather. The use of the harnessed horse considerably facilitated land transport and this was further helped by the laying of trackways across bogs (Raftery 1990, 22–8). Foreign contacts were also crucial and substantial, these were wide-ranging, from south Scandinavia to Iberia and eastwards to British and continental lands.

GOLD-WORKING: TECHNOLOGY

To a large extent this was similar to that used during the Beerhackett-Taunton/Bishopsland Phases as most objects were made from either bar or sheet-gold but there were some additions or revivals, an important one being the cladding of a surface by foil, a technique that was already in use during the Earlier Bronze Age (*cf.* p. 28). This is best exemplified by the heads of disc-pins with bent stems from the Ballytegan, Co. Laoghais, "South of Ireland" and Arboe/ Killycolpy, Co. Tyrone hoards (Eogan 1983a, Nos. 94, 157, 138). For the use of this technique the decorated pin-head was first cast but in doing so preparations were made for attaching the foil by leaving a groove around the slightly thickened edge. When the pin was cast, the foil was placed over the surface of the head and pressed into the ornamental grooves and its edge inserted into the groove in the side of the head. The socket of a leaf-shaped spearhead from Lough Gur, Co. Limerick has foil covering (Coles in Coles, Coutts and Ryder 1964, 188–93) which consists of three panels and is less elaborate than the circular decoration on the pinheads. The broadest panel is in the middle and consists of horizontal grooves in the bronze into which strips of gold, 9 mm long and 1 mm wide were set. The strips must have been attached by adhesive but out of the forty eight grooves only four strips survive. The flanking panels consist of five bands of alternating vertical and horizontal lines. Each has a separate cladding which is apparently seamless, it was inserted over the already grooved surface of the bronze and then secured in place by hammer-welding into the grooves. Somewhat similar decoration is found on the typologically earlier spearhead with lunate-shaped openings in the blade from an unrecorded location in Ireland (Wilde 1861, 499, Fig. 372; Coles 1971, 94–95). At one point the decoration is interrupted by a vertical channel.

This technique is also used in Britain (Coles, Coutts, Ryder 1964). A spearhead with basal loops of the string form from Pyotdykes, Angus has a decorated sheet-gold band, 2–6 cm broad, surrounding the socket externally. There is no evidence for a joint. How this was achieved is not certain but it appears to have been either by hammer-welding a strip or by hammer thinning a ring. The decoration on the band was formed by engraving and it consists of zones – three zones of horizontal lines with two zones of hatched triangles in between. Before applying the band the pattern was engraved on the surface and it was secured by forcing its corresponding portions into the grooves. This spearhead was found with two swords of Ewart Park type. A leaf-shaped spearhead from near Harrogate, Yorkshire has similar decoration. A spearhead with rapier-shaped blade and basal loops from the River Thames at Taplow, Berkshire has gold false rivets in the butt of the blade (British Museum 1920, 38, Fig. 25). A Class 5 bronze sword, possibly from the Bog of Cullen, Co. Tipperary assemblage, may have had gold cladding around the hilt (Eogan 1965, 140).

A related technique is the encasing of an entire object in gold sheet. This is carried out to perfection on the thick penannular rings with a core of lead or bronze but the overlying sheet is highly decorated (Fig. 37:1–4). It is also the technique used in the manufacture of hair-rings, although some of these are solid. But the latter objects are of further interest as on a number of examples the gold sheet is decorated with inlay resembling niello. This consists of applying, apparently in solder-like fashion, electrum or silver-like material.

Most of the objects were formed by firstly hammering out an ingot (as was the case during previous stages), and an ingot survives in the hoards from Askeaton, Co. Limerick (Eogan 1983a, 102) and Llanarmon-yn-Iâl, Denbighshire (Green 1983; see Fig. 36:4). Two unfinished objects both from Ireland survive, these show that the first stage was partial manufacture by producing a rough working as is demonstrated by the unfinished 'dress-fastener', possibly from Inchigeelagh, Co. Cork, and a bracelet with evenly expanded terminals without a recorded find-place (Armstrong 1933, 70, No 177, Pl. 16:299; 77, No 251, Pl. 18:369). The manufacture of objects with hollowed body, possibly some examples of thick penannular bracelets, 'dress-fasteners', and 'sleeve-fasteners,' demanded greater skill. This involved casting as the body is in the form of a tube, which reduces in size from the centre to the terminals. Others were made from sheet gold bent around and joined with molten gold. Sheet-gold was now used to perfection and large objects such as gorgets were made from it.

From the technological and manufacturing points of view, the most remarkable achievement of all is displayed in the manufacture of the 'lock-rings', especially the face-plates (Eogan 1969). The most elaborate specimens come from Ireland where up to ten separate pieces of gold were used on some examples. While the face-plates have the appearance to have been made of grooved sheet this is not in fact the case. On the contrary, each sheet is created by placing individual wires side-by-side and soldering. These wires average 1 mm in diameter and despite their small size those on the Rathfarnham (Co. Dublin) piece are twisted.

Composite construction was common. As already mentioned up to ten individual pieces were used in the manufacture of some 'lock-rings'. Several pieces were also used in the make-up of the Enniscorthy discs, on some boxes, but in particular on the gorgets. All of these four types share a number of structural features such as the strengthening of a joint by inserting a wire along it and then securing the edge by clamping it with a C-sectioned binding strip itself of sheet gold. Another method of securing an edge was to project outwards one edge and then lapp or fold the edge of the other piece over it. On the body of the Shannongrove gorget where it adjoins the discs there are tab-like projections but those appear to be decorative rather than functional, in fact on that gorget the terminals were attached to the body by rivets (Powell 1973, 6–7, Fig 2; see Pl. 25). On other examples terminals were secured by the use of wire. As has been shown wire was used in the manufacture of the face plates of 'lock-rings'. The use of wires to constitute a form of filigree was occasionally used, a good example being the bulla from Kinnegoe, Co. Armagh (Eogan 1983a, 60–l). In the amber bead from Milmorane, Co. Cork the central perforation is lined with a sheet-gold cylinder around the mouth of which is a band consisting of four thin twisted wires (N.M.I 1944:226–7). On some objects, such as the sides of boxes, the joint was effected by fusing the edges together under heat.

The application of the art also involved a range of techniques. Many of the circular motifs were laid out by the use of a compass. The art was applied either by incision (as for instance on Box No 2 – Eogan 1981b, 346), or by repoussé, although on some examples, the gold may have been stamped into a die. Repoussé was the technique mainly used in creating the elaborate decoration, the ridges vary from prominent, as on the gorget bodies, to refined examples as on the terminals. In addition to incision, tracer work, by which a tool was employed like a punch, and chasing were also used (Maryon 1938, 187–8).

DECORATION

Decoration was not common in Britain on ornaments of Late Urnfield/western continental derivation and when present mainly consisted of incised angular motifs. In contrast it was frequently used in Ireland and to a large extent the techniques already described were employed in its application. Two main forms were used – angular and circular. The former consists of zig-zags, lozenges, triangles (plain or hatched), hexagonal and kite-shaped compartments. For the latter the main shapes were a conical boss (either slender or prominent) or a depression surrounded by concentric circles, a "ladder" pattern (or short radial lines constituting a band), ridges either plain or obliquely notched ("cord" moulding) and rows of bosses. On bracelets and 'dress-fastners' the decoration usually consisted of ridges or grooves surrounding the mouth of the terminals. The body of both 'sleeve-fasteners' and striated rings is decorated on the outside by deep longitudinal scoring, at the end of which there is a band of criss-cross hatching enclosed by lines. A feature of the decoration is its overall arrangement on some objects such as gorgets and discs. When this is the case it is applied in an ordered and systematic way, for instance, individual motifs often occur in bands. It was usual to apply the decoration on the front or other visible part of the objects, although it is known from "hidden" parts such as the back of gorget terminals or the Enniscorthy discs.

THE OBJECTS

These fall into two main groups, British and Irish. Each can be distinguished from the other mainly on the grounds of form, background and distribution.

The British Group

During the final stage of the Bronze Age practically all the ornaments were made from metal, either gold or bronze. There is approximately one hundred and forty gold objects (the Coul, Argyll 'hoard' is taken as one find) from about seventy find-places. These include about forty of Irish origin (penannular bracelets with body of round cross-section and solid or hollowed evenly expanded terminals, thick penannular bracelets and dress-fasteners) and also objects common to both Britain and Ireland ('lock-rings,' 62 examples and 'hair-rings', *c.* 170 examples). The characteristic British object is the penannular bracelet. This is represented by nine varieties. In their manufacture the use of the bar-gold was a feature and as a result their bodies and terminals are solid except for Forms 3 and 4 which have hollowed bodies. Close to ninety examples from almost sixty find-places are known but the overwhelming number, almost eighty, comes from England (list p. 154–8).

Despite their simple shape penannular bracelets differ considerably in form. Therefore, the groups isolated below are not intended as a classification, only an aid to description. In order to keep coherence the bracelets, whether belonging to the British or Irish groups, are numbered sucessively from 1–12. Varieties 1–9 are British while varieties 10–12 are Irish. Some of the varieties can be correlated with Needham's classification (Hook and Needham 1990). His Class A equates with Variety 12; B1 with Variety 1; B2 with Variety 2; C with Variety 4 and D with Variety 5.

(1) *Flat body, solid terminals generally evenly expanded* (*cf.* Fig. 36:2–3). In England this variety and Varieties 5 and 9 are the most common types.

(2) *Flat body, ends coiled to form terminals* (*cf.* Pl. 11:1,2,6).

(3) *Large body that is deeply hollowed to produce a C-shaped cross-section and flat outwardly-projecting terminals* (*cf.* Pl. 11:4–5). The gold examples are plain; but the bronze piece from Shoebury, Essex is decorated with angular designs (*Inv. Arch.* G.B. 38.1, 6th Set, 1958).

(4) *Internally hollowed body and solid outwardly-expanding terminals* (*cf.* Pl. 12:2).

(5) *Solid body of D-shaped cross-section and evenly expanded solid terminals* (*cf.* Pl. 12:1).

(6) *Solid body round or lozenge-shaped cross-section and evenly-expanded solid terminals* (*cf.* Pl. 15:1). Although the terminals are unexpanded one of the bracelets from the Caister-on-Sea, Norfolk hoard the body cross-section is lozenge-shaped (Pl. 13:2).

(7) *Solid body of rounded cross-section and outwardly-expanding solid terminals* (*cf.* Pl. 16:5). More frequently made from bronze, they are common in north-east Scotland where they constitute part of the Covesea complex (Coles 1959–60). Examples made from gold are rare, *cf.* Alloa, Clackmannanshire.

(8) *Solid body of rounded cross-section and having elongated evenly expanded solid terminals* (*cf.* Pls. 10:1; 15:4).

(9) *Solid body with almost rounded cross-section but normally with slight flattening along the inner circumference and ends expanded into solid terminals* (*cf.* Pl. 10:2–5; Fig. 35:3–5).

Irish Gold

Ireland had an extensive and varied range of ornaments, including those made from material other than gold. Amongst the bronze ornaments, pins with disc-shaped decorated heads were particularly common and occur in two forms, with a straight or a bent stem, as well as a smaller and apparently later group of cup-headed pins (Eogan 1974a, 98–100). Plain bronze annular rings, such as those in the ornament hoard from Meenwaun (Banagher), Co. Offaly (Pl. XVI top) may have served as bracelets, as could jet rings like the Ballinderry No 2, Co. Offaly examples (Hencken 1942, 13–15).

Another item that is comparable to gold, at least colour-wise, is amber and this was also popular in Ireland during the Dowris Phase (Feeney 1976) but rare in Britain at this time (Beck and Shennan 1991, 101–4). In Ireland there are over thirty find-places; all comprise beads varying in shape with spherical, oval and disc shapes being common. A small number come from habitation sites but in the main they form necklaces which were found either individually or as parts of hoards. The most splendid necklace is that from Derrybrien, Co. Galway (Prendergast 1960, 61–4) which was formed from about 500 beads (Pl. 20). This was a multiple stranded necklace, six strands in all, with beads decreasing in size not only from the centre to the ends but also from the outer to the inner strand. A necklace from Kurin, Co. Derry consisted of 421 beads and appears to have been single stranded, as there is a single large bead 45 mm in diameter and 34 mm thick (Pl. 21). This would have been the central bead with the beads to each side

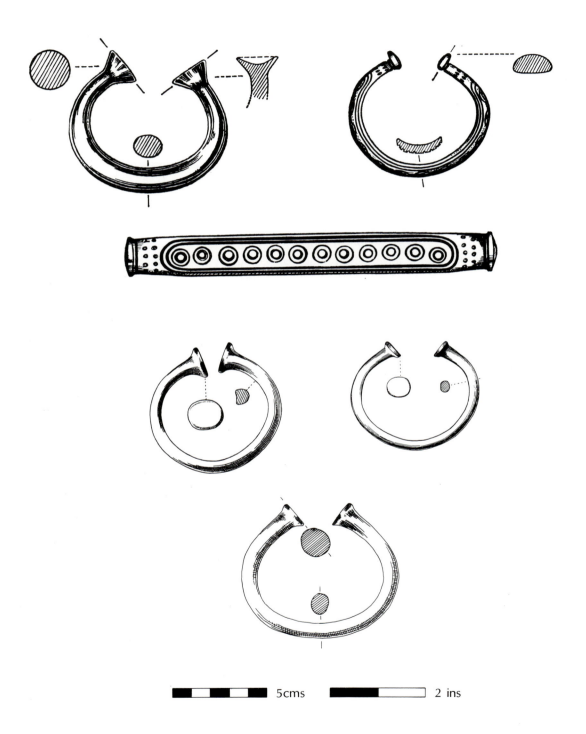

5cms   2 ins

Figure 35. Hoards, Wanderslade, Kent (1–2) (After Longworth, British Mus. Quarterly, 31 (1966–67), Figs. 1–2). Selsey, Sussex (3–5); (After Ant. Journal, 6 (1926), 308; 17 (1937), 322, and Karen Hughes).

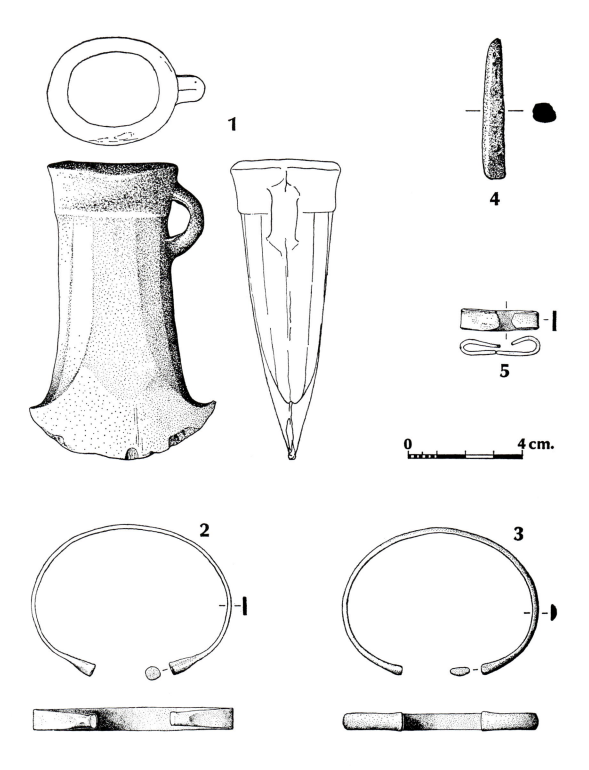

Figure 36. Hoard. Llanarmon-yn-Iâl, Denbighshire. (After Green, 1983).

of it diminishing in size towards the end where they are reduced to 7 mm in diameter and 3 mm thick (Flanagan 1964, 92–3). What was probably the longest necklace comes from Whitegates, Co. Meath. It consists of 278 beads and when strung out the length would be very close to 3 metres. Amber has been found in association with gold in eight hoards. A good example of an ornament hoard is that from Meenwaun (Banagher), Co. Offaly, where the graded single-stranded necklace was associated with a gold 'dress-fastener', a penannular bracelet with solid evenly expanded terminals and two bronze rings (Pl. XVI top). As already remarked the dating of the Cruttenclough, Co. Kilkenny necklace is problematic but if it dates to this period, rather than earlier, it presents an interesting combination of gold and amber beads.

The material most commonly used for ornaments was gold. Approximately seven hundred gold items survive or have been recorded from this period. These include bracelets but the range of artifacts was much more extensive than is found in the British series and includes neck ornaments, garment fasteners, vessels, discs and bullae. Only a small percentage of those ornament types was made from bronze, the most common bronze form being bracelets.

Penannular Bracelets
(10) Thin body of rounded cross-section and evenly expanded solid terminals (*cf.* Pl. XVI top).
(11) As (10) but with hollowed terminals (*cf.* Pl. 24:2–3).
(12) Thick body of rounded or oval cross-section and hollow terminals and has a much greater diameter than the bodies of the other bracelet types. The body which is usually hollowed is bent to a semi-circular shape and it has evenly expanded terminals that are set at a marked inclination to the plane of the body (*cf.* Pl. 24:1).

Neck ornaments
In addition to necklaces of amber beads there was also a range of neck ornaments in gold.
(i)   *Penannular neckring with solid body of rounded cross-section and evenly expanded solid terminals*. The only known specimens come from the Mooghaun assemblage. A bronze neckring with similar body but with solid oval terminals set at an oblique angle to the body forms part of the Ballykeaghra, Co. Galway hoard (Eogan 1983a, 88, No 83).
(ii) *Collar*. This term is being applied to a group of ornaments from the Mooghaun hoard. The body is of C-shaped cross-section. It narrows towards each end which finishes in an evenly expanded terminal that is usually hollowed. Sometimes parts of the surface are decorated with engraved designs, angular in shape.
(iii) *Gorgets* (*cf.* Pls. XIV; 25). These, always made from gold, consist of a body that narrows from the centre to each end. The body is highly decorated by a series of ridges, "rope" patterns and small bosses all formed by the repoussé technique. A disc-shaped terminal is attached at each end. These have a conical central projection that is surrounded by bands of ornament, usually concentric circles. At least ten specimens are known, all from Ireland, the localised examples are concentrated in the Lower Shannon region.

Other Objects
'Dress-fasteners' (Pl. 19:1–2; 22:1). In Ireland, with one exception, all these ornaments are made from gold. The bow takes the form of a broad curve and is usually of round or oval cross-section and springs in nearly all cases from the apex of the terminals. The latter are large, usually evenly expanded and hollowed. The mouths of each are placed horizontally, or almost so, and therefore rest on the same plane. A number of 'dress-fasteners' are ornamented. This normally consists of ridges that were placed concentrically with the edge of the mouth opening, a small number are more elaborately decorated such as the over-all pattern of multiple concentric circles on the Clones, Co. Monaghan piece (Pl. XIX top).

'Sleeve-fasteners' (*cf.* Pl. 23:1). These objects have been termed 'sleeve-fasteners' by Hawkes (in Hawkes and Clarke 1963, 223) but in fact their precise use is not known. They consist of

an arched body the ends of which are attached peripherally to the terminal which is flat, usually circular and undecorated. Each terminal is set at an angle to the plane of the body. The body is decorated on the outside by longitudinal grooving and the part adjoining the disc has criss-cross hatching. Up to ninety 'sleeve-fasteners' are known and they are exclusively Irish type (Eogan, 1972).

Small penannular rings with external longitudinal striations on the body. The body tapers on both ends and these are unexpanded. The body is solid. At each end there is criss-cross hatching, delimiting the grooves. These ornaments are similar in shape and decoration to the body of the 'sleeve-fastener', they have not been recorded outside Ireland where at least fifteen are known.

'Hair-rings' (*cf.* Pl. 14) are small penannular rings of rounded cross-section. They usually consist of a solid lead core covered by gold foil, on some examples this is decorated with 'niello' placed in transverse lines. They have also been known as 'ring-money'.

Decorated thick penannular rings (Fig. 37:1–4) consist of a leaden or occasionally clay core that is covered by a thin gold plate. At each end and at the top and bottom the covering plate bears ornamental designs. These mainly consist of dotted linear and diaper patterns. These ornaments probably developed (in Ireland) out of the 'hair-rings' which they resemble closely in method of manufacture and two of the Tooradoo pieces are sort of "transitional" between the 'hair-rings' (one of which occurs at Tooradoo) and the decorated thick penannular rings.

Discs (Eogan 1981a). Only one example of a single sheet disc is known, from the Lattoon hoard, Co. Cavan. It is a sheet that is highly, but elegantly, decorated with concentric and angular motifs and as it was made from very thin sheet it must have been attached to a backing. The four disc-mounts from Enniscorthy (Pl. 26) are heavier, multi-piece objects that were attached and therefore formed part of a larger composite object. Each is manufactured from three pieces, *viz* front-plate, back-plate and binding strip. They also have all-over decoration, this is prominent as it was formed by distinctive repoussé work. The face-plate is the most highly decorated, the motifs consisting of a conical boss, concentric circles, X-shaped motifs and plain ridges. The motifs on the back are either lozenge- or kite-shaped.

Bullae. These ornaments are somewhat heart-shaped in form. All bear some ornament but one, which consists of a leaden core covered by a thin plate of gold, is highly ornamented with motifs consisting of concentric circles, lines, dots and chevrons (Pl. XIX bottom).

'Lock-rings' (Pl. 23:2) are penannular ornaments of triangular cross-section that are nearly always made from gold plate (Eogan 1969). A total of sixty-two have been recorded. Of these eighteen have been found in Ireland, thirty-two in Britain and twelve in France. In Ireland, apart from one definite exception, the conical face-plates are made from individual gold wires soldered together. These are held in place by a binding strip along the edge. Outside Ireland, except for examples from Castle Cary (Somerset) and Glenluce (Wigtownshire), the face-plates are made from sheet gold. A tube closes the interior of the ring. In Ireland 'lock-rings' are mainly found in the lower Shannon area of Co.Limerick and Clare. Distributionally the British examples fall into two groups – northern and southern. The ornament is also known in France where the distribution is western (Fig. 41). The concentrations in north Munster suggest that 'lock-rings' may have developed in Ireland, though prototypes do not exist there.

Vessels – All sheet-gold
Boxes (Pls. 27, 28). These circular objects average 60 mm in diameter. They were made from three main pieces, the side and a 'lid' at both ends. The terminals of the vertical sides were joined by 'fusing'. The lids are either flat or domed and they are usually attached to the sides by bending

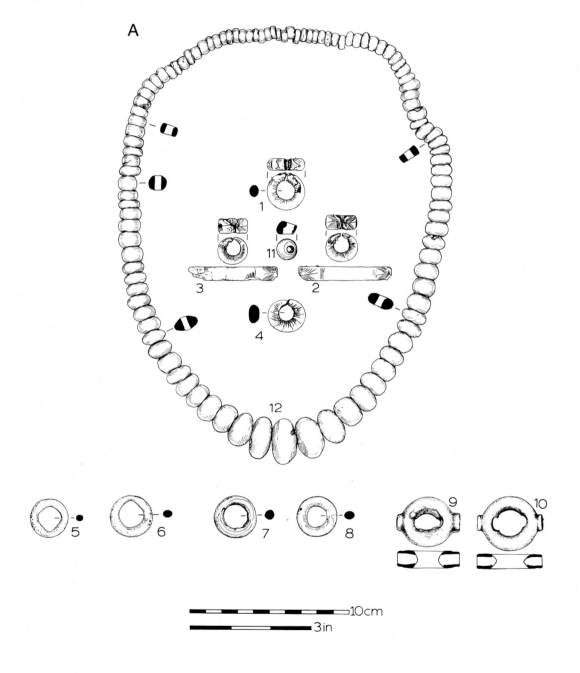

Figure 37. Hoard. Tooradoo, Co. Limerick, decorated thick penannular rings (1–4), plain solid bronze rings (5–8), rings with lateral buffer-shaped perforated projections (9–10), lignite bead (11) and amber necklace (12). (After Eogan, 1983a)

over their edges. A more elaborate method of fastening was used on the Ballinclemesig, Co. Kerry box. There the joint was achieved by gripping the edges of the lids and side by a C-sectioned binding strip, similar to the method employed on some gorgets and 'lock-rings'. Seven boxes are known (add two, discovered in 1990 at Ballinesker, Co. Wexford to Eogan's list (1981b, 346–48). In all examples the lids are decorated, usually with a central conical projection surrounded by concentric circles. This is surrounded by one or more bands of individual motifs, smaller but similar to the central one. It is also usual to have one or two rows of cord moulding at the junction between the lids and the edge. Boxes did not function as accessible containers and their lids are fixed. It has been stated that boxes Nos 2 and 3 contained a penannular bracelet with evenly expanded terminal.

The object with constricted sides and having lids, one of which is larger than the other, from near Cashel, Co. Tipperary may be related to boxes (Armstrong 1933, 47, 98). Both lids are decorated. The ornamentation is applied by dots and the larger disc consists of circles or V-shaped motifs; on the smaller there is a central circle with eight lines radiating out from it. There are two further lines parallel to the edge. Internally there was a small ball of solid gold.

Bowls (Pl. 29). Only one example survives and its find place has not been recorded but from published accounts it appears that there were at least four others (Eogan 1981b, 348–50). The decoration on the surviving piece is similar to that occurring on the box lids.

DISCUSSION

On the continent during the early Urnfield stage (Hallstatt A, 12th–11th centuries BC) and the approximately equivalent Period IV in northern Europe, the manufacture and use of gold objects continued (i.e gold bowls associated with a sheet-bronze amphora from Mariesminde, Denmark (*cf.* Eogan 1981b, 371). In some areas an unbroken continuity existed. That does not appear to have been the case in either Britain or Ireland. As has been previously discussed gold bar torcs were being deposited during the English Penard Phase (= Hallstatt A) but this represents continuity from the Beerhackett-Taunton Phase. None of the classic Penard Phase hoards such as Ambleside or Appleby (Jockenhövel 1975, Abb. 20–22) contain ornaments. Neither were ornaments in any material a feature of the southern British Wilburton Complex or the Irish Roscommon Phase, a small number of bronze bracelets do occur in the north of England during the Wallington stage (Burgess 1968, 19).

A feature of the 'carp's-tongue'/Ewart Park complex in Britain is a re-emphasis on personal ornaments. Most were made from bronze but some from gold and the latter are mainly found in the south and east, in the counties adjacent to the Channel and North Sea. Although 'lock-rings' and 'hair-rings' also occur in the region these are not an exclusive British type, that consists of distinctive forms of penannular bracelets (p. 154–8). There are close to one hundred examples but there are variations, about nine different varieties being present. By far the greatest number has been found in England, close to eighty, while in Scotland ten or so definite examples are extant. Although isolated finds are known, most occur in hoards; amongst these about two dozen consist exclusively of bracelets and all were found on dry land. Sometimes the bracelet or bracelets occur as a minority item in a hoard in which bronze objects predominate as at Portfield, Lancashire (Blundell and Longworth 1967; Schmidt-Burgess 1981, 232 (1480), Pl.150:A) but they were not incorporated into the great founders' hoards of the period. Heathery Burn (Durham) is the only large assemblage that contains gold bracelets. The average hoard content is three as at Little Chart (Kent) Patcham and Selsey (Sussex) or Stonehill Wood (Lanarkshire). There are also larger hoards, for instance from Tisbury, Wiltshire with seven bracelets while the combined contents of the two hoards from Bexley Heath, Kent amount to seventeen bracelets (Pls. 8, 9). Apart from numbers weight clearly shows that gold was available in some quantities. The combined weight of the two Bexley Heath hoards was 34.316 oz. troy

(1067.3477 grammes), an average of about two ounces per bracelet (62.207 grammes). Other bracelets are much heavier, one of the Beachy Head (Sussex) pieces is about three ounces while examples from Selsey (Sussex) and Aylesford (Kent) weigh over 4 oz. (124.44 grammes) each.

The greater concentration of the bracelets in the south-east clearly places them within the primary 'carp's-tongue' region and in regions strongly influenced by it. Within it the Kent-Sussex region was a main bracelet-wearing area but there are other groupings such as in Wiltshire and Cornwall; in the latter place tin would have been a wealth-creating factor. There is also a dispersed horizontal and linear distribution of bracelets, principally the type with flat body and evenly-expanded ends (1 above), from eastern Norfolk to north Wales. Northwards the distribution is predominantly eastern but there are few examples between south-east Yorkshire and Berwick (Fig. 38). From there northwards to eastern Scotland, and to a lesser extent westwards, there is a scatter. However the bulk of the British varieties were made from bronze and mainly consisted of the form with a solid body of round or lozenge-shaped cross-section and solid terminals that normally expanded outwards (Variety 6). Such bracelets are known from nine or so hoards and a cave habitation site. Some of the hoards, like Balmashanner, Angus (Coles 1959–60, 98–9; see Pl. 14), contain a dozen examples, indeed the Braes of Gight (Aberdeenshire) hoard with the neckring in addition to bracelets and a razor can be considered as the personal paraphernalia of a male. These hoards containing bracelets and other bronze objects (hoards of Covesea type, Coles 1959–60, 41–2) concentrate in that triangular-shaped area of eastern Scotland between the Moray Firth in the north, the Firth of Forth in the south and Rattray Point in the east.

The prototypes of the British type bracelets, more commonly manufactured from bronze, are frequently found in west-central European Late Urnfield contexts but also westwards to the Atlantic lands of France and northward to the Low Countries (*cf.* De Laet 1982, Fig 195 hoard from Jemeppe-sur-Sambre in Belgium). The principal forms are common in hoards of the 'carp's-tongue' stage, such as Saint Genouph, Indre-et-Loire (Cordier *et al.* 1960, 122–7) or Prairie de Mauves at Nantes (Briard 1966). By and large such bracelets constitute part of the Late Urnfield contribution to the emerging 'carp's tongue' industry in the west of France. As this industry in its complete form also spread to the south of England and other elements of it, such as socketed knives spread throughout Britain the presence of centre to west continental bracelets in Britain is to be expected. As Christopher Hawkes was the first to recognise, Britain, especially in the lowland parts, had "goldsmiths of its own" (Hawkes and Clarke 1963, 234). The extent of production and the weight of gold used has been underestimated.

It is clear from the distribution of British types of gold ornaments that they were worn by people that lived in areas of good agricultural land which would have sustained well-off farming families as is confirmed by the already-mentioned evidence from the homesteads. Kent and Sussex would appear to have been particularly wealthy. The rich lands would have been a major factor but so would the region's close proximity to the continent; that was probably the area, under continental inspiration, that saw the rise of a British school of gold-working and which was economically vibrant enough to sustain a materially well-off society.

The ornament aspect of this west-Continental/British industry was based on solid or bar metal and its produce was consumed locally. There is no clear evidence for a reflux influence back to the mainland. Neither were Continental/British gold types favoured in Ireland. There are no more than half a dozen definite pieces and these include two bracelets with flat bodies and solid, evenly-expanded terminals, Variety 1 (Fore, Co. Westmeath and an unprovenanced piece from Co. Cork) and two coilended bracelets, Variety 2 (Dunbrody, Co. Wexford and an unprovenanced piece), (for distribution see Fig. 38). If however, bracelets of Variety 10, a common Irish type, arose due to stimulus from Britain, say from Variety 9, then the British contribution would have been more significant.

In Ireland, at the end of the Bishopsland Phase, gold-working became dormant, so why did it re-emerge? At least part of the answer can be attributed to the fact that this was a time of economic expansion over most of Europe and also a time of social and ritual changes. The

Figure 38. Distribution of British type penannular bracelets with expanded terminals (see p. 85). (Find-places of hoards are encircled).

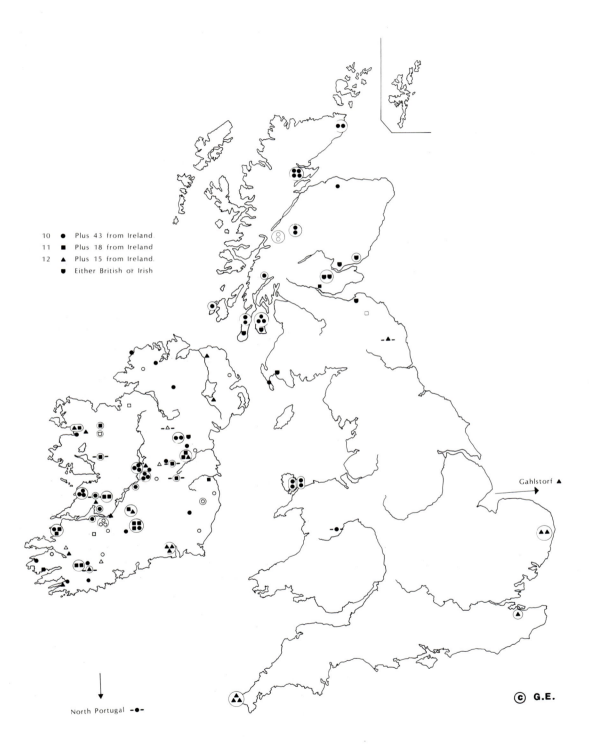

10 ● Plus 43 from Ireland.
11 ■ Plus 18 from Ireland.
12 ▲ Plus 15 from Ireland.
◗ Either British or Irish

Gahlstorf ▲

North Portugal -●-

© G.E.

Figure 39. Distribution of Irish type penannular bracelets with expanded terminals (see p. 88).
(Find-places of hoards are encircled; flanking horizontal lines indicate bronze).

Dowris Phase (Eogan 1964, 293–320), is characterised by radical industrial changes that affected the manufacture and production of metal objects. Ireland emerged as a leading economic centre; furthermore, it became integrated into an international network of contacts. A revival of gold-working was part of these changes. That raises the question of the origins of the types that emerged. Unlike the British series of gold ornaments, which have their origins in the west continental area, the background to the Irish series is not so straight-forward, more than one factor contributing to their origin.

Native Development

As some of the items have no clear-cut immediate background, they must have arisen as virtual inventions to meet specific needs. Amongst these are discs, gorgets, collars, neckrings, boxes and possibly bullae. Further modification of introduced types produced thick penannular bracelets (Variety 12), striated rings and thick rings with incised decoration.

Continuity

Some features of Dowris Phase gold-working also resemble those of the Bishopsland Phase. These include the deposition of hoards of gold objects, usually on dry land, the use of both bar and sheet-gold, the latter having repoussé formed decoration but now more elaborate and rivalling the best produced in any other part of Europe. Neckrings and penannular bracelets with solid evenly-expanded terminals and possibly the bracelet with hollow terminals might also be due to native typological development. But if there are some similarities between Bishopsland and Dowris gold-working, there are also contrasts. Gold was now present in quantity, about seven hundred known objects in contrast to less than two hundred pieces from the Bishopsland Phase, a greater variety in forms, about eighteen in contrast to six, the widespread distribution, new techniques and new art styles, and the use of composite objects were characteristic features.

Introduced Types

While gold-work of the Bishopsland and Dowris Phase share features in common the latter cannot be considered as a direct development from the former. Therefore, outside influence must be considered and this had different sources. While Britain was the immediate place of origin of bronze weapons, tools, vessels and the technique of sheet-bronze working, that was not generally so with ornaments. Britain and Ireland shared 'hair-rings' and 'lock-rings'. On the Continent only small numbers of both types have been found, all in the Belgian/north-west French area and in contexts that can be dated to the Late Urnfield or an equivalent stage, 'hair-rings' coming from graves (Toupet 1979, 35–9); 'lock-rings' from hoards (Eogan 1969).

'Hair-rings' have been considered as derivative from the Egyptian-Palestinian wig-rings (Hawkes 1961a, 453–4) but except for a possible piece in the earlier Lanrivoaré (Finistère) hoard (Eluère 1982, Pl. 171) no intermediate finds are known. In Britain they are mainly found in southern England, from Wessex to East Anglia, while in Scotland there is a scatter in the north-east, however, the type is most commonly found in Ireland where it has a wide distribution (Fig. 42).

'Lock-rings' also present a problem with regard to origins. Their distribution in Britain is largely eastern but the main concentration is in Ireland, in north Munster, where the largest and most spectacular specimens were made (Fig. 41). This would have been a prime area of manufacture (Eogan 1969). Bullae also lack forerunners but their shapes vaguely recall the form of some bronze one-piece pendants that occur in 'carp's-tongue' contexts on the continent and in England. These have been termed Lyzel pendants by O'Connor (1980, 571; Evans 1881, 405).

An external area that may have made an important contribution to the emergence of Dowris Phase gold working is the west Baltic land of northern Europe centred on Denmark. As has been previously mentioned the penannular bracelets with evenly-expanded solid terminals could represent native typological development from the unexpanded terminal type of the Bishopsland Phase, the hollow terminal type (Variety 11) representing further development. Nevertheless, it must be borne in mind that a type of penannular bracelet with evenly-expanded hollow terminals, the so called 'oath-rings' made from both gold and bronze, came into existence in Nordic lands during Period IV but were most popular during Period V (Baudou 1960, 64–7). Even if it is difficult to prove a connection between 'oath-rings' and bracelets, other Irish objects are close in form to certain north European types. These include bowls, which were particularly prominent in Denmark and adjoining areas throughout the Later Nordic Bronze Age (Periods III–V) with small numbers in southern Germany and France and also in north-western Spain (Eogan 1981b). None of the Irish bowls have positive associations but their art and the distribution in north Munster suggest a Dowris Phase date. Although difficult to prove the boxes may also have a background in the Danish area. At least in that region circular belt boxes made from bronze and having concentric circle decoration were current (Brøndsted 1939, 101–2, Fig. 93:c; 94). The 'dress-fasteners' appear to be a modification of Periods IV–V fibulae with large hollow terminals which are often decorated with motifs that include concentric circles and which were on occasions embellished with gold leaf. The origin of the 'sleeve-fasteners' is difficult to establish, the flat outwardly-projecting terminals recall those on the Late Urnfield/'carp's tongue' thick bracelets with internally hollowed body (No. 3 above), but in view of their shape, arched bow decorated with parallel lines, and size they could be considered as a modification of another Nordic type, the caterpillar brooch which dates to Period IV (Randsborg 1972, 29–33, Maps 7–8), a brooch that is mainly found in northern Zealand and northern Jutland.

But these ornaments do not stand alone, they were part of a wider Nordic influenced assemblage. Although amber has been found in the coastal areas of East Anglia in England (Beck and Shennan 1991, 16–19) in view of the quantity used in Ireland it is likely that it was imported from Jutland or other Baltic lands; fashioning would have taken place in Ireland. Other Nordic inspired types are bronze disc-headed pins with either straight or bent stem, and later cup-headed pins, annular bracelet with ring, toggle, shields (or moulds) of wood or leather with boss and concentric rib concentration that are interrupted with a U-shaped notch, and bronze horns. What is interesting is that apart from a small number of pins within the primary series (Eogan 1974a, 84) and the amber, none of the other items can be considered as imports; what exists are Irish renderings or modifications. No doubt the native craftsman must initially have seen originals but these need only have been available in small numbers. It would also have been the importation of some Nordic types that enriched the art, the new motifs include conical projections, concentric circles and possibly the more lavish "diadem-vessel" style.

As already discussed gold discs were popular in the Nordic area and even earlier this region also had broad neckrings (*halskragen*). While concrete proof is lacking, it is tempting to think of these two further Irish types, discs and gorgets, as having a background in the north of Europe but there is a considerable chronological gap to fill. It is just possible that the Irish pieces represent a vague reflection of earlier Nordic types but how such memories would have lingered cannot be established. In view of these difficulties, perhaps discs and gorgets should be considered as native developments. The body of the gorget retains the concept of a multi-stranded neck ornament, a concept that previously existed elsewhere, for instance in Britain, with the multiple-stranded gold bar torcs or on the continent with the Sintra collar (Hawkes 1971; Powell 1973) or the Nordic *halskragen*. The gorget could then have emerged by adding discs to each end of the body. The collar is another native type but reflecting less elaborate workmanship and creativity in design than the gorget.

Modification

The thick ring with incised geometric decoration could have developed out of the 'hair-ring'. In view of the similarity of the body decoration striated rings could have emerged out of the 'sleeve-fastener'. A parallel development produced the thick penannular bracelet, Variety 12, and its emergence can be attributed to interaction between penannular bracelets with hollow terminals and 'dress-fasteners'.

Geographical Locations

The wearing of ornaments made from gold and other materials was, of course, only one of the wide-ranging changes that took place during the Dowris Phase. The widespread distribution of certain types, 'dress-fasteners' for instance (Fig. 40), shows that the population was dispersed throughout the land. The hoards of gold objects like those during the Bishopsland Phase may be considered as personal ornament sets, and as such they confirm the presence of wealthy persons or families. However, an important aspect of this phase is the correlation of some artifact types with specific geographical locations.

During the Bishopsland Phase, gold ornaments, either as individual finds or associated with others in hoards, concentrated in Leinster in a triangle that was widest along the coast and narrowing to the centre. There was also a scatter of ornaments in the north-east and less so in the south. The use of gold became more widespread during the Dowris Phase and shifts in distributional patterns took place. Leinster lost its prominence; north-east Ulster strengthened its position, while in north Munster a flourishing gold industry emerged. Ireland can now be considered as a socio-economic unit but with regions and sub-regions within it that had their own characteristics. There were three principal industrial regions each of which was characterised by the presence of artifacts of unusual type; some were items of prestige and luxury but these were not autonomous or exclusive to each other and interchange was a feature.

1. *Midland.* This emerged on the foundations of the Bishopsland Phase. Its principal gold type is the penannular bracelet with evenly-expanded terminals represented by two main varieties, *viz.* solid thin body and evenly-expanded terminals that may be solid or hollowed (Varieties 10–11) and Variety 12 which has a thick body and hollowed evenly-expanded terminals. The arrival of bronze objects from Britain was important, the most prominent being the slender faceted axehead and its developed form, the thick faceted axehead. Harnessed horses may also have been a feature (e.g. rattle-pendants from Lissanode, Co. Westmeath, Eogan 1964, 307, Fig 16:15). Bronze rings some of which might have been associated with horse harness also concentrate in this region (Eogan 1983a, Fig 3:D for distribution of hoards with rings). Finds of bronzes from Keeloge on the Shannon and Kildrinagh on the Nore may indicate fording places and, therefore, the importance of communication (for sword finds see Eogan 1965, 64, 67–8). The basic family unit would have been the single farmstead with mixed farming practised as was the case at Ballinderry No. 2, Co. Offaly (Hencken 1942, 6–27). For a background for the British material north Wales was important as the hoards from Tŷ Mawr and Llangwyllog in Anglesey testify (Lynch 1970, Figs. 68–69) and the hoard with horse-harness trappings from Parc-y-Meirch found further east close to the coast in Denbighshire (Savory 1980, 119, Fig 39). This midland province must also have been a source for export of gold objects, not only a reflex trade to north Wales as the hoards from Castell Crwn, Gaerwen and Beaumaris show (Lynch 1970, 203–6, Fig 67) but further afield (see Figs. 39–41). This postulated province may have had centres of formation within it, such as the Port Laoghais area with its Ballytegan and other hoards (Eogan 1983a, Nos 94–9) and westwards in the Shannon valley around Banagher, Co. Offaly (Eogan 1983a, No. 117). This seems to have been an important area of industrial expansion, the items from Lusmagh, Co. Offaly may have constituted a hoard of specialist tools (Eogan 1983a, 192–3; No 22), but also of ritual change. Included would have been the "sacred" lake of Dowris into which quantities of bronze objects were deposited but also indicating, for the first time, the emergence of a new type of hoard, the so called 'Founders' hoard, which had an immediate background in 'carp's-tongue' complex Britain.

In a modified fashion this new industry of the midland region can be considered as a revival

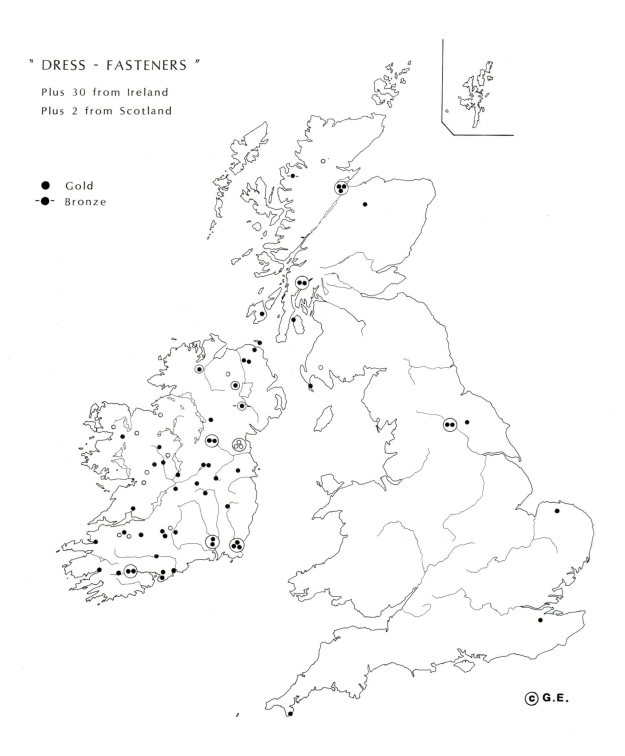

" DRESS - FASTENERS "

Plus 30 from Ireland

Plus 2 from Scotland

●   Gold

-●-   Bronze

Figure 40. Distribution of 'dress-fasteners'.
(Enclosed symbol indicates a hoard. Open symbol indicate that only county of origin is known).

of Bishopsland Phase events (p. 77–8). Those were explained as the result of demands for metal from Beerhackett-Taunton communities in southern England. Now the 'carp's-tongue'/Ewart Park Phase was a large consumer of copper and to a lesser extent gold. These materials were probably being acquired from the continent as some 'carp's-tongue' scrap hoards suggest but that supply need not have been sufficient to meet all of the needs; to achieve this perhaps Irish resources were again resorted to. This could have involved a resumption of contacts with the area of previous connections, the east and midlands, with its gold and copper in Wicklow. The 'carp's-tongue' complex could have been anxious to have had access to foreign supplies of metal and in turn producers of metal objects in the Midlands province would have had access to a foreign market.

2. *North-east.* Territorially this is a more coherent region from the point of view of find distribution. The regional personal ornaments were gold 'sleeve-fasteners', striated rings (Fig. 43) and bronze disc-headed pins of the primary series (Eogan 1974a, 84). Further items were the splendid sheet-bronze buckets and cauldrons, especially Class A (Hawkes and Smith 1957) as well as cast bronze objects notably the wind instruments termed horns of Class 1 (Coles 1963, 326–30). New types of socketed axeheads with a British background were concentrated in the north-east. These include axes with a prominent mouth moulding, ridge at base of neck and having either a plain or rib-decorated body (Eogan forthcoming). Razors of Class 2 are also common (C.M. Piggott 1946, Fig. 2). These regional objects manifest a new social and ritual order but what was its nature and how did it come about? The facts are that the region received external types and it created others, principally the striated gold rings. The introduced types have backgrounds in two different regions – Britain and northern Europe. The former was the immediate homeland of the bronze vessels and socketed axes but the 'sleeve-fasteners', horns and disc-headed pins of the primary series have their background in the Danish area. The inhabitants of the north-east province may also have been the first to use other novel types such as small tools (e.g. gouges and chisels) from Britain and amber from Denmark.

The Nordic influence appears to have been more than just a source of inspiration for gold ornaments and other metal types. New fashions in clothing may also have been introduced. After all 'dress-fasteners', and 'sleeve-fasteners' and pins are accessories to clothing and we know that in Early Christian Ireland, clothing acted as a symbol of an individual's wealth and status (Fitzgerald 1991, 85). And it is just in the north-east, at Cromaghs (Co. Antrim) that good evidence for clothing has come to light. This includes parts of a woven woollen cloak (Eogan 1983a, 53), some of its features such as a selvedge on the top and bottom of the cloth can be paralleled on Danish prehistoric textiles (Henshall 1950, 135). The other related object appears to have been part of a belt, it was woven from black horse-hair and is finished off at the ends with tassels. In its own right this is a splendid and outstanding example of handicraft. In form, including tasselled terminals, as well as in aspects of its weaving the belt shows some resemblance to the woven woollen belts for some Danish burials dating to Period II (Henshall 1950, 138–9; for illustration of Borum Eshøj woman's belt and accompanying costume, see Glob 1970, fig 10, for Trindhøj man's costume, see Fig. 31). Belted garments were also worn in north-western Germany at the same time (Jacob-Friesen 1963, 304–9). Perhaps this tradition of costume continued on into Periods IV and V; evidence would not have survived in graves due to change to the cremation burial rite and lack of coffin burials. The north-east regional gold ornaments are not spectacular but Class 1 horns and the buckets and cauldrons are. They constitute sumptuary items and, as such, reflect a concentration of wealth but personal aggrandisement need not have been its main feature. However, it is likely that there were well-off and prominent citizens. The Cromaghs hoard could have been the paraphernalia of a master wood-worker – a vital craft in Dowris Phase Ireland as already noted. The presence of the buckets and cauldrons and the splendid flesh-fork from Dunaverney, Co. Antrim, as well as Class I horns indicate feasting and entertainment, perhaps periodic festivals of a communal nature, rather than events that involved the adulation of a leader. Of course commercial transactions could have been

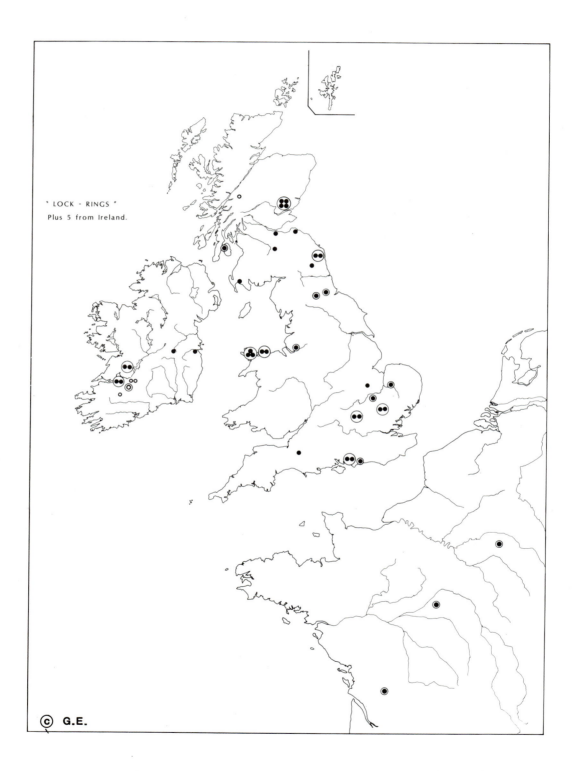

Figure 41. Distribution of 'lock-rings'.
(Enclosed symbol indicates a hoard. Open symbols indicate that only county of origin is known).

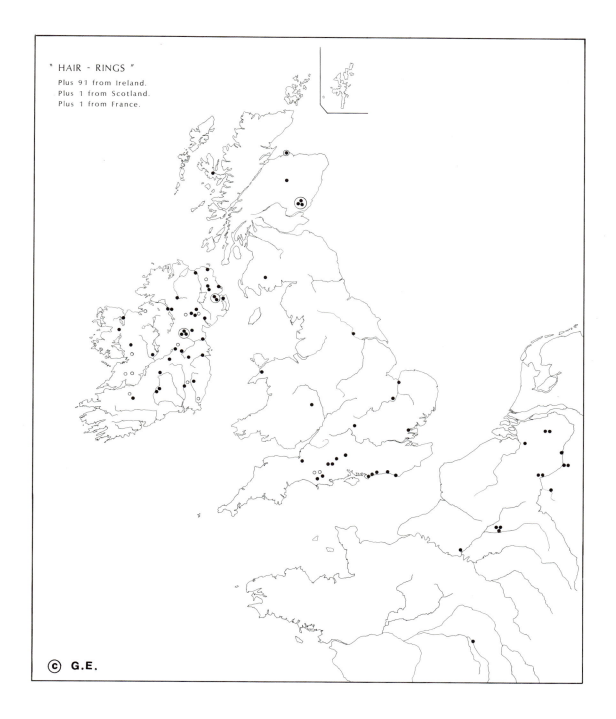

Figure 42. Distribution of 'hair-rings'.
(Enclosed symbol indicates a hoard. Open symbols indicate that only county of origin is known).

carried out on such occasions, such as the buying and selling of produce but also "legislative" matters that affected the tribe as a whole. Ritual too may have been a feature and this could have involved the deposition of hoards of metal objects or individual objects. In this connection a relevant site is the King's Stables, Co. Armagh (Lynn 1977). This was an artificially constructed water-logged basin-shaped pool 25 m in diameter and about 4 m deep, with a bank on the outside. It contained clay mould fragments, sherds of pottery, part of a human skull, animal bones and other objects. Dr. Lynn has suggested that this was a specially constructed ritual pool. The absence of outstanding gold ornaments and the presence of items such as bronze vessels may suggest that north-east Ulster had a communally-organised social structure, rather than one governed by a leader.

The north-east was an area of entry for Nordic and some British types but why was this so? Present evidence does not present a clear-cut answer, certainly it had no particular resource advantage. Nordic items in Ireland are predominantly personal ornaments but with a limited warrior element (U-notched shields) or objects associated with feasting or communal gatherings (horns). Even so it is unlikely that these objects emerged as a result of some casual or haphazard occurrences, such as the bartering of personal belongings by visiting Nordic fishermen in return for provision or shelter (Hodges 1956, 49). It is more likely that the arrival of prototypes or at least a knowledge of Nordic types was the result of emerging commercial activities, such as trade in bronze and gold. As has been mentioned already Period V was a time of large-scale metal consumption in Nordic lands and of importation of types from the Alpine region. That area lacked natural sources of metal; Ireland could supply this and in so doing was benefiting economically. The already postulated communal gatherings may also have been drawing people from afar. May one speculate that amongst them were salesmen and buyers from 'carp's-tongue'/ Ewart Park lands on the one hand and from the more distant Danish region on the other? The north-eastern province is of further significance as it influenced the central province; most of the disc-headed pins from the latter province belong to the developed series.

The midland province has been explained as a virtual revival of the commercial and trading activities that existed during the Bishopsland Phase consequent to the export of Irish metal to the Beerhackett-Taunton complex. But the problem with the north-east region is that the forerunners of the tools concentrate in southern Britain, so why was an area in the Irish north-east receiving types from afar? Taking one aspect, the socketed axes, did the forests of Antrim provide special types of wood and for its more efficient working new and improved types of socketed axes were introduced? Perhaps the answer should be more general. Could it be the continued growth and expansion of the 'carp's-tongue'/Ewart Park Phase occasioned the seeking out of new trading areas? Precise chronology is insecure but perhaps one can speculate that the midland economic zone was the first to come into existence and therefore had to be by-passed. There is clear evidence for direct contact between north-east Ireland and England; the contents of the Crevilly-valley (Co. Antrim) hoard could have been English imports.

North Munster. Since the time of the wedge-shaped tomb builders of about 2000 BC, information about human activity in north Munster is limited but at the end of the Bronze Age a considerable upsurge in activity took place. As elsewhere the region has a fair amount of good agricultural land, bisected by a prominent river, direct access to the Atlantic and copper deposits in the Silvermines Mountains (Jackson 1979, 108, Map 1) but there is no evidence that these were exploited during the Dowris Phase. The general range of Late Bronze Age metal types circulated throughout Munster but with some of the prestige types there was an exclusiveness in distribution (*cf.* Eogan 1964, Fig. 19; see Fig. 44). Class B cauldrons and Class II horns, both of bronze, occur almost exclusively in the south-western parts. In view of their possible function, one group acting as containers or as cooking vessels the other as wind instruments, they may have been used during communal ceremonies. In a more geographically restricted area centred around the lower Shannon in north Munster, there is a concentration of artifacts of unusual type some of which were objects of prestige and luxury. This is especially so with the gorgets, 'lock-rings', bowls and boxes, objects that were costly to produce, difficult to manufacture and profuse in decoration. Gorgets and 'lock-rings' were lavish ornaments, supreme types without competitors and as such indicate the presence of significant persons. Already, in dealing with *c.*13th century BC gold-working, it was pointed out that gold discs were worn by persons of rank in the Danish area. They can, therefore, be considered as indicators of authority and status held by certain males who must also have had access to wealth. Whether this is relevant to the Dowris Phase in Ireland, cannot be conclusively established but what can be established is that in north Munster

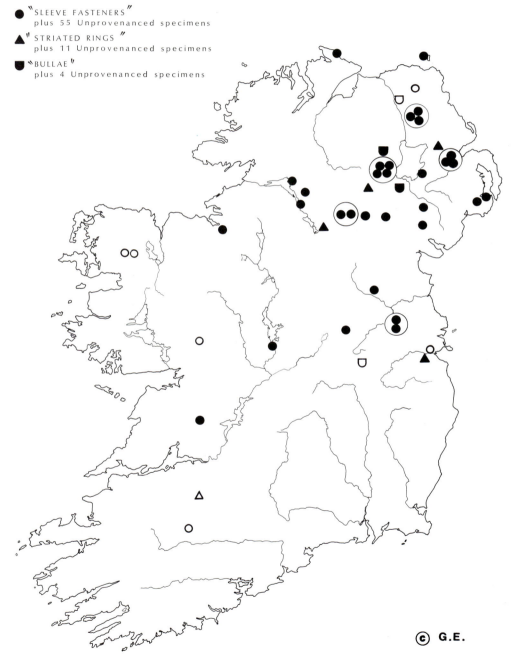

● "SLEEVE FASTENERS"
plus 55 Unprovenanced specimens

▲ "STRIATED RINGS"
plus 11 Unprovenanced specimens

▌ "BULLAE"
plus 4 Unprovenanced specimens

Ⓒ G.E.

Figure 43. Distribution of 'sleeve-fasteners', striated rings, and heart-shaped bullae.
(Enclosed symbol indicates a hoard. Open symbols indicate that only county of origin is known).

discs, serving as terminals for gorgets, took on a new role and became part of a sumptuous piece of composite construction. The creation of gorgets may at least in part be due to a wish or need to wear discs in a prominent manner as beheld their significance. As already noted the concept of the broad body already existed in the multi-stranded torcs for instance (p. 96). For north Munster, one could suggest that the lavish gold ornaments were manifestations of a hierarchical order, in other words north Munster society was presided over by chieftains or magnates who were part of a new social fabric that was different to that of the south-west Munster. Ritual was also important in that area. In this regard the bowls and boxes could have had a role. There may also have been sacred places at which objects were deposited in honour of deities, perhaps over a period of time. Southwards from Dowris these are the great collections from Mooghaun, Askeaton and Cullen (Eogan 1983a, 117–42; 69–72; 101–2; 154–56). At least some of these were wet-places. At this time Cullen could have been a small natural lake, larger but fulfilling a similar role to the artificial pool at the King's Stables.

Taking the Irish evidence firstly it may be that the north Munster province was the last to emerge. This is suggested by the fact that useful everyday items such as small tools only occur in limited numbers in that region, indeed in the western part of the country as a whole (Eogan 1974b, Abb. 6), and that the main socketed axe type is the native bag-shaped form. However, there need not be a long time-lag, as a slender faceted axehead and a "Thorndon" type socketed knife occur in the Enagh wood-worker's hoard from Co. Clare (unpublished N.M.I.) which also contained bag-shaped socketed axeheads and other tools. The presence of two broad faceted axes in the central Cork hoard of Mountrivers (Pl. XVI bottom) indicates penetration even further south.

The rise of the north Munster province is not easy to explain fully. The background to the gold bowls is likely to have been the Danish region and that may also have been the case with the boxes as previously mentioned, but from the point of view of both technology of manufacture and prototypes gorgets and 'lock-rings' stand apart. If these items were due to the arrival of highly skilled and creative craftsmen, where did they come from? In the absence of such information they have to be attributed to local innovation. For other items there is a native Irish background, in fact in part it is due to contributions from the other two provinces. Perhaps the north-eastern province was the source of the horns which were modified (Class 2) in Munster. The Class B cauldrons present problems with regard to origin. Generally they have been considered as a contribution from north-western Iberia (Hawkes and Smith 1957, 176–85) and while somewhat similar cauldrons occur in that region (Eogan 1990, 160–2) nevertheless, could it be that they emerged in Ireland out of Class A as is postulated in parallel fashion for Class 2 horns? The Midland province also paved the way for the emergence of the north Munster province. None of the varieties of the penannular bracelet with evenly-expanded terminals have their forerunners in that area but a case has already been made for a background in the east of the country, if so the north Munster specimens appear to be an extension southwards.

North Munster now became incorporated into the Irish Late Bronze Age and as a result it obtained a position within the wider Irish complex. Did it also have a relationship with wider external complexes? This seems to have been so. The gold bowls reflect influence from the continent, probably its northward part, but despite the north European concentration they were also accepted, due to a process of diffusion not yet understood, in Atlantic lands, not only north Munster but well to the south. This is clear from the finds from Axtroki in the Basque lands (Eogan 1981b, 375) and supported by a subsequent find from Rixano on the Atlantic corner of north-west Spain close to La Coruña (Cardozo 1976). Some reorientation of contacts could have been taking place with north Munster in direct receipt of north European types but also achieving a role within long distance exchange networks that embraced the wider territories and larger socio-economic systems of the Atlantic Bronze Age. Within its southern regions the Atlantic Bronze Age of Iberia was undergoing transformations which included the incorporation of new elements. An important area was in southern Spain in the region of, and inland from, Huelva (p. 106). There the Tartessos complex emerged partly as a result of new elements arriving from

PLATE XIII

General view of Bog of Cullen, Co. Tipperary. Photo: Eoin Grogan.

PLATE XIV

Gorget, Shannongrove, Co. Limerick. Photo: Victoria and Albert Museum, London.

PLATE XV

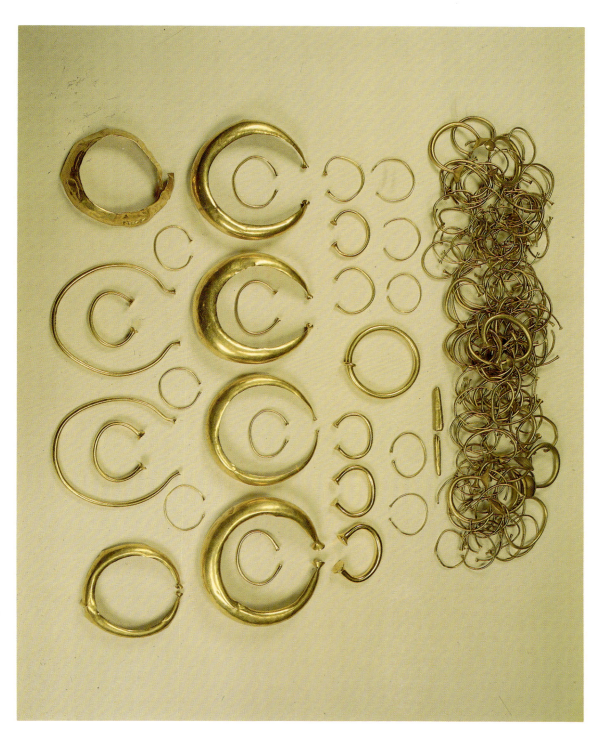

Part of hoard from Mooghaun, Co. Clare. Photo: National Museum of Ireland.

PLATE XVI

Hoards from Meenwaun (Banagher), Co. Offaly (top), and Mountrivers, Co. Cork (bottom).
Photos: National Museum of Ireland.

PLATE XVII

Hoards from Killymoon, Co. Tyrone (top) and New Ross, Co. Waterford (bottom).
Photos: National Museum of Ireland.

PLATE XVIII

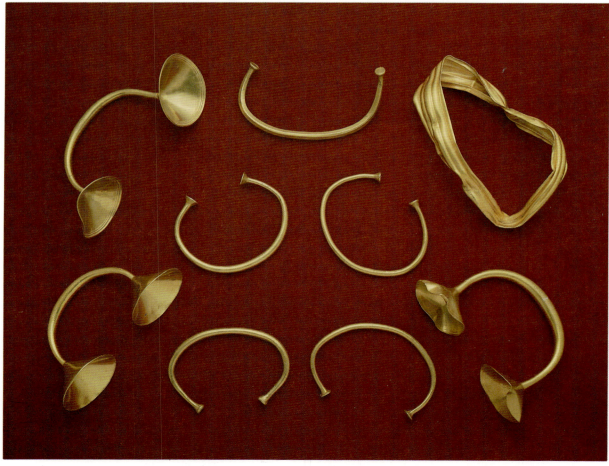

Hoards from Morvah, Cornwall (top) and Heights of Brae, Ross-Cromarty (bottom).
Photos: British Museum and National Museum of Scotland.

PLATE XIX

'Dress-fastener', Clones, Co. Monaghan (top) and bulla, Bog of Allen, Co. Kildare area (bottom).
Photos: National Museum of Ireland.

PLATE XX

The Messingwerk (Eberswalde) hoard, Brandenburg, Germany. Photo: Museum für Ur- und Frühgeschichte, SMPK Berlin

Mediterranean lands. These involved fibulae of the elbow type, wagons with four-spoked wheels, V-notched shields and helmets. The practice of erecting pictorial stones was also a feature (Almagro 1966). The re-opening of contacts to the south was possibly achieved by the 'carp's-tongue' people and the deposit of bronzes from Huelva harbour (M. Almagro-Basch, *Invent. Archeo.* España. Fas. 6. Madrid, 1962, E.7 (1–2) largely consisted of northern types, possibly contents of a merchantman that may have set out from a Breton or southern English port, more likely the latter in view of the presence of spearheads with lunate-shaped openings in the

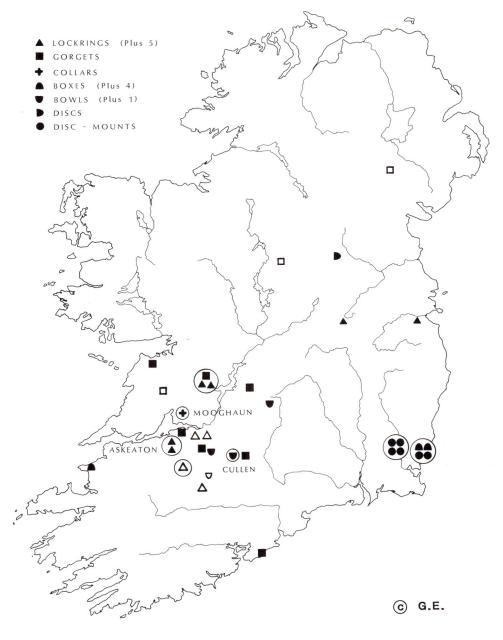

Figure 44. Distribution in Ireland of sheet-gold objects of the Dowris Phase. (Collars, gorgets, boxes, bowls, discs and disc-mounts). The place-names refer to the large assemblages. (Enclosed symbol indicates a hoard. Open symbols indicate that only county of origin is known).

blade. But Tartessos might also have been contributing to areas northwards and it is interesting that Christopher Hawkes (1969) suggested that the wooden boat model with gold inlay from Caergwrle in north Wales was based on Phoenician ships. Another important area was the north-west of Iberia. As already noted this area has gold bowls possibly with a north Munster background. Even if some doubt can be cast on the place of origin of the bowls there is no doubt about the penannular bracelet of bronze with evenly-expanded hollowed terminals from an unrecorded location in north Portugal (Silva 1986, 185, Fig. XCIX: 7); it is a typical Irish type. Could these connections be even more fundamental. A feature of northern Portugal and north-west Spain is a distinctive type of fortified settlement – the *Castro*. These are a most common monument in north-western Iberia and some have multi-vallation. There is a problem with their dating. Certainly some hill-tops on which *castros* were built had Later Bronze activity but the construction of *castros* may date from a later time. The north-Munster area may have been incorporated into a wider cultural zone. As a result of an increase in commercial and other activities by Atlantic communities to the south, it took on a personality of its own but yet remained very much part of the Irish Late Bronze Age (Eogan 1993, 125–32).

Irish Gold for Export

As natural gold is rare in Britain it seems likely that the objects used there were either imported or manufactured from introduced raw material. In view of the continental origins of the British varieties of penannular bracelets perhaps they, or the material from which they were manufactured, originated there. The results of analysis do not provide a solution. In Britain metal groups M/N/MC/NC contain ornaments of different date; some belong to the Beerhackett-Taunton Phase, others to the 'carp's-tongue' sword complex. However, in Ireland most Dowris Phase ornaments can be assigned to that grouping (Hartmann 1970, 90–97; 1982, 104–7). On the other hand definite Irish types have been found in Britain, sometimes in the same hoard, as at Morvah (Cornwall) or Caister-on-Sea (Norfolk) (Pls. XVIII top and 13).

The Morvah ornaments may be linked with barter for Cornish tin and, since that hoard also contained British pieces, 'carp's tongue' people may have been on the same errand. Morvah is of further interest as its location is 'Atlantic' and may represent a stage on the way south to Iberia. Assuming at least that north Munster was a main area of 'lock-ring' manufacture, their distribution could indicate a route outwards from that region (Fig. 41). Firstly, this led to the Dublin area, within the Midland Province, and then across the Irish Sea to Anglesey, a route that could have taken not only 'lock-rings' but possibly also penannular bracelets with evenly-expanded terminals, since examples occur in the Gaerwen (associated with 'lock-rings'), Beaumaris and Castell Crwn hoards (Lynch 1970, 203–6). Some of the contents of the Llyngwollog and Ty Mawr hoards, such as the amber beads may, too, have had an Irish source. Eastwards and northwards, 'lock-rings' have a strung-out distribution along north Wales, over the Pennines to South Yorkshire and then northwards to Balmashanner in eastern Scotland, north of the Tay. South-west Scotland also has a couple of 'lock-rings' but in the Atlantic area of Britain the best evidence is provided by penannular bracelets of Varieties 10–12 and less so by 'dress-fasteners'. The principal region of contact was in the western part, especially in the coastal lands (Figs. 39, 40). There are a number of finds in the southern islands of Arran and Islay and it is interesting that one of the more important finds of Irish gold – a hoard mainly consisting of bracelets and 'dress-fasteners' – was found at the Heights of Brae near Dingwall in Ross and Cromarty just to the north of the mouth of the Great Glen indicating that the Glen may have been a route to the north-east (Pl. XVIII bottom). In addition to the dozen or so pieces from Heights of Brae an even more substantial hoard was found at Coul, Argyll. This contained thirty six bracelets (Clarke and Kemp 1984; Taylor 1980, 90).

In the English midlands and north Wales the transporters or traders were part of the southern English 'carp's-tongue' sword complex, their 'badge of office' or talisman being the penannular bracelet with evenly-expanded solid terminals and flat body (No 1 above). The distribution of this type suggests a route from Anglesey to East Anglia (or visa-versa) with its Caister-on-Sea hoard and other finds (Hawkes & Clarke 1963). This concept of traders also receives support from the fact that a gold ingot forms part of the Llanarmon-yn-Iâl (Denbighshire) hoard and that a similar type bracelet was found with a 'lock-ring' in the hoard from Portfield, Lancashire (Blundell and Longworth 1967). There may have been a corresponding southern route, possibly from Wexford to the Bristol channel area and then eastwards to Kent with its Irish gold ornament finds from Aylesford and Wanderslade (see list p. 145, 153). The Irish gold trade did not stop in eastern England; in fact this region was a stepping stone to the northern continent and was the immediate background to the thick penannular bracelet from Gahlstorf in Lower Saxony near Bremen. The reason that the Gahlstorf bracelet is the only Irish gold object in the north of continental Europe may be due to the fact that others could have been treated as ingots and melted down. As has previously been mentioned this was a time of major industrial expansion and social development in west Baltic lands, especially Denmark. As part of this the use of gold increased enormously. What was probably a mutually beneficial trade network was established and that can explain the range of north European types in Ireland and Irish gold in the North. The south Scandinavian area and Britain were the leading markets but in Britain the nature of the distribution of types suggest that they may also reflect a route to the Baltic.

ASSESSMENT

In the early centuries of the first millenium BC most of Europe participated in a major industrial revolution. On both sides of the English Chanel the 'carp's-tongue' sword complex arose, this was influenced by Late Urnfield cultures to the east, the Rhineland-Alpine areas and also further afield. Regardless of the origin of 'lock-rings' and 'hair-rings' the Channel region was a source of the most prominent gold type that emerged in England and extended over the south and up the east coast of Scotland. This is the penannular bracelet in its different varieties (Nos. 1–9).

Britain, in particular western Scotland, was also indebted to Ireland for personal ornaments especially penannular bracelets, 'dress-fasteners' and possibly raw gold. Ireland now became one of the main centres of gold production in Europe. This was part of a country-wide revitalised metal industry which produced a variety of objects in abundance including superb pieces in sheet-gold. In addition to Britain its produce was exported to northern Europe and possibly to Atlantic Iberia. One can tentatively identify three industrial provinces each of which by and large had its own distinctive gold objects. In the north this was the 'sleeve-fastener' and striated ring, in the midlands penannular bracelets with evenly expanded terminals and in the south-west the flashy items of sheet-gold such as gorgets, 'lock-rings' and vessels. Detailed chronology is lacking but the main periods of external contacts after 1000 BC mainly parallel with Period V in the west Baltic area and the west continental British 'carp's-tongue' (Ewart Park) stage with its late Urnfield element. In view of the concentrated use of gold ornaments in the eastern midlands during the Bishopsland Phase, including penannular bracelets and also such factors as the association of narrow faceted axes with "Middle" Bronze Age forms of looped spearhead at Kish, Co. Wicklow and Ballinliss, south Armagh (Eogan 1983a, Nos 155 and 43) during the Dowris Phase, perhaps this was the initial area of change. The north-east province could have emerged about the same time in view of the presence of some types with a Nordic Period IV background, i.e. disc-headed pins. The north east also received strong influences from Britain, indeed the contents of the Crevilly-valley hoard may have been imported. Socially, in both the northern and midland provinces, one can picture well-off farming families but North Munster may have been different. The sumptuous sheet-gold pieces suggest a higher social order, perhaps a priesthood but just as readily, probably more so, powerful secular individuals. This province was stimulated from the other two but it also may have had relationships with the southern

Atlantic zone from which it was also enriched. Considering the insular Late Bronze Age from the point of view of its gold items one can conclude that in both Britain and Ireland but more particularly in the latter, possibly due to native supplies, gold objects constitute an important body of information that throws light not only on technology and manufacturing achievements but also on the nature of a society that is seen to be talented and artistic and at least in the south of Ireland stratified also. Above all gold demonstrates not only regional independence but also regional interdependence.

THE END

About 700 BC changes took place in the Late Bronze Age complexes (Cunliffe 1978, 32–8, 137–50, 330–31). An obvious development is the appearance in Britain and Ireland of continental Hallstatt C elements especially the smaller, *Gündlingen*, bronze swords and the contemporary winged and boat-shaped chapes (Cowen 1967) and looped razors. New varieties of socketed axes also emerged, the Armorican and Sompting types (Burgess 1969). Important hoards are those of Sompting in Sussex (Curwen 1948) and Llyn Fawr in Glamorgan (Fox and Hyde 1939). These hoards show that cauldrons of Class B were current but in particular Llyn Fawr demonstrates changes in horse-harness and in particular in technology; iron-working was now being established. It is usual to take a minimal view of this Hallstatt C element, some continental elements becoming incorporated into Late Bronze Age contexts, but this may be underestimating its significance. After all the Court-Saint-Etienne burials and their grave goods shows that Bavarian cavaliers arrived in Belgium close to the Channel coast (Mariën 1958). This site provides many parallels for the continental element found at Llyn Fawr, Glamorganshire. If the Hallstatt C element is in general an addition or enrichment of the existing Late Bronze Age, this is not so from the gold point of view. Taking gold as a criteria it was a time of impoverishment since it was at this time that gold-working ceased possibly as a consequence of the technological dislocation caused by the spread of iron-working. But Hallstatt C may have brought about much greater changes than it is credited with, and more wide-ranging than merely technological, for the first time since the Penard Phase there is the possibility that people who were engaged in non-commercial or non-domestic activities arrived, and amongst them could have been cavaliers.

In Ireland the Hallstatt C element, Athlone phase, is less prominent than in Britain but it may still be significant in contributing to the demise of the old Bronze Age culture. Were aliens prowling the land and even dominating the indigenous population? In this connection it can be noted that two small Hallstatt C swords (Class 5) may have been found in the bog of Cullen (Eogan 1983, 155, No. 3 or 4). As such types are foreign to the contents of the assemblage could they have been thrown into this great and established sacred site as a deliberate deed of mortification of a secret site and its rituals by culturally different people so as to deprive it of character and significance. These were probably not the only changes that were taking place, social alterations may have been more fundamental. While the significance of Hallstatt C is not yet fully appreciated certainly throughout Britain and Ireland from now on the age of gold-working was temporarily over.

Chapter VI

Conclusions

On four separate occasions during the "Bronze Age" of Britain and Ireland gold-working was a significant feature as apparently it indicates wealth in society and the high status of certain individuals or groups within it. Objects made from it could also have served as trappings during political or ritual ceremonies. Gold throws light on autonomous insular creativity and also on external contacts, notably commerce and trade. This is especially so with Ireland where the export of gold must have been an important economic factor. The initial working of gold in Britain and Ireland during the late 3rd millenium BC can be attributed to Beaker-using people with a continental background possibly in the area of the lower Rhine. The wearing of gold objects was the prerogative of the male leaders. In turn this society and this practice underwent further development during the Early Bronze Age when, especially in the Wessex area, society was characterised by influential and powerful individuals. Males continued to play a prominent and significant role but females were also accorded status. In Ireland evidence for the deposition of gold objects with burials is scanty. Predominantly the finds consist of individual objects, mainly lunula, although a couple of objects occurring together and forming a small hoard are known. In view of the absence of skeletal associations the sex of the wearers cannot be determined but perhaps it should be noted that the lunula related spacer-plate necklaces from Scotland, northern England (of jet) and Wessex (of amber) are in the main found with female remains.

Changes in the overall cultural composition of Britain and Ireland took place about 16th–17th centuries. The use of gold ornaments was only a minor part of this newly emerging complex and it was some centuries later, around the 13th and the 12th that a major revival or re-introduction of gold-working took place. While the emergence of this second main phase of the gold usage appeared, new techniques, new technologies and new types emerged, the latter including sheet gold objects and heavy ornaments made from bar gold. The re-emergence of gold-working at this time was part of much wider cultural changes that took place not only in Britain and Ireland but on the continent as well. The initiation can have been due to southern English farming communities benefiting from or participating in the creation of greater wealth by continental communities. In gold-working regional development and innovation took place, but in some cases the development was local as is demonstrated by the Irish 'tress-rings'. The use of sheet gold continued, now more elaborately decorated and the use of bar gold was introduced and often skilfully worked.

After the 12th century gold ornaments faded from the scene but a couple of centuries or so later a new phase of gold-working emerges. During the 9th and 8th centuries, south-eastern England in particular came under strong continental influence which went back to the Late Urnfield complexes of west-central Europe. Personal ornaments in the form of bracelets, in both bronze and gold, were worn in considerable numbers, especially in Kent and Sussex which must have been the home of well-off farming families. British type gold ornaments were of course, known as far west as Cornwall and northwards in the eastern counties up to Scotland. In Ireland the expansion in gold-working was more marked and goldsmiths created some of Europe's most superb pieces. The Irish series of gold ornaments now in use owes a great deal to native innovation, even to native creation, nevertheless stimulus from abroad was important. The Danish region was relevant but unless penannular bracelets with evenly expanded solid terminals have an origin there, influence from British gold-working was limited. Some ornaments have a wide distribution throughout the country but the distribution of others is more restricted and concentrates in two principal areas, in the north-east and in the lower Shannon area of North Munster. Penannular bracelets occur frequently in the eastern midlands. Gold objects may therefore throw light on aspects of society. For instance in the north-east communal gatherings may have been a feature while in north Munster the sumptuous ornaments suggest the presence of communal leaders, either secular or religious. Of course, in all regions the main economic stay would have been farming.

The 7th century saw the demise of insular gold-working. New and exotic influences, again emanating from the western Continent, were a feature (Hallstatt C, Athlone Phase) though it cannot be conclusively proved that Hallstatt C elements brought about far reaching changes including the termination of gold-working. At least the use of gold and its manufacture into ornaments for personal use was no longer relevant. The long history, in its various stages, of the use of gold during the insular Bronze Age came to an end. With the disappearance of this ancient tradition of accomplished art and craft a period of craftsmanship that brought into existence some of the greatest creations of European artisans and artists faded from the scene.

Bibliography

Abbreviations
JRSAI Journal of the Royal Society of Antiquaries Ireland, Dublin.
PPS Proceedings of the Prehistoric Society, London.
PRIA Proceedings of the Royal Irish Academy, Dublin.
PSAS Proceedings of the Society of Antiquaries of Scotland, Edinburgh.
UJA Ulster Journal of Archaeology, Belfast.

ALCOCK, L. 1971. Excavations at South Cadbury Castle 1970. *Antiquaries Journal* 51 (1971), 1–7.

ALMAGRO, Martín. 1966. *Las Estelas Decoradas del Suroeste Peninsular*, Bibliotheca Prehistorica Hispaña VIII, Madrid.

ALMAGRO, Martín. 1974a. The Bodonal de la Sierra Gold Find, *JRSAI*, 104 (1974), 44–51.

ALMAGRO, Martín. 1974b. Los Tesoros de Sagrajas y Berzocana y los torques de oro macizo del Occidente Peninsular. III Congreso Nacional de Arqueología, Oporto, (1974), 259–82.

ALMAGRO, Martín. 1977. *El Bronce Final y el Período Orientalizante en Extremadura*. Bibliotheca Prehistorica Hispaña Vol. XIV, Madrid.

ANDERSON, Joseph. 1886. *Scotland in Pagan Times: The Bronze and Stone Ages*. Edinburgh.

ANNABLE, F.K. & SIMPSON, D.D.A., 1964. *Guide Catalogue of the Neolithic and Bronze Age Collections in Devizes Museum*. Devizes.

ARMSTRONG, E.C.R. 1917. The Great Clare Find of 1854, *JRSAI*, 47 (1917) 21–36.

ARMSTRONG, E.C.R. 1922. Notes of some Irish Gold Ornaments, *JRSAI*, 52 (1922), 133–42.

ARMSTRONG, E.C.R. 1933. *Catalogue of Irish Gold Ornaments in the Collections of the Royal Irish Academy*, 2nd edition. Dublin.

BAUDOU, Evert. 1960. *Die regionale und chronologische Einteilung der jüngeren Bronzezeit im Nordischen Kreis*. Stockholm.

BECK, Curt & SHENNAN, Stephen. 1991. *Amber in Prehistoric Britain*. Oxbow Monograph 8. Oxford.

BENTON, S. 1930–31. The Excavation of the Sculptor's Cave, Covesay, Morayshire, *PSAS*, 65 (1930–31), 177–216.

BLUNDELL, J.D. & LONGWORTH, I.H. 1967. A Bronze Age Hoard from Portfield Farm, Whalley, Lancashire, *British Museum Quarterly*, 32 (1967), 8–14.

BOGNÁR-KUTZIÁN, Ida. 1963. *The Copper Age Cemetery of Tiszapolgár-Baatanya*. Budapest.

BRIARD, Jacques. 1965. *Les Dépôts Bretons et l'Age du Bronze Atlantique*. Rennes.

BRIARD, Jacques. 1966. *Dépôts de l'Age du Bronze de Bretagne: La Prairie de Mauves à Nantes*. Travaux du Laboratoire d'Anthropologie Préhistorique, Rennes.

BRIARD, Jacques, CORDIER, Gérard & GAUCHER, G. 1969. Un Dépôt de la Fin du Bronze Moyen à Malassis, Commune de Chery (Cher), *Gallia Préhistorie* 12 (1969), 37–82.

BRIGGS, Stephen, BRENNAN, James & FREEBURN, George. 1973. Irish Prehistoric Gold-working: some Geological and Metallurgical Considerations, *Bull. Historical Metallurgy Group* 7 (1973), 18–26.

BRITISH MUSEUM. 1920. *A Guide to the Antiquities of the Bronze Age in the Department of British and Medieval Antiquities*. London.

BRITTON, Denis. 1960. The Isleham Hoard, Cambridgeshire, *Antiquity*, 34 (1960), 279–82.

BRITTON, Denis. 1963. Traditions of metal-working in Later Neolithic and Early Bronze Age Britain, *PPS*, 29 (1963), 258–325.

BROHOLM, H.C. 1948. The Midskov Find, *Acta Archaeologia* (København), 19 (1948), 189–204.

BRØNDSTED, Johannes. 1939. *Danmarks Oldtid: II. Bronzealderen*. København.

BURGESS, Colin. 1968. *Bronze Age Metalwork in Northern England c.1000–700 BC*. Newcastle upon Tyne.

BURGESS, Colin. 1969. Some decorated socketed axes in Canon Greenwell's Collection. *Yorkshire Archaeological Journal* 43 (1969), 267–72.

BURGESS, Colin 1980. *The Age of Stonehenge*. London.

BURGESS, Colin. & GERLOFF, Sabine. 1981. *The Dirks and Rapiers in Great Britain and Ireland*. Prähistorische Bronzefunde, Abteilung IV, 7. München.

BUTLER, J.J. 1963. Bronze Age Connections across the North Sea, *Palaeohistoria* 9 (1963), 1–286.

CALLANDER, J. Graham. 1922–23. Scottish Bronze Age Hoards, *PSAS*, 57 (1922–23), 123–66.

CARDOZO, Mário. 1976. Valioso Archado Arqueológico em Espanha, *Revista de Guimarães* 86 (1976), 173–76.

CASE, H.J. 1966. Were Beaker-people the first Metallurgists in Ireland? *Palaeohistoria* 12 (1966), 141–77.

CASE, H.J. 1977. An early accession to the Ashmolean Museum, in Vladimir Markotic (ed) *Ancient Europe and the Meditteranean*. Warminster, 18–34.

CATLING, H.W. 1964. *Cypriot Bronze-work in the Mycenaean World*. Oxford.

CHILDE, V. Gordon. 1951. Bronze Dagger of Mycenaean Type from Pelynt, Cornwall, *PPS*, 17 (1951), 95.

CHROPOVSKÝ, B., DUŠEK, M. & POLLA, B. 1960. *Pohrebiská zo Staršej Doby Bronzovej na Slovensku (Gräberfelder aus der Älteren Bronzezeit in der Slowakei)*. Bratislava.

CLARK, J.G.D. 1932. Fresh evidence for the Dating of 'Lunalae', *Man* 32 (1932), 40–1.

CLARKE, D.L. 1970. *Beaker Pottery of Great Britain and Ireland*. Cambridge.

CLARKE, D.V. & KEMP, M.M.B. 1984. A Hoard of late Bronze Age gold objects from Heights of Brae, Ross and Cromarty District, *PSAS*, 114 (1984), 189–198.

CLARKE, D.V., COWIE, T.G. & FOXON, A. 1985. *Symbols of Power at the Time of Stonehenge*. Edinburgh.

CLIBBORN, Edward. 1860a. On the Gold Antiquities found in Ireland, *UJA*, 8 (1860), 36–98.

CLIBBORN, Edward. 1860b. Historical argument on the origin of the Irish Gold Antiquities, *UJA* 8 (1860), 88–98.

COFFEY, George. 1895. On a double-cist grave and remains at Oldbridge, Co. Meath, *PRIA*, 3 (1895), 747–92.

COFFEY, George. 1909. The Distribution of Gold Lunulae in Ireland and North-Western Europe, *PRIA*, 27C (1909), 251–58.

COFFYN, André. 1985. *Le Bronze Final Atlantique dans la Pénnisule Ibérique*. Paris.

COLES, J.M. 1959–60. Scottish Late Bronze Age Metalwork, *PSAS*, 93 (1959/60), 16–134.

COLES, J.M. 1963. Irish Bronze Age Horns and their relations with Northern Europe, *PPS*, 29 (1963), 326–56.

COLES, John M. 1963–64. Scottish Middle Bronze Age Metalwork, *PSAS*, 97 (1963–4), 82–156.

COLES, John M. 1968–69. Scottish Early Bronze Age Metalwork, *PSAS*, 101 (1968–69), 1–110.

COLES, John M. 1971. Bronze Age Spearheads with gold decoration, *Antiquaries Journal*, 51 (1971), 94–5.

COLES, John M., COUTTS, Herbert & RYDER, M.L. 1964. A Late Bronze Age Find from Pyotdykes, Angus, Scotland, *PPS*, 30 (1964), 186–98.

COLES, John M., & HARDING, A.F. 1979. *The Bronze Age in Europe*. London.

COLES, John M., & TAYLOR, Joan. 1971. The Wessex Culture: a Minimal View, *Antiquity*, 45 (1971), 6–14.

CORDIER, G. MILLOTTE, J.P. & RIQUET, R. 1960. Trois chachettes de bronze de l'Indre-et-Loire, *Gallia Préhistorie* 3 (1960), 109–28.

COWEN, J.D. 1967. The Hallstatt Sword of Bronze: on the Continent and in Britain, *PPS*, 33 (1967), 377–454.

CRAW, James Hewat. 1928–29. On a Jet Necklace from a Cist at Poltalloch, Argyll, *PSAS*, 63 (1928–29), 154–89.

ČUJANOVÁ-JÍLKOVÁ, Eva. 1970. *Mittelbronzezeitliche Hügelgräberfelder in Westböhmen*. Prague.

ČUJANOVÁ-JÍLKOVÁ, Eva. 1975. Zlaté předměty v hrobech českofalcké mohylové kultury (Gegenstände aus Gold in Gräbern der Bohmisch-Oberpfälzischen Hügelgräber Kultur), *Památky Archeologické*, 66 (1975, 74–132.

CUNLIFFE, B.W. 1978. *Iron Age Communities in Britain*. Second Edition. London.

CURWEN, E.C. 1948. A bronze cauldron from Sompting, Sussex, *Antiquaries Journal*, 28 (1948), 157–63.

CURWEN, E.C. 1954. *The Archaeology of Sussex*, 2nd edition. London.

DE LAET, Sigfried J. 1982. *La Belgique d'Avant les Romains*. Wetteren.

DÉCHELETTE, Joseph. 1924. *Manuel d'archéologie préhistorique, celtique et gallo-romaine*, 2nd edition. Paris.

DONALDSON, Peter. 1977. The Excavation of a Multiple Round Barrow at Barnack, Cambridgeshire 1974–1976, *Antiquaries Journal*, 57 (1977), 197–231.

ELUÈRE, Christiane. 1980–81. Réflexions à propos de 'boucles d'oreilles' torsadées en or de types connus à l'Age du Bronze, *Antiquités Nationales*, 12–13 (1980–81), 34–9.

ELUÈRE, Christiane. 1982. *Les Ors Préhistoriques*. Paris.

EOGAN, George. 1957. A Hoard of Gold Objects from Drissoge, Co. Meath, *JRSAI*, 87 (1957), 125–34.

EOGAN, George. 1964. The Later Bronze Age in Ireland in the light of recent research, *PPS*, 30 (1964), 268–351.

EOGAN, George. 1965. *Catalogue of Irish Bronze Swords*. Dublin.

EOGAN, George. 1967. The Associated finds of Gold Bar Torcs, *JRSAI*, 97 (1967), 129–75.

EOGAN, George. 1969. 'Lock-rings' of the late Bronze Age, *PRIA*, 67C (1969), 93–148.

EOGAN, George. 1972. 'Sleeve-fasteners' of the Late Bronze Age, in Frances Lynch & Colin Burgess (eds). *Prehistoric Man in Wales and the West*, Bath, 189–209.

EOGAN, George. 1974a. Pins of the Irish Late Bronze Age, *JRSAI*, 104 (1974), 74–119.

EOGAN, George. 1974b. Regionale Gruppierungen in der Spätbronzezeit Irlands, *Archäologisches Korrespondenzblatt*, 4 (1974), 319–27.

EOGAN, George. 1981a. Gold Discs of the Irish Late Bronze Age, in Donnchadh Ó Corráin (ed.) *Irish Antiquity*. Cork 1981, 147–62.

EOGAN, George. 1981b. The Gold Vessels of the Bronze Age in Ireland and Beyond, *PRIA*, 81C (1981), 345–82.

EOGAN, George. 1983a. *The Hoards of the Irish Later Bronze Age*. Dublin.

EOGAN, George. 1983b. Ribbon Torcs in Britain and Ireland, in Anne O'Connor & D.V. Clarke (eds). *From the Stone Age to the Forty-Five*. Edinburgh.

EOGAN, George. 1986. *Knowth and the Passage Tombs of Ireland*. London.

EOGAN, George. 1990. Possible Connections between Britain and Ireland and the East Mediteranean region during the Bronze Age, in *Orientalisch-Ägäische Einflusse in der Europäischen Bronzezeit*. Bonn. Monographien Band 15: Römisch-Germanisches Zentralmuseum, Mainz.

EOGAN, George. 1993. The Late Bronze Age: Customs, Crafts and Cult, in Elizabeth Shee Twohig and Margaret Ronayne (eds) *Past Perceptions: The Prehistoric Archaeology of South-West Ireland*, Cork.

EOGAN, George. Forthcoming. *The Socketed Bronze Axehead in Ireland*. Prähistorische Bronzefunde, München.

EVANS, John. 1881. *The Ancient Bronze Implements, Weapons and Ornaments of Great Britain and Ireland*. London.

FEENEY, Catherine. 1976. *Aspects of Irish Amber Finds*. Unpublished MA Thesis, Dept. of Archaeology, University College, Dublin. Dublin.

FITZGERALD, Maria. 1991. *Dress Styles in Early Ireland (5th-12th centuries AD)*. Unpublished MA Thesis, Dept. of Archaeology, University College, Dublin. Dublin.

FLANAGAN, L.N.W. 1964. Necklace of Amber beads, Kurin, Co. Derry, *UJA*, 27 (1964), 92–3.

FOX, C.F. & HYDE, H.A. 1939. A second cauldron and an Iron sword from the Llyn Fawr hoard, Glamorganshire, *Antiquaries Journal*, 19 (1939), 369–404.

FRAZER, William. 1897a. On Gold Lunulae, *JRSAI*, 27 (1897), 53–66.

FRAZER, William. 1897b. On Irish Gold Ornaments, *JRSAI*, 27 (1897), 359–70.

GERLOFF, Sabine. 1975. *The Early Bronze Age Daggers in Great Britain*. Prähistorische Bronzefunde, Abteilung VI. Band 2. München.

GIMBUTAS, Marija. 1965. *Bronze Age Cultures in Central and Eastern Europe*. The Hague.

GLOB, P.V. 1974. *The Mound People*. London.

GREEN, H. Stephen. 1983. A Late Bronze Age gold hoard from Llanarmon-yn-Iâl, Clwyd, *Antiquaries Journal*, 63 (1983), 384–87.

GREEN, H. Stephen, GUILBERT, G., COWELL, M. 1983. Two Gold Bracelets from Maesmelan Farm. Powys, *Bulletin Board of Celtic Studies* 30 (1983), 394–8.

GROHNE, Ernst. 1939. Der Goldring von Gahlstorf, *Jahresschrift des Focke-Museums Bremen* 1939, 29–47.

HACHMANN, Rolf. 1954. Ein frühbronzezeitlicher Halskragen aus der Altmark, *Jb. Mittel Deutschland Vorgeschichtsblatter*, 38(1954), 92.

HACHMANN, Rolf. 1957. *Die frühe Bronzezeit im westlichen Ostseegebiet und ihre mittel- und sudösteuropäischen Beziehungen*. Hamburg.

HARBISON, Peter. 1969a. *The Daggers and Halberds of the Early Bronze Age in Ireland*, Prähistorische Bronzefunde, Abteilung VI, I Band. München.

HARBISON, Peter. 1969b. *The Axes of the Early Bronze Age in Ireland*, Prähistorische Bronzefunde, Abteilung IX, I Band. München.

HARBISON, Peter. 1971. Hartmann's Gold Analysis: A Comment, *JRSAI*, 101 (1971), 159–60.

HARBISON, Peter. 1976. *Braces and V-perforated buttons in the Beaker and Food Vessel Cultures of Ireland*. Archaeologia Atlantica, Research Reports 1. Bad Bramstedt.

HARDMEYER, Barbara. 1976. *Prähistorisches Gold Europas im 3. und 2. Jahrtausend vor Christus*. Wädemswil.

HARRISON, Richard J. 1980. *The Beaker Folk*. London.

HARTMANN, Axel. 1970. *Prähistorische Goldfunde aus Europa*, Studien zum den Anfängen der Metallurgie 3. Berlin.

HARTMANN, Axel. 1979. Irish and British Gold types and their west European counterparts, in M. Ryan (editor). *The Origins of Metallurgy in Atlantic Europe*. Dublin, 215–28.

HARTMANN, Axel. 1982. *Prähistorische Goldfunde aus Europa, II*. Studien zu den Anfängen der Metallurgie 5. Berlin.

HAWKES, C.F.C. 1942. The Deveral Urn and the Picardy Pin, *PPS*, 8 (1942), 26–47.

HAWKES, C.F.C. 1961a. Gold Ear-rings of the Bronze Age, East and West, *Folklore* 72 (1961), 438–74.

HAWKES, C.F.C. 1961b. The newly-found gold torc from Moulsford, Berkshire, *Antiquity* 35 (1961), 240–2.

HAWKES, C.F.C. 1962. Archaeological significance of the Moulsford Torc analysis, *Archaeometry*, 5 (1962), 33–7.

HAWKES, C.F.C. 1969. Las relaciones atlanticas del Mundo Tartesico, in J. Malquer de Motes (ed.), *Tartessos y sus Problemas*. Barcelona, 179–97.

HAWKES, C.F.C. 1971. The Sintra Gold Collar, *British Museum Quarterly* 35 (1971), 38–50.

HAWKES, C.F.C. 1981. The Lansdown Sun-disc, *Studien zur Bronzezeit: Festschrift für Wilhelm Albert v. Brunn*. Mainz, 119–30.

HAWKES, C.F.C. & CLARKE, R.R. 1963. Gahlstorf and Caister-on-Sea: Two finds of Late Bronze Age Irish Gold, in I.Ll. Foster & Leslie Alcock (eds.), *Culture and Environment: Essays in Honour of Sir Cyril Fox*. London, 193–250.

HAWKES, C.F.C. & SMITH, M.A. 1957. On some Buckets and Cauldrons of the Bronze and Early Iron Ages, *Antiquaries Journal* 37 (1957), 131–98.

HENCKEN, Hugh. 1942. Ballinderry Crannog No. 2, *PRIA*, 47C (1942), 1–76.

HENCKEN, Hugh. 1971. *The Earliest European Helmets*. Harvard.

HENNESSY, J.B. 1966. Excavation of a Bronze Age Temple at Amman, *Palestine Exploration Quarterly* 98 (1966), 155–62.

HENSHALL, Audrey S. 1950. Textiles and Weaving Appliances in Prehistoric Britain, *PPS*, 16 (1950), 130–62.

HENSHALL, Audrey S. 1968. Scottish dagger graves. In J.M. Coles & D.D.A. Simpson (eds), *Studies in Ancient Europe*. Leicester, 173–95.

HENSHALL, Audrey S. & WALLACE, J.C. 1962–3. A Bronze Age Cist Burial at Masterton, Pitreavie, Fife, *PSAS*, 96 (1962–63), 145–54.

HERITY, Michael. 1969a. Irish Antiquarian Finds and Collections of the early nineteenth century, *JRSAI*, 99 (1969), 21–37.

HERITY, Michael. 1969b. Early finds of Irish Antiquities, *Antiquaries Journal* 49 (1969), 1–21.

HERITY, Michael & EOGAN, George. 1977. *Ireland in Prehistory*. London.

HERNANDO GONZALO, A. 1983. La orfebrería durante el Chalcolítico y el Bronce Antiguo en la Península Ibérica, *Trabajos de Prehistoria* 40 (1983), 85–138.

HERRMANN, Fritz-Rudolf & JOCKENHÖVEL, Albrecht. 1990. *Die Vorgeschichte Hessens*. Stuttgart.

HODGES, H.W.M. 1956. Studies in the Late Bronze Age in Ireland: 2. The typology and distribution of Bronze Implements, *UJA*, 19 (1956), 29–56.

HOOK, D.R. & NEEDHAM, Stuart. 1990. A comparison of recent analysis of British Late Bronze Age goldwork with Irish parallels, *Jewellery Studies*, 3 (1990), 15–24.

HOWARTH, E. 1899. *Catalogue of the Bateman Collection of Antiquities in the Sheffield Public Museum.* London.

IRELAND, Aideen. 1989. A Seventeenth-century find of Gold Ornaments, *Journal of Irish Archaeology* 5 (1989), 35-6.

IRELAND, Aideen. 1992. The finding of the 'Clonmacnoise' Gold Torc, *PRIA*, 92C (1992), 123-46.

JACKSON, J.S. 1979. Metallic Ores in Irish Prehistory: Copper and Tin, in Michael Ryan (ed.) *The Origins of Metallurgy in Atlantic Europe.* Dublin, 107-25.

JACOB-FRIESEN, K.H. 1963. *Einfrührung in Niedersachsens Urgeschichte, II. Teil, Bronzezeit.* 4th edition, ed. by G. Jacob-Friesen. Hildesheim.

JENSEN, Jørgen. 1967. Voldtofte-fundet: Boplandsproblemer i yngre bronzealder i Danmark, *Aarbøger for Nordisk oldkyndighed og historie,* (1967), 91-154

JENSEN, Jørgen. 1981. Et rigdomscenter fra yngre bronzealdar på Sjaelland, *Aarbøger for Nordisk oldkyndighed og historie*, (1981), 48-96.

JOCKENHÖVEL, Albrecht. 1975. Zum Beginn der Jungbronzezeitkultur in Westeuropa, *Jahresbericht des Inststituts für Vorgeschichte der Universität Frankfurt A.M.*, 134-81.

JOCKENHÖVEL, Albrecht. 1980. *Die Rasiermesser in Westeuropa.* Prähistorische Bronzefunde, Abteilung VIII. Band 3. München.

JOPE, E.M. 1951. A Crescentic Jet Necklace from Rasharkin, Co. Antrim, *UJA*, 14 (1951), 61.

JOPE, E.M. & WILSON, B.C.S. 1957. A burial group of the first century A.D. from 'Loughey', Co. Down, *UJA*, 20 (1957), 73-95.

KALB, Philine. 1991. Die Goldringe vom Castro Senhora da Guia, Baioes (Co. São Pedro do Sul), Portugal, *Internationale Archäologie*, 1 (1991), 185-200.

KAVANAGH, Rhoda M. 1976. Collared and Cordoned Cinerary Urns in Ireland, *PRIA*, 76C (1976), 293-403.

KAVANAGH, Rhoda M. 1991. A reconsideration of Razors in the Irish Earlier Bronze Age, *JRSAI*, 121 (1991), 77-104.

KERSTEN, Karl. 1935. *Zur älteren Nordischen Bronzezeit.* Neumünster.

KIEKEBUSCH, Albert. 1928. *Das Königsgrab von Seddin.* Augsburg.

KINNES, I.A., LONGWORTH, I.H., McINTYRE, I.M., NEEDHAM, S.P. & ODDY, W.A. 1988. Bush Barrow Gold, *Antiquity*, 62 (1988), 24-39.

KOSSINNA, Gustaf. 1913. *Der Goldfund von Messingwerk bei Eberswalde.* Würzburg.

KOSSINNA, Gustaf. 1917. *Die golden, 'Eidringe' und die jungere Bronzezeit in Ostdeutschland.* Mannus 8. Würzburg.

LALOR, M.W. 1879. Discovery of Kists and Human Remains at Luggacurren, Queen's Co. *JRSAI*, 15 (1879-82), 446-7.

LEVY, J. 1982. *Social and Religious Organisation in Bronze Age Denmark: An Analysis of Ritual Hoard Finds.* British Archaeological Reports (International Series, 124). Oxford.

LIVERSAGE, G.D. 1968. Excavations at Dalkey Island, Co. Dublin 1956-59 *PRIA*, 66C (1968), 53-233.

LONGELY, David. 1980. *Runnymede Bridge 1976: Excavations on the site of a Late Bronze Age Settlement.* Research volume of Surrey Archaeological Society, No. 6. Guildford.

LONGWORTH, Ian H. 1972. The Ickleton Gold Neckring, *Antiquaries Journal*, 52 (1972), 358-63.

LONGWORTH, Ian H. 1984. *Collared urns of the Bronze Age in Great Britain and Ireland.* Cambridge.

LYNCH, Frances. 1970. *Prehistoric Anglesey.* Llangefni.

LYNN, C.J. 1977. Trial Excavations at the King's Stables, Tray townland, County Armagh, *UJA*, 40 (1977), 42-62.

MACWHITE, Eoin. 1944. Amber in the Irish Bronze Age, *Jour. Cork Hist. Archaeol. Soc.*, 49 (1944), 122-7.

MACWHITE, Eoin. 1951. *Estudios sobre las relaciones Atlanticas de la Península Hispanica en la Edad del Bronce.* Madrid.

MAJNARÍC-PANDŽÍC, Nieves. 1974. Der Goldfund aus Orolik bei Vinkovci, *Archaeologia Jugoslavica* 15 (1977), 21-6.

MALLET, J.W. 1853. Report on the chemical examination of Antiquities from the Museum of the Royal Irish Academy, *Transactions of the RIA*, 22 (1853), 313-42.

MANBY, T.G. 1980. Bronze Age Settlement in Eastern Yorkshire, in J.C. Barrett & R.J. Bradley (eds.), *Settlement and Society in the British Later Bronze Age*, British Archaeological Reports (BS, 83). Oxford.

MANNING, C. & EOGAN, George. 1979. A find of Gold Torcs from Coolmanagh, Co. Carlow, *JRSAI*, 109 (1979), 20-7.

MARIËN, M.E. 1958. *Trouvailles du champ d'urnes et des tombelles hallstattienes de Court-Saint-Etienne.* Brussels.

MARYON, Herbert. 1938. The technical methods of the Irish Smiths in the Bronze and Early Iron Ages, *PRIA*, 44C (1938), 181–228.

MEGAW, J.V.S. 1964. An Irish Gold Neck-Ring in the Nicholson Museum, Sydney, *Jour. Cork Hist. Archaeol. Soc.*, 69 (1964), 94–100.

MEGAW, J.V.S. & SIMPSON, D.D.A. 1979. *British Prehistory*. Leicester.

MENGHIN, Wilfried & SCHAUER, Peter. 1977. *Magisches Gold: Kultgerät der späten Bronzezeit*. Nürnberg.

MONTEAGUDO, Luis. 1953. Orfebreria del NW. Hispánico en la Edad del Bronce, *Archivo Español de Arqueologia*, 26 (1953), 269–312.

MONTELIUS, Oscar. 1916. Guldarbeten från bronsåldern funna i Sverige, *Fornvännen* II(1916), 1–62.

MORRISON, A. 1979. A bronze age burial site near South Mound, Houston, Renfrewshire, *Glasgow Archaeological Journal*, 6 (1979), 20–45.

MOZSOLICS, Amália. 1950. Der Goldfund von Velem-Szentvid. *Praehistorica* I, Basel.

MOZSOLICS, Amália. 1964. Der Goldfund aus dem Kom. Bihar. *Mitteilungen der Anthropologischen Gesellschaft in Wien*, 93–4 (1964), 104–114.

MOZSOLICS, Amália. 1965–66. Goldfunde des Depotfundhorizontes von Hajdúsámson, 46–47 *Bericht der Römisch-Germanischen Kommission*, 1–76.

MOZSOLICS, Amália. 1967. *Bronzefunde des Karpatenbeckens: Depotfundehorizonte von Hajdúsámson und Kosziderpadlás*. Budapest.

MOZSOLICS, Amália. 1973. *Bronze und Goldfunde des Karpatenbeckens: Depotfundhorizonte von Forró und Opályi*. Budapest.

MÜLLER-KARPE, Hermann. 1959. *Beiträge zur Chronologie der Urnenfelderzeit Nördlich und Sudlich der Alpen*. Römisch-Germanische Forschungen, Band 22. Berlin.

NEEDHAM, Stuart P. 1990a. Bronze Age Metalwork: The gold bracelets and Class B1 bracelets in Britain, In Martin Bell, *Brean Down Excavations 1983–87*. English Heritage Archaeological Report No. 15. London.

NEEDHAM, Stuart P. 1990b. The Penard-Wilburton Succession: New Metalwork Finds from Croxton (Norfolk) and Thirsk (Yorkshire), *Antiquaries Journal* 70 (1990), 253–70.

NEEDHAM, Stuart P. 1990c. *The Petters Late Bronze Age Metalwork*. British Museum Occasional Paper No. 70. London.

NEEDHAM, Stuart P. 1991. *Excavation and Salvage at Runnymede Bridge, 1978: The Late Bronze Age Waterfront Site*. London.

NORTHOVER, J.P. 1989. The Gold Torc from Saint Helier, Jersey, *Annual Bulletin Société Jersiaise* 25[1] (1989), 112–37.

O'CONNELL, Martin. 1986. *Petters Sports Field, Egham, Surrey*. Research Volume of the Surrey Archaelogical Society, No. 10.

O'CONNOR, Brendan. 1980. *Cross-channel relations in the Later Bronze Age*. British Archaeological Reports (International Series, 91). Oxford.

O'KELLY, M.J. 1950. Two Burials at Labbamolaga, Co. Cork, *Jour. Cork Hist. Archaeol. Soc.*, 55 (1950), 15–20.

O'KELLY, M.J. & SHELL, Colin A. 1979. Stone objects and a Bronze axe from Newgrange, Co. Meath, in M. Ryan (ed.) *The Origins of Metallurgy in Atlantic Europe*. Dublin, 127–44.

Ó RÍORDÁIN, Seán P. 1951. Lough Gur Excavations: The Great Stone Circle (B) in Grange Townland, *PRIA*, 54C (1951), 37–74.

Ó RÍORDÁIN, Seán P. 1954. Lough Gur Excavations: Neolithic and Bronze Age Houses on Knockadoon, *PRIA*, 56C (1954), 297–459.

Ó RÍORDÁIN, Seán P. 1955. A Burial with Faience Beads at Tara, *PPS*, 21 (1955), 163–73.

OTTO, Helmut. 1939. Die chemische Untersuchung des Goldringes von Gahlstorf und seine Beziehungen zu anderen Funden, *Jahresschrift des Focke-Museums Bremen* 1939, 48–62.

PIGGOTT, C.M. 1946. The Late Bronze Age Razors of the British Isles, *PPS*, 12 (1946), 121–41.

PIGGOTT, C.M. 1949. A Late Bronze Age Hoard from Blackrock in Sussex and its significance, *PPS*, 15 (1949), 107–21.

PIGGOTT, Stuart. 1938. The Early Bronze Age in Wessex, *PPS*, 4 (1938), 52–106.

PIGGOTT, Stuart. 1965. *Ancient Europe from the beginnings of Agriculture to Classical Antiquity*. Edinburgh.

PIGGOTT, Stuart. 1983. *The Earliest Wheeled Transport*. London.

PINGEL, Volker. 1992. *Die Vorgeschichtlichen Goldfunde der Iberischen Halbinsel*, Madrider Forschungen 17. Berlin.

POWELL, T.G.E. 1953. The Gold Ornament from Mold, Flintshire, North Wales, *PPS*, 19 (1953), 161–179.

POWELL, T.G.E. 1973. The Sintra Collar and the Shannongrove Gorget: aspects of Late Bronze Age goldwork in the west of Europe, *Nth. Munster Antiquarian Journal* 16 (1973), 3–13.

PRENDERGAST, Ellen. 1960. Amber Necklace from Co. Galway, *JRSAI*, 90 (1960), 61–6.

PROUDFOOT, V. Bruce. 1955. *The Downpatrick Gold Find*, Archaeological Research Publications No.3. Belfast.

PROUDFOOT, V. Bruce. 1957. A Second Gold Find from Downpatrick, *UJA*, 20 (1957), 70–2.

RAFTERY, Barry. 1990. *Trackways Through Time*. Rush.

RAFTERY, Joseph. 1961. The Derrinboy Hoard, Co. Offaly, *JRSAI*, 91 (1961), 55–8.

RAFTERY, Joseph. 1970. Two Gold Hoards from Co. Tyrone, *JRSAI*, 100 (1970), 169–74.

RAFTERY, Joseph. 1971a. A Bronze Age Hoard from Ballytegan, Co. Laois, *JRSAI*, 101 (1971), 85–100.

RAFTERY, Joseph. 1971b. Irish Prehistoric Gold Objects: New Light on the Source of the Metal, *JRSAI*, 101 (1971), 101–5.

RANDSBORG, Klaus. 1970. Eine kupferne Schmuckscheibe aus einem Dolmen in Jütland, *Acta Archaeologica* (København), 41 (1970), 181–90.

RANDSBORG, Klaus. 1972. *From Period III to Period IV*. Copenhagen.

RANDSBORG, Klaus. 1974. Social Stratification in Early Bronze Age Denmark, *Praehistorische Zeitschrift* 49 (1974), 38–61.

RANDSBORG, Klaus. 1987. The Neolithic Copper Discs from Rude, Jutland and Hřivice, Bohemia, *Acta Archaeologica* (København), 58 (1987), 234–36.

RASCHKE, G. 1954. Ein Goldfund der Bronzezeit von Ezelsdorf-Buch bei Nürnberg, *Germania* 32 (1954), 1–6.

REEVES, T.J. 1971. Gold In Ireland, *Geological Survey of Ireland Bulletin*, 1 (1971), 73–85.

ROE, F.E.S. 1966. The Battle-Axe Series in Britain, *PPS*, 32 (1966), 199–245.

ROWLANDS, M.J. 1971a. A Group of Incised Decorated Armrings and their significance for the Middle Bronze Age of Southern Britain, *British Museum Quarterly*, 35 (1971), 183–99.

ROWLANDS, M.J. 1971b. The archaeological interpretation of prehistoric metalworking, *World Archaeology*, 3 (1971), 210–24.

ROWLANDS, M.J. 1976. *The Organisation of Middle Bronze Age Metalworking*. British Archaeological Reports (British Series, 31). Oxford.

RUIZ-GÁLVEZ, Marisa. 1978. El tesoro de Caldas de Reyes, *Trabajos de Prehistoria* 35 (1978), 173–92.

RUIZ-GÁLVEZ, Marisa. 1991. Songs of a Wayfaring Lad, *Oxford Journal of Archaeology* 10 (1991), 277–306.

SAVORY, H.N. 1958. The Late Bronze Age in Wales, *Archaeologia Cambrensis*, 107 (1958), 3–63.

SAVORY, H.N. 1968. *Spain and Portugal*. London.

SAVORY, H.N. 1977. A new Hoard of Bronze Age Gold ornaments from Wales, *Archaeologia Atlantica*, 2 (1977), 37–53.

SAVORY, H.N. 1980. *Guide catalogue of the Bronze Age collections in the National Museum of Wales*. Cardiff.

SCHAUER, Peter. 1978. Die Urnenfelderzeitlichen Bronzepanzer von Fillingres, Dép. Haute Savoie, Frankreich, *Jahrbuch des Römisch-Germanischen Zentralmuseums Mainz*, 25 (1978), 92–130.

SCHAUER, Peter. 1982. Die Beinschienen der späten Bronze und frühen Eisenzeit, *Jahrbuch des Römisch-Germanischen Zentralmuseums Mainz*, 29 (1982), 100–55.

SCHAUER, Peter. 1983. Orient im spätbronze-und früheisenzeitlichen Occident, *Jahrbuch des Römisch-Germanischen Zentralmuseums Mainz*, 30 (1983), 175–94.

SCHAUER, Peter. 1985. *Goldene Kultdenkmäler der Bronzezeit*. Mainz.

SCHAUER, Peter. 1986. *Die Gredblechkegel der Bronzezeit*. Bonn.

SCHMIDT, Peter Karl & BURGESS, Colin B. 1981. *The Axes of Scotland and Northern England*. Prähistorische Bronzefunde, Abteilung IX, 7 Band. München.

SCOTT, B.G. 1976. The occurrence of platinum as a trace element in Irish Gold, *Irish Archaeological Research Forum*, 3(2) (1976), 21–4.

SCOTT, Lindsay. 1951. The Colonisation of Scotland in the Second Millennium B.C. *PPS*, 17 (1951), 16–82.

SCHUCHHARDT, Carl. 1914. *Der Goldfund von Messingwerk bei Eberswalde*. Berlin.

SHEPPARD, T. 1929. *Catalogue of the Mortimer Collection of Prehistoric Remains from East Yorkshire Barrows*. Hull Museum Publication 162. Hull.

SHERRATT, Andrew. 1986. The Radley 'earrings' revisited, *Oxford Journal of Archaeology* 5 (1986), 61–6.

SHERRATT, Andrew. 1987. 'Earrings' again, *Oxford Journal of Archaeology* 6 (1987), 119.

SILVA DA, Armando Coelho Ferreira. 1986. *A Cultura Castreja No Noroeste de Portugal*. Paços de Ferreira.

SIMPSON, D.D.A. & THAWLEY, J.E. 1972. Single Grave Art in Britain, *Scottish Archaeological Forum* 4 (1972), 81–104.

SMITH, Aquila. 1858. *JRSAI*, 5 (1858), 207.

SMITH, M.A., 1959. Some Somerset Hoards and their place in the Bronze Age of Southern Britain, *PPS*, 25 (1959), 144–87.

SOLER GARCÍA, José María. 1965. *El tesoro de Villena*. Excavaciones arqueológicas en España 36. Madrid.

SOTHEBY'S. 1990. *Ancient Glass, Egyptian, and Middle Eastern Antiquities, Irish Bronze Age Gold Ornaments… sale 13th December 1990*. London.

SPROCKHOFF, Ernst. 1939. Zur Entstehung der altbronzezeitlichen Halskragen im nordischen Kreise, *Germania* 23 (1939), 1–7.

STEAD, I.M. 1991. The Snettisham Treasure, *Antiquity* 65 (1991), 447–64.

STOUT, Geraldine. 1991. Embanked enclosures of the Boyne region, *PRIA*, 91C (1991), 245–84.

TAYLOR, Joan J. 1968. Early Bronze Age Gold Neckrings in Western Europe, *PPS*, 34 (1968), 259–65.

TAYLOR, Joan J. 1970. Lunulae Reconsidered, *PPS*, 36 (1970) 38–81.

TAYLOR, Joan J. 1979. The relationship of British Early Bronze Age Goldwork to Atlantic Europe, in M. Ryan (ed.) *The Origins of Metallurgy in Atlantic Europe*. Dublin, 229–50.

TAYLOR, Joan J. 1980. *Bronze Age Goldwork of the British Isles*. Cambridge.

TAYLOR, Joan J. 1985. Gold and Silver, in Clarke, Cowie and Foxton 1985, 182–92.

THEVENOT, Jean-Paul. 1991. *Le dépôt de Blanot (Côte d'Or)*. Dijon.

THRANE, Henrik. 1975. *Europaeiske forbindelser*. København.

THRANE, Henrik. 1984. *Lusehøj ved Voldtofte*. Odense.

THRANE, Henrik. 1990. The Mycenaean Fascination: A Northerner's View, *Orientalisc-Ägäische Einflüsse in der Europäischen Bronzezeit*, Monographien, Band 15. Römisch Germanisches Zentralmuseum Mainz. Bonn.

TOČÍK, Anton & PAULÍK, Jozef. 1960. *Vyskum Mohyly v Čake* (Die Ausgrabung eines Grabhügels in Čaka), *Slovenska Archaeologie* 8 (1960), 59–124.

TORBRÜGGE, Walter. 1959. *Die Bronzezeit in der Oberpfalz*. Kallmünz.

TORBRÜGGE, Walter & UENZE, Hans P. 1968. *Bilder zur Vorgeschichte Bayerns*. Konstanz.

TOUPET, Ch. 1979. *Rapport des fouilles d'une necropole à incinérations à Longuesse, Val d'Oise*, Service Departemental d'Archeologie, Val d'Oise.

TYLECOTE, R.F. 1962. *Metallurgy in Archaeology*. London.

VANDKILDE, Helle. 1988. A Late Neolithic Hoard with objects of Bronze and Gold from Skeldal, Central Jutland, *Journal of Danish Archaeology*, 7 (1988), 115–35.

VON BRUNN, Wilhelm Albert. 1959. *Die Hortfunde der frühen Bronzezeit aus Sachsen-anhalt, Sachsen und Thüringen*. Berlin.

VON MERHART, Gero. 1969. *Hallstatt und Italien* (ed. G. Kossack). Mainz.

WALLACE, Colin R. 1986. A note on two lunulae, *PSAS*, 116 (1986), 566–67.

WALLACE, J.N.A. 1938. The Golden Bog of Cullen, *Nth. Munster Antiquarian Journal*, 1 (1938), 89–101.

WILDE, W.R. 1857. *A Descriptive Catalogue of the Antiquities of Stone, Earthen and Vegetable Materials in the Museum of the Royal Irish Academy*. Dublin.

WILDE, W.R. 1861. *A Descriptive Catalogue of the Antiquities of Animal Materials and Bronze in the Museum of the Royal Irish Academy*. Dublin.

WILDE, W.R. 1862. *A Descriptive Catalogue of the Antiquities of Gold in the Museum of the Royal Irish Academy*. Dublin.

WOOD-MARTIN, W.G. 1888. *The Rude Stone Monuments of Ireland*. Dublin.

WOOD-MARTIN, W.G. 1895. *Pagan Ireland*. London.

WRIGHT, E. Perceval. 1900. Address delivered at the Annual General Meeting (Royal Society of Antiquaries) 30th January 1900, *JRSAI*, 30 (1900), 1–21.

Appendix

Figure 30. Map of Britain and Ireland showing county locations. For Britain the pre-1974 names and boundaries are given. (Tom Condit and Paul Synott, Discovery Programme, Dublin)

List of British-Irish Gold Objects Plotted on Distribution Maps

Lunula
Bar Torcs
Ribbon torcs
British Type Penannular Gold Bracelets
Irish Type Penannular Bracelets
Penannular Bracelets, type uncertain
'Dress-Fasteners'
'Lock-Rings'
Straited Rings
'Sleeve-Fasteners'
Hair-Rings (Ring-money)

Enclosed symbol indicates a hoard
Open symbol indicates only county (or equivalent) of origin is known

List of Museums and Abbreviations used

Aberdeen Anth. Mus.	Anthropological Museum (Marischal College), Aberdeen, Scotland.
Aberdeen Cit. & Dist. Mus.	Aberdeen City and District Museum, Aberdeen, Scotland.
Alnwick Cas.	Alnwick Castle, Northumberland, England.
Armagh Mus.	The County Museum, Armagh, Ireland.
Ash. O.	The Ashmolean Museum, Oxford, England.
Aylesford	Aylesford Museum, Aylesford, England.
Barber Institute	The Barber Institute, Birmingham, England.
Birmingham Mus.	The City Museum and Art Gallery, Birmingham, England.
BM	The British Museum, London, England.
Boston Mus.	Boston Museum of Fine Arts, Boston, United States of America.
Bowes Mus.	The Bowes Museum, Barnard Castle, Durham, England.
Brighton Mus.	Brighton Art Gallery and Museums and the Royal Pavilion, County Borough of Brighton, England.
Bucks. Museum	Buckingham County Museum, Aylesbury, England.
Cab. des Med. Biblia. Nat. Paris	Cabinet des Medailles Bibliothèque Nationale, Paris, France.
Chicago	Field Museum of Natural History, Chicago, Illinois, United States of America.
Devizes Mus.	The Wiltshire Archaeological and Natural History Society, The Museum, Devizes, Wiltshire, England.
Detroit Inst. of Arts	The Detroit Institute of Arts, Detroit, United States of America.
Dorchester	Dorset Natural History and Archaeological Society, Dorset County Museum, Dorchester, England.
Dover Mus.	Dover Museum, Kent, England.
Elgin	Elgin Museum, Morayshire, Scotland.
Folke Mus. Bremen	Folke Museum, Bremen, Germany.
Glasgow Mus. & Art Gall.	Art Gallery and Museum, Glasgow, Scotland.
Hannover Landesmuseum	Hannover Landesmuseum, Hannover, Germany.
Hunt Mus.	The Hunt Museum, University of Limerick, Ireland.
Hunterian	Hunterian Museum, University of Glasgow, Scotland.
Inveraray Cas.	Inveraray Castle, Argyll, Scotland.
Israel Mus.	The Israel Museum, Jerusalem, Israel.
Liverpool Mus.	The Merseyside County Museums, Liverpool, England.
Maidstone Mus.	Museum and Art Gallery, Maidstone, Kent, England.

Manchester Mus.	The Museum, University of Manchester, England.
Metropolitan Mus.	The Metropolitan Museum of Art, New York, United States of America.
MN St Germain	Musée des Antiquitiés Nationale, Saint-Germain-en-Laye, Paris, France.
MRAH.	The Royal Museum of Art and History, Brussels, Belgium.
Moyses Hall Mus.	The Moyses Hall Museum, Bury St. Edmunds, England.
Mus. Archeol. Namur	Musée Archéologique, Namur, Belgium.
Mus. de Cherbourg	Musée de Cherbourg, Cherbourg, France.
Mus. de Cluny	Musée de Cluny, Paris, France.
Mus. Dept. Breton Quimper	Musée Départment Breton, Quimper, Brittany.
Mus. Saint Raymond	Musée de Saint Raymond, Toulouse, France.
Mus. Soc. Hist et Arch de la Charente	Musée de Société Histoire et Archéologique de la Charente, Charente, France.
Mus. Soc. Jersiaise	Musée de la Société Jersiaise, St. Helier, Channel Islands.
Mus. Jn. Dobree	Musée Jn. Dobree, Nantes, Brittany.
Mus. Préhistoire Epernay	Musée Préhistoire, Epernay, France.
Newcastle Mus.	Newcastle Antiquarian Museum, University of Newcastle-Upon-Tyne, England.
NMI.	The National Museum of Ireland, Dublin, Ireland.
NMS.	The National Museum of Scotland, Edinburgh, Scotland.
NMW.	The National Museum of Wales, Cardiff, Wales
Norwich Cas.	Castle Museum of Art, Archaeology and Natural History, City of Norwich Museums, Norwich, England.
PRO.	The Pitt-Rivers Museum, Oxford, England.
Reading	Museum and Art Gallery, County Borough of Reading, Berkshire, England.
ROM.	The Royal Ontario Museum, Toronto, Canada.
Salisbury Mus.	The Salisbury Museum, South Wiltshire and Blackmore Museum, Salisbury, Wiltshire, England.
South Australian Mus.	The South Australian Museum, Adelaide, South Australia.
Stoke-on-Trent Mus.	Stoke-on-Trent Museum, Stoke-on-Trent, Staffordshire, England.
Taunton Cas. Mus.	Somerset County Museum, Taunton, England.
Truro	The Royal Institution of Cornwall, County Museum and Art Gallery, Truro, Cornwall, England.
UM.	The Ulster Museum, Belfast, Ireland.
UMAEC.	The University Museum of Archaeology and Ethnology, Cambridge, England.
Walters Art Gall.	The Walters Art Gallery, Baltimore, United States of America.

LUNULAE (Figure 13)

Classical

COUNTY	FIND PLACE	COLLECTION	PRINCIPAL REFERENCES. AFTER TAYLOR 1970, 1980, WITH ADDITIONS	WEIGHT Grammes
		IRELAND		
Cavan	nr. Baileborough	B.M. 71. 4–1. 2	----	48.47
Cavan	Lisanover, nr. Bawnboy	N.M.I. 1910:45	----	53.20
Cavan	Newtown, Crossdoney	N.M.I. 1884:494	----	34.99
Clare	Rehey or Rey Hill, west of Carrigholt, nr. Loop Head	Lost	----	----
Cork	Middleton	Detroit Inst. of Arts. 53.268	----	----
Cork	Middleton	Ash. O. 1927:2931	----	34.90
Down	Castlereagh	Private	----	----
Down	Kilwarlin	Not known	Walker, (1788), *Historical Essay on the dress of the Ancient and Modern Irish*, 159–60, Fig. 1.	----
Galway	Mr. Trench's Estate (There was a landed family of Trench that has estates at Clonfert, east Co. Galway, in the last century)	N.M.I. W. 10	Clarke et al., (1985), No.64.	35.77
Kerry	Banmore, Kilfeighny, Clanmaurice	N.M.I. R. 1756	----	42.38
Kerry	Banmore, Kilfeighny, Clanmaurice	N.M.I. R. 1757	----	31.10
Kerry	Mangerton	B.M. 71. 4–1. 1	----	57.9
Kerry	Killarney(?)	N.M.I. W.2	----	99.53
Mayo	West coast of Mayo (another, lost, see below under "Uncertain Lunulae")	N.M.I. 1909:4	----	46.33
Monaghan	Rossmore Park, (3 miles S/SW of Monaghan Town)	N.M.I. S.A. 1928:715	----	58.12
Roscommon	nr. Athlone	N.M.I. 1893:4	----	48.31
Tyrone	nr. Carrickmore	N.M.I. 1900:50	----	54.95
Tyrone	nr. Trillick	N.M.I. 1884:495	----	47.89
Tyrone	Tullynafoile, nr. Clogher	U.M. A. 254:1946	----	57.5
Tyrone	----	N.M.I. W.5	----	124.99
Westmeath	nr. Mullingar	N.M.I. 1884:7	----	46.66
Westmeath	Ross, nr. Lough Ree, Kilkenny West	N.M.I. 1896:15	----	43.09
Westmeath	----	N.M.I. 1920:32 (Formerly Killua Castle Coll.)	----	40.43
Wicklow	Blessington	B.M. W.G. 31	Clarke et al., (1985), No.63.	67.3
Ireland	----	N.M.I. W.1	----	47.30
Ireland	----	N.M.I. W. 11	----	42.90
Ireland	----	N.M.I. R. 4023	----	61.37
Ireland	----	N.M.I. R. 4024	----	32.72
Ireland	----	N.M.I. 1881:90	----	51.65
Ireland	----	N.M.I. 1946:392	----	43.4

Ireland	----	B.M. 38. 12–19. 1	----	65.1
Ireland	----	B.M. 45. 1–22. 1	----	81.13
Ireland	----	N.M.S. F.F. 1	Clarke et al., (1985), No.65.	----
ENGLAND				
Cornwall	Gwithian, nr. Hayle, nr. Penzance	B.M. 38. 5–19. 1	----	68.69
Cornwall	Harlyn Bay, Merryn, nr. Padstow	Truro	Clarke et al., (1985), No.58:2.	----
Cornwall	Lesnewth, nr. Boscastle, Hennet, St. Juliot	Truro	----	----
ATTRIBUTED TO SCOTLAND				
Perthshire*	Monzie Estate, Comrie, Strathern	N.M.S. L. 1963:30	----	----
No Location Scotland*	Probably Ayr or Lanark	N.M.S. F.E. 63	Clarke et al., (1985), No.60.	----

* N.B. Two 'Classical' lunulae attributed to Scotland, Monzie, Perthshire, and Ayr or Lanark may have been modern imports from Ireland. (See Eogan, 1969; Wallace, 1986). See p. 148.

Provincial

COUNTY	FIND PLACE	COLLECTION	PRINCIPAL REFERENCES. AFTER TAYLOR 1970, 1980, WITH ADDITIONS	WEIGHT Grammes
IRELAND				
Fermanagh	Coltrain, Wheathill	U.M. A. 157:1926	----	55.0
ENGLAND				
Cornwall	Harlyn Bay, Merryn, nr. Padstow	Truro	Clarke et al., (1985), No.58:3.	----
WALES				
Caernarvonshire	Llecheiddior, Dolkenmaen ("Llanllyfni")	B.M. 69.6–19.1	Savory, *Guide Catalogue of the Bronze Age Collections* (1980), 125.	185.4
SCOTLAND				
Dumfriesshire	Auchentaggert, Sanquhar	N.M.S. F.E. 3	Clarke et al., (1985), No.59.	----
Morayshire	Orbliston Junction Station, Speymouth	N.M.S. F.E. 2	----	----
Peeblesshire	Southside Farm, nr. Coulter	N.M.S. F.E. 1	Clarke et al., (1985), No.61:1.	44.39
Peeblesshire	Southside Farm, nr. Coulter	N.M.S. F.E. 74	Clarke et al., (1985), No.61:2.	----
FRANCE				
Côtes-du-Nord	Kerivoa, nr. Bourbriac, Ar. Guingamp	M.N. St. Germain 76.492 Chatellier Coll.	Eluère, (1982), 254–55, Fig.144.	----
Côtes-du-Nord	Kerivoa, nr. Bourbriac, Ar. Guingamp	M.N. St. Germain	Eluère, (1982), 254–55, Fig.144.	----
Côtes-du-Nord	Kerivoa, nr. Bourbriac, Ar. Guingamp	M.N. St. Germain	Eluère, (1982), 254–55, Fig.144.	----
Côtes-du-Nord	Saint-Potan, Ar. Dinan, C. Matignon	M.N. St. Germain 72.399	Eluère, (1982), 257, Fig.73.	----
Manche	Saint-Cyr between Valonges and Montebourg	Melted down	Eluère, (1982), 268, Fig.7:2.	----
Manche	Montebourg, Cherbourg	Mus. de Cherbourg	Eluère, (1982), 268, Fig.7:3.	----

GERMANY				
Hannover	Schulenburg, Kr. Marienburg	Hannover Landesmuseum Inv. Nr. 18370	----	----
LUXEMBURG				
----	Fauvillers	Musée Royal d'Art et Histoire, Brussels	----	----

Unaccomplished

COUNTY	FIND PLACE	COLLECTION	PRINCIPAL REFERENCES. AFTER TAYLOR 1970, 1980, WITH ADDITIONS	WEIGHT Grammes
IRELAND				
Antrim	Cairnlochran, Magheramesk	Not known	----	----
Antrim	Cairnlochran, Magheramesk	Not known	----	----
Antrim	Cairnlochran, Magheramesk	Not known	----	----
Clare	Carrowduff, nr. Ennistimon	N.M.I. 1877:52	----	70.76
Derry	Draperstown	Private	----	----
Derry	----	N.M.I. 1909:7	----	36.42
Donegal	Ardragh	Detroit Inst. of Arts. 53. 273	----	----
Donegal	Naran	N.M.I. 1909:6	----	21.77
Fermanagh	Enniskillen	U.S.A. (? Private) ex. Day Collection	----	----
Galway	----	N.M.I. 1990:71 ex. Northumberland Collection	Sotheby, (1990), 62.	41
Kerry	Ballinagroun	N.M.I. IA/L/1964:1	----	78.17
Kerry	Banmore, Kilfeighny, Clanmaurice	N.M.I. R. 1755	----	46.72
Kildare	Dunfierth, Grange	N.M.I. W. 15	----	12.12
Kildare	Dunfierth, Grange	N.M.I. W. 4 ; R. 136	----	16.33
Kildare	Dunfierth, Grange	N.M.I. W. 8	----	69.40
Kildare	Dunfierth, Grange	N.M.I. W. 9	----	6.35
Kilkenny	Coolaghmore	N.M.I. 1992:5	----	----
Mayo	Rathroeen	N.M.I. 1965:31	Clarke et al., (1985), No.66:2.	34.2
Monaghan	Ballybay	U.M. A. 200:1913	Clarke et al., (1985), No.62.	43.7
Sligo	nr. Sligo	B.M. 49. 3–1. 21	Clarke et al., (1985), No.67.	40.76
Sligo	nr. Sligo	B.M. 49. 3–1. 22	----	22.68
Tipperary	Glengall, Ballingarry	B.M. 35. 10–26. 1	----	40.8
Waterford	----	N.M.I. W. 3	----	65.32
Ireland	----	N.M.I. W. 6	----	28.12
Ireland	----	N.M.I. W. 7	----	31.69
Ireland	----	N.M.I. W. 12? (Number badly worn)	----	28.25
Ireland	----	N.M.I. W. 13	----	21.97
Ireland	----	N.M.I. P. 817	----	44.52
Ireland	----	N.M.I. R. 625	----	25.35
Ireland	----	N.M.I. R. 2611	----	33.18
Ireland	----	N.M.I. R. 2612	----	3.11

County	Find Place	Collection	Principal References	Weight Grammes
Ireland	----	N.M.I. 1881:91	----	34.99
Ireland	----	N.M.I. 1975:229	----	51.97
Ireland	----	N.M.I. 1991:70 ex. Dunraven Collection, Limerick City Museum.	----	48.49
Ireland	----	Private	----	----
Ireland	----	Liverpool Mus. M 6417	Nicholson, *Prehistoric Metalwork* (1980), No. 74.	46.5061
Ireland	----	Liverpool Mus. M6386	Nicholson, *Prehistoric Metalwork* (1980), No. 75.	33.275
Ireland	----	U.M. A. 669:1910	----	42.3
Ireland	----	B.M. 49. 3–1. 23	----	56.96

Plain

COUNTY	FIND PLACE	COLLECTION	PRINCIPAL REFERENCES. AFTER TAYLOR 1970, 1980, WITH ADDITIONS	WEIGHT Grammes
IRELAND				
Donegal	Trenta, between Carriagans and Saint Johnstown	N.M.I. 1889:20	----	43.22
Mayo	Rathroeen	N.M.I. 1965:30	Clarke et al., (1985), No.66:1.	37.43
Ireland	----	Ash. O. 1927:2930	----	41.20
Ireland	----	N.M.I. W. 14	----	24.36
Possibly Ireland	----	R.O.M. 909.14.1	----	----
FRANCE				
Manche	Tourlaville	Not known	Eluère, (1982), 268, Fig.7:1.	----
GERMANY				
Butzbach (Hessen)	----	Denkmalpflege, Wiesbaden	Herrmann & Jockenhvel,(1990), 335, Alb. 104.	----

Not Known/Uncertain

COUNTY	FIND PLACE	COLLECTION	PRINCIPAL REFERENCES. AFTER TAYLOR 1970, 1980, WITH ADITIONS	WEIGHT Grammes
IRELAND				
Derry	Dungiven	Not known	----	----
Mayo	West coast of Mayo	Lost	----	----
Sligo	----	Private	----	----
Ireland	----	Private	----	----
Ireland	----	Private	----	----
Ireland	----	Private	----	----
Ireland	----	Private	----	----
Ireland	----	Private	----	----
FRANCE				
?Ille-et-Vilaine	Saint-Méloir-des-Ondes	Not known	Eluère, (1982), 59, 264.	(small lunula)
Manche	Montebourg, ar. Cherbourg	Not known	Eluère, (1982), 268, Fig.7:3.	----

Manche	Tourlaville, ar. Cherbourg, c. Octeville	Not known	Eluère, (1982), 59, 268.	----
Manche	Saint-Cyr, between Valonges and Montebourg	Not known	Eluère, (1982), 59, 268.	----
Manche	Saint-Cyr, between Valonges and Montebourg	Not known	Eluère, (1982), 59, 268.	----
Vendée	Le Bourneau	Not known	Eluère, (1982), 279.	----
Vendée	Nesmy, ar. et c. La Roche-sur-Yon	Not known	----	----
?Vienne	Chalais, Les Mazeaux	Not known	Eluère, (1982), 59, 280.	(small lunula)

BAR TORCS (Figure 32)

COUNTY	FIND PLACE	COLLECTION	PRINCIPAL REFERENCES. AFTER EOGAN 1967, WITH ADDITIONS	WEIGHT Grammes
IRELAND				
Antrim	Carrickfergus	Melted down	----	23.72
Antrim	Priestland, nr. Giants Causeway	N.M.I. 1878:30	----	341.62
Antrim	Island Magee	Not known	----	----
Antrim	Ballycastle	Not known	----	----
Armagh	----	Not known	Eogan, (1983a), p.28, No.8:1.	283.79
Armagh	----	Not known	Eogan, (1983a), p.28, No.8:2.	139.45
Carlow	Coolmanagh	N.M.I. 1978:338	Manning & Eogan, 109(1979), 20–27; Eogan, (1983a), p.29, No.9:1.	295.48
Clare	? Mooghaun North	N.M.I. 1948:44	----	(Part only)
Donegal	Fahan	Melted down	----	290.82
Down	Carrowdore	Barber Institute, Birmingham	Taylor, (1980), 104.	----
Down	Drumsallagh	Private, on loan to U.M.	Cahill, *U.J.A.*, 48(1985), 116; Cahill, *U.J.A.*, 52(1989), 10–12.	----
Down	----	N.M.I. R. 1680	----	175.35
Galway	nr. Aughrim	N.M.I. W.174	----	389.44
Kildare	Kingsfurze (Previously referred to as Tipper)	N.M.I. 1946:391	Eogan, (1983a), p.38–9, No.18:1.	567
Kilkenny	nr. Thomastown	B.M. 49.3–1.1	----	123.90
Laoghais(?)	Ballymorris	Not known	Eogan, (1983a), p.39–40, No.19:1; Ireland, 1989–90.	----
Mayo	Kilmutt (?)	N.M.I. 1881:84	----	26.94
Mayo	----	N.M.I. R.2605	----	186.69
Meath	Newgrange	N.M.I. E.56:945	Carson & O'Kelly, *P.R.I.A.*, 77 C(1977), pl. 7a.	----
Meath	Tara	N.M.I. W.192	Eogan, (1983a), p.40–1, No.21:1.	851.83
Meath	Tara	N.M.I. W.173	Eogan, (1983a), p.40–1, No.21:2.	384.90
Meath	Tara	Not known	Eogan, (1983a), p.40–1, No.21:3.	----
Roscommon	nr. Athlone	N.M.I. 1893:6	----	32.92
Roscommon/ Westmeath	nr. Athlone	N.M.I. 1893:5	----	35.96
Westmeath	nr. Mullingar	N.M.I. 1884:6	----	336.89

Wexford	nr. Enniscorthy	N.M.I. W. 180	Eogan, (1983a), p.45–6, No.30:1.	306.69
Wexford	Gorey	N.M.I. R. 1668	----	389.44
Ireland	----	N.M.I. W. 179	----	99.27
Ireland	----	N.M.I. W. 183	----	12.51
Ireland	----	N.M.I. W. 187	----	7.52
Ireland	----	N.M.I. W. 189	----	19.63
Ireland	----	N.M.I. 1881:102, 102a	----	9.98
Ireland	----	N.M.I. R. 4029	----	257.12
Ireland	----	Not known. Formerly in the possession of Lord Charleville.	----	----
Ireland	----	Not known. Formerly in the possession of Lord Charleville.	----	----
Ireland	----	Hunt Museum, Limerick B 1951:3251	----	----
Ireland	----	Not known	----	----
Ireland	----	Not known	----	----
ENGLAND				
Berkshire	Moulsford	Reading	----	373
Cambridgeshire	Grunty	U.M.A.E.C. Z.15078	----	166
Cambridgeshire	Soham	U.M.A.E.C. Z.15082	Taylor, (1980), 8–13.	----
Cambridgeshire	Stretham	Hunt Museum, Limerick	----	----
Cambridgeshire	----	U.M.A.E.C. 1973:1	Taylor, (1980),78.	----
Cheshire	Hampton	Manchester Mus., 0.9180/1.	----	210
Cheshire	Hampton	Manchester Mus., 0.9180/2.	----	----
Cornwall	Towednack	B.M. 1932.5–11.1	----	94.61
Cornwall	Towednack	B.M. 1932.5–11.2	----	96.55
Dorsetshire	Beerhackett	Not known	----	----
Dorsetshire	Ansty, nr. Hilton	Birmingham Mus. 284 64.	----	202
Essex	Woodham Walter	Colchester Mus.	----	(part only)
Essex	Woodham Walter	Colchester Mus.	----	(part only)
Hampshire	Blackwater	Private in 1912	----	(part only)
Hampshire	Romsey	Private in 1912	----	363.65
Hampshire	Ropley	Truro Mus.	----	182.67
Kent	River Medway, Aylesford.	Maidstone Mus.	Roach Smith, *Archaeologia Cantiana* 9(1874), 11, Pl.A, Fig.1.	152.08
Kent	River Medway, Aylesford.	Maidstone Mus.	Roach Smith *op. cit.,* p. 11, Pl.A, Fig. 3.	157.59 (part only)
Kent	River Medway, Aylesford.	Maidstone Mus.	Roach Smith *op. cit.,* p. 11, Pl.A, Fig. 2.	88.19 (part only)
Kent	nr. Canterbury	Not known	----	----
Kent	Chatham	B.M. 73.2–12.1	----	685.00 (part only)
Kent	Dover (Castlemount)	B.M. 91. 4–17. 1	----	367.09
Kent	Gillingham	Maidstone Mus.	Roach Smith, *Archaeologia Cantiana* 9(1874), 2.	(part only)
Lincolnshire	Haxey	B.M. 80. 8–20. 36	----	94.22
Lincolnshire	Holkham	Private	----	----

Norfolk	Ashill	B.M. 66. 12–1. 1	----	142.24
Norfolk	Bittering Common, Foulsham	Norwich Cas. 5.947 (loan).	----	143.07 (part only)
Norfolk	Croxton	Norwich Cas.	----	38.4
Norfolk	Scultorphe	Norwich Cas. 253, 986	Northover 1989, 132, 136, No. 16.	216
Norfolk	Sporle	Norwich Cas. 400.961.3	----	(part only)
Somerset	Yeovil	Taunton Cas. Mus.	----	167.18
Staffordshire	Fantly Hill, Pattingham	Melted down	----	1180
Staffordshire	Stanton	B.M. W.G. 1	----	183
Suffolk	Boyton	B.M. 46. 6–22. 1	----	68.87
Sussex	Mountfield	Melted down	----	78.47
Wiltshire	Allington	Private in 1912	----	----
Wiltshire	Monkton Deverell	Salisbury Mus.	----	----
Yorkshire	Scalby, Cam-Boots, Hackness	Not known	----	----
WALES				
Brecknockshire	Llanwrthwl	N.M.W. 54. 306/1	----	214.6
Brecknockshire	Llanwrthwl	N.M.W. 54. 306/3	----	44.48
Brecknockshire	Llanwrthwl	N.M.W. 54. 306/4	----	60.03
Brecknockshire	Llanwrthwl	N.M.W. 54. 306/2	----	100.46
Denbighshire	Tan-y-Ilwyn	Not known	----	----
Flintshire	Bryn Siôn Bach, Ysgeifiog	Sold at Sotheby's 14/11/1966. Whereabouts not known December 1967.	----	772.92
Glamorgan/ Brecknock border	----	B.M. 38. 1–28. 1	----	231.46
Merionethshire	Gilfachwdd, Brithdtir	Not known	----	261
Merionethshire	nr. Harlech Castle	Private (Mostyn Hall, Flintshire) in 1925.	----	295.48
Merionethshire	Llyn Gwernan, Calder Idris.	Sold Sotheby's 27/11/1967. Whereabouts not known December 1967.	----	261.27
Pembrokeshire	Tiers Cross	N.M.W. 93.77H	----	125.15
Pembrokeshire	Tiers Cross	N.M.W. 93.77H	----	176.15
Pembrokeshire	Tiers Cross	N.M.W. 93.77H	----	178.45
Central Wales	----	N.M.W. 66.511/1.	----	237.94
SCOTLAND				
Inverness	Leys, Culloden	Not known	----	----
Midlothian	Slateford	Melted down. Cast in N.M. Scotland.	----	----
Wigtown	Stoneykirk	Not known	----	----
Outer Hebrides	The Minch	N.M.S. FE 108	Cowie, *Hebredian Naturalist* 12 (1994), 19–21	----
CHANNEL ISLANDS				
Jersey	St. Helier	Mus. Soc. Jersaise	----	746
FRANCE				
Allier	Jaligny-sur-Besbre	M.N. St. Germain 8579	Eluère, (1982), 248, Fig. 84, 150.	69.93
Allier	Jaligny-sur-Besbre	M.N. St. Germain 9602	Eluère, (1982), 248, Fig. 84, 150.	28.24 (part only)

Aude	Carcassonne	Ash. O. 1927:2323	Eluère, (1982), 250, Fig. 151.	----
Aude	Serviès-en-Val	Not known	Guilaine, *L'Age du Bronze en Languedoc...* (1972), 300, Fig. 117.	----
Aude	Serviès-en-Val	Not known	Guilaine, *L'Age du Bronze en Languedoc...* (1972), 300, Fig. 117.	----
Aude	Serviès-en-Val	Not known	Guilaine, *L'Age du Bronze en Languedoc ...* (1972), 300, Fig. 117.	---
Calvados	Fresné-la-Mère	Ash. O. 1927:2315	Eluère, (1982), 252–53, Fig.166.	355.23
Charente-Maritime	Cressé, Comparait	Private Coll.	Eluère, (1982), 253, Fig.94.	610
Finistère	Kerdrin, nr. Plouguin	Not known	Eluère, (1982), 260.	456
Finistère	Daoulas area	Mus. Dept. Breton, Quimper	Abbaye do Daoulas, *L'Europe a l'Age du Bronze*, (1988), 92.	320
Gironde	?Talais, Le Pérey	Not known	Eluère, (1982), 263.	----
? Haute-Garonne	Haute-Garonne	Mus. Saint-Raymond, Toulouse	Eluère, (1982), 263, Fig.85.	----
Ille-et-Vilaine	Cesson-Sévigné region, Le Pual sur le Touche	Mus. de Cluny	Eluère, (1982), 264, Fig.95.	389
Loire-Atlantique	Nozay-Abbartez	Mus. Jn. Dobree, Nantes	Eluère, (1982), 266, Fig.83.	----
Manche	Flamanville	Not known	Eluère, (1982), 268, Fig.8.	353
Morbihan	Augan	Not known	Eluère, (1982), 270.	458
Oise	Saint-Leu-d'Esserent	Cab. ds Medailles, Bibliothèque Nationale, Paris.	Eluère, (1982), 274.	344
----	River Seine	M.N. St. Germain 26.655	Eluère, (1982), 79, 277 Fig.93.	96 (part only)
France	----	M.N. St. Germain 35.809	Eluère, (1982), 281, Fig.86.	----
France	----	Louvre (salle des bijoux)	----	----
France	----	Louvre (salle des bijoux)	----	----
? France	----	B.M. 2766 (Greek and Roman Dept.)	----	----
SPAIN				
**Extremadura	Bodonal de la Sierra	Mus. Arqueológico Nacional 1970.3.1–19	Almagro, (1966), 43–8. Almagro, (1974), 44–51.	1278.15 (total weight)
Burgos	Castrogeriz	----	----	----

** The number of torcs cannot be determined but there are twelve individual terminals and four body fragments.

RIBBON TORCS (Figure 33)

COUNTY	FIND PLACE	COLLECTION	PRINCIPAL REFERENCES. AFTER EOGAN (1983b), WITH ADDITIONS	WEIGHT Grammes
IRELAND				
Antrim	Ballylumford	Not known. Several were found.	Eogan, (1983a), p.26-7.	----
Antrim	Ballywindland	N.M.I. 1919:10	----	28.32
Antrim	Lisnacroghera	U.M. A. 631:1924	----	6.6 & 1.0

Antrim/Down	nr. Belfast	N.M.I. R. 2606	----	125.71
Carlow	Coolmanagh	N.M.I. 1978:339	Manning & Eogan, 109(1979), 20-27; Eogan, (1983a), p.29, No.9:2.	69.8
Cavan	Derryvony ('Derravonna')	N.M.I. W.195	Eogan, (1983a), p.30, No.10:1.	2.79
Cavan	Derryvony ('Derravonna')	N.M.I. W.196	Eogan, (1983a), p.30, No.10:2.	9.27
Cavan	Derryvony ('Derravonna')	N.M.I. W.197	Eogan, (1983a), p.30, No.10:3.	8.16
Cavan	Derryvony ('Derravonna')	N.M.I. W.198	Eogan, (1983a), p.30, No.10:4.	6.93
Cavan	Derryvony ('Derravonna')	N.M.I. W.199	Eogan, (1983a), p.30, No.10:5.	8.49
Cavan	Derryvony ('Derravonna')	N.M.I. W.200	Eogan, (1983a), p.30, No.10:6.	11.47
Cavan	Derryvony ('Derravonna')	N.M.I. W.201	Eogan, (1983a), p.30, No.10:7.	1.49
Cavan	Derryvony ('Derravonna')	N.M.I. W.202	Eogan, (1983a), p.30, No.10:8.	1.88
Cavan	Derryvony ('Derravonna')	N.M.I. W.203	Eogan, (1983a), p.30, No.10:9.	6.48
Cavan	Derryvony ('Derravonna')	N.M.I. W.204	Eogan, (1983a), p.30, No.10:10.	5.90
Cavan	Derryvony ('Derravonna')	N.M.I. W.205	Eogan, (1983a), p.30, No.10:11.	5.05
Cavan	Derryvony ('Derravonna')	N.M.I. W.206	Eogan, (1983a), p.30, No.10:12.	4.02
Cavan	Derryvony ('Derravonna')	N.M.I. W.207	Eogan, (1983a), p.30, No.10:13.	5.64
Derry	----	N.M.I. 1909:8	----	30.39
Donegal	Ballyshannon	U.M. A. 202:1913	----	16.0
Donegal	Bundrews	N.M.I. 1990:73 ex. Northumberland Coll.	Sotheby (1990), 61.	33.75
Donegal	Inishowen	Ash.O. 1927:2944	Eogan, (1983a), p.31-3, No.12:1.	12.28
Donegal	Inishowen	Ash. O. 1927:2945	Eogan, (1983a), p.31-3, No.12:2.	11.15
Donegal	Inishowen	Ash. O. 1927:2946	Eogan, (1983a), p.31-3, No.12:3.	11.88
Donegal	Inishowen	Ash. O. 1927:2947 a, b	Eogan, (1983a), p.31-3, No.12:4.	3.85
Donegal	Inishowen	B.M. W.G. 2	Eogan, (1983a), p.31-3, No.12:5.	20.22
Donegal	Inishowen	B.M. W.G.4	Eogan, (1983a), p.31-3, No.12:6.	1.17
Donegal	Inishowen	Chicago Museum?	Eogan, (1983a), p.31-3, No.12:7.	----
Donegal	Inishowen	Hunt Museum, Limerick	Eogan, (1983a), p.31-3, No.12:8.	----
Donegal	Inishowen	N.M.I. 1913:34	Eogan, (1983a), p.31-3, No.12:9.	11.60
Donegal	Inishowen	N.M.S. FF.24	Eogan, (1983a), p.31-3, No.12:10.	----
Donegal	Inishowen	U.M. A. 201:1913	Eogan, (1983a), p.31-3, No.12:11.	10.0
Donegal	Inishowen	Not known	Eogan, (1983a), p.31-3, No.12:12.	----
Donegal	Inishowen	Not known	Eogan, (1983a), p.31-3, No.12:13.	----
Donegal	Inishowen	Boston Museum of Fine Arts 50:10	Eogan, (1983a), p.31-3, No.12:14.	----
Donegal	Largatreany	N.M.I. 1918:375	Eogan, (1983a), p.33-4, No.13:1.	12.38
Donegal	Largatreany	N.M.I. 1918:376	Eogan, (1983a), p.33-4, No.13:2.	11.86
Donegal	Largatreany	N.M.I. 1918:377	Eogan, (1983a), p.33-4, No.13:3.	12.31
Donegal	Largatreany	N.M.I. 1918:378	Eogan, (1983a), p.33-4, No.13:4.	15.81
Donegal	Largatreany	N.M.I. 1918:379	Eogan, (1983a), p.33-4, No.13:5.	9.00
Donegal	Largatreany	N.M.I. 1918:380	Eogan, (1983a), p.33-4, No.13:6.	7.32
Donegal	----	N.M.I. 1877:120	----	12.25
Down	Carrowdore	U.M. A. IA. 1968	Eogan, (1983), No. 31, p. 120.	32.8

Down	Neighbourhood of Strangford	Formerly in N.M.I. The group was apparently disposed of in the 1930's and may have been melted down.	Eogan, (1983b), No. 32.	84.60
Galway	Somerset	N.M.I. 1958:156	Raftery, *JRSAI*, 90 (1960), 2. (Iron Age)	18.66
Mayo	Lisadroone	N.M.I. 1888:14	----	22.16
Mayo	Swineford	B.M. 73. 6-2.1	----	123.77
Roscommon	Knock	N.M.I. W. 291	Ireland, *PRIA.*, 92c (1992), 123–46. (Iron Age)	65.45
Roscommon	Ballinameen	B.M.49. 3-1. 24	----	----
Sligo	Carrowmore	N.M.I. 1990:72 ex. Northumberland Coll.	Sotheby (1990), 60.	32.5
Sligo	Curry Bog	B.M. 1926. 4-18. 1	----	42.96
Tipperary	Ballinatogher	Private	----	----
Westmeath	Mullingar	N.M.I. 1929:277	----	----
May have been in Co. Clare.	----	Detroit Institute of Arts 54.35	----	----
Ireland	----	N.M.I. W. 181	----	30.65
Ireland	----	N.M.I. W. 182	----	27.22
Ireland	----	N.M.I. R. 4028	----	8.62
Ireland. May have come from Donnybrook, Dublin.	----	N.M.I. R. 1821	----	6.87
Ireland	----	N.M.I. R. 2613	----	6.16
Ireland	----	B.M. 38. 7-18. 1	----	10.95
Ireland	----	U.M.A.E.C. FB.437	----	----
Ireland	----	Hunterian. B. 1951:3249	----	----
Ireland	----	In Vize Collection, England, in the 1920's. Sold Sotheby's at a date not ascertained.	----	----
Ireland	----	Wells, Sudbury. Sotheby's sale 21.6.20	----	----
Ireland	----	Wells, Sudbury	----	----
Ireland	----	Wells, Sudbury	----	----
Possibly Ireland but not proven	----	R.O.M. AF. 305 (909.14.5)	----	----
ENGLAND				
Norfolk (?)	----	B.M. 1921. 6-21. 2	----	----
Somerset	Winterhay Green	Not known	----	----
Somerset	Edington Burtle	Somerset, Co. Museum, Taunton 24-9.	----	----
Somerset	Wedmore	Not known. Other objects from hoard in Ashmolean	----	----
Possibly England	----	R.O.M. AF. 304 (952 × 184.1)	----	----
WALES				
Radnorshire	Heyope	N.M.W. 55.543.3	----	88.96
Radnorshire	Heyope	N.M.W. 55.543.1	----	118.81

Radnorshire	Heyope	N.M.W. 55.543.2	----	121.30
BRITAIN OR IRELAND				
----	----	Birmingham Mus. A. 113 1964	----	----
SCOTLAND				
Aberdeenshire	Belhelvie	N.M.S. F.E. 33	----	28.9
Aberdeenshire	Belhelvie	N.M.S. F.E. 59	----	----
Aberdeenshire	Belhelvie	N.M.S. F.E. 66	----	----
Aberdeenshire	Belhelvie	N.M.S. F.E. 73	----	----
Fife	Lower Largo	N.M.S. F.E. 53	----	11.99
Fife	Lower Largo	N.M.S. F.E. 54	----	11.86
Fife	Lower Largo	N.M.S. F.E. 55	----	12.57
Fife	Lower Largo	N.M.S. F.E. 56	----	3.5 (part only)
Lanarkshire	Coulter	N.M.S. F.E. 75	----	----
Morayshire	Law Farm	N.M.S. F.E. 35	----	13.44
Morayshire	Law Farm	N.M.S. F.E. 36	----	13.6
Morayshire	Law Farm	N.M.S. F.E. 37	----	14.05
Morayshire	Law Farm	N.M.S. F.E.38	----	12.55
Morayshire	Law Farm	N.M.S. F.E. 38a	----	fragment
Morayshire	Law Farm	N.M.S. F.E. 67	----	13.51
Morayshire	Law Farm	N.M.S. F.E. 68	----	14.02
Morayshire	Law Farm	N.M.S. F.E. 77	----	12.73
Morayshire	Law Farm	N.M.S. F.E. 87	----	13.52
Morayshire	Law Farm	N.M.S. F.E. 88	----	12.62
Morayshire	Law Farm	B.M. W.G.12	----	12.1
Morayshire	Law Farm	B.M. W.G.13	----	13.75
Morayshire	Law Farm	B.M. W.G.14	----	12.8
Morayshire	Law Farm	B.M. 57.7-29.1	----	13.3
Morayshire	Law Farm	B.M. 58.3-20.1	----	13.93
Morayshire	Law Farm	B.M. 58.3-10.2	----	12.41
Morayshire	Law Farm	B.M. 58.3-20.3	----	7.71
Morayshire	Law Farm	U.M.A.E.C. Z.15077a	----	13.1
Morayshire	Law Farm	U.M.A.E.C. Z.15077b	----	13.85
Morayshire	Law Farm	U.M.A.E.C. Z.15077c	----	13.1
Morayshire	Law Farm	Elgin 1888.10	----	13.35
Morayshire	Law Farm	P.R.O. P.R. 1661	----	12.8
Morayshire	Law Farm	P.R.O. P.R.1661	----	12.2
Morayshire	Law Farm	Hunterian A.141	----	13.42
Morayshire	Law Farm	Ash. O. 1927:2964	----	13.4
Morayshire	Law Farm	Walters Art Gallery, Baltimore, 57.1847	----	13.52
Morayshire	Law Farm	Walters Art Gallery, Baltimore, 57.1848	----	12.53
Morayshire	Law Farm	Anthropological Museum, Aberdeen	----	11.4
Morayshire	Law Farm	Formerly Lady Reay	----	----

Morayshire	Law Farm	Formerly Mrs. Stevenson	----	----
Morayshire	Law Farm	Formerly Miss M. Young	----	----
Morayshire	Law Farm	Formerly Mrs. Burg	----	----
Morayshire	Law Farm	Formerly Sir William Gordon-Cunningham	----	----
Morayshire ?	Possibly Law Farm	Art Gall. & Mus., Glasgow	----	----
Perthshire	Rannoch Moor	N.M.S. F.E. 32	----	(Cast)
Ross-shire	Little Lochbroom	N.M.S. F.E. 34	----	----
Scotland (incorrectly attributed to Burghead, Morayshire)	----	Burrell Coll. Glasgow 301 n.	Scott, *PSAS.*, 87 (1952–53), 191–2; Coles, *Antiquaries Jour.*, 48(1968), 166.	
SCOTLAND Possible Ribbon Torcs				
Argyll	----	Not known	----	----
Banff	Alvah	Not known	----	----
Galloway	----	Not known	----	----
Galloway	----	Not known	----	----
Lanarkshire	Carmichael	Not known	----	----
Lanarkshire	Carmichael	Not known	----	----
Perthshire	Crieff (?)	Not known	----	----
Wigtownshire	Stoneykirk	Not known	----	----

'SLEEVE FASTENERS' (Figure 43)

COUNTY	FIND PLACE	COLLECTION	PRINCIPAL REFERENCES. AFTER EOGAN 1972, WITH ADDITIONS	WEIGHT Grammes
IRELAND				
Antrim	Ballynagard, Rathlin Island	U.M. L.A. 1.1943	----	6.9
Antrim	Ballinderry	N.M.I. 1874:70	----	11.28
Antrim	Belfast	Ash. O. 1927:2937	Eogan, (1983a), 56:2.	26.29
Antrim	Belfast	Ash. O. 1927:2938	Eogan, (1983a), 56:3.	15.95
Antrim	Belfast	Ash. O. 1927:2939	Eogan, (1983a), 56:4.	5.74
Antrim	Craighilly	Ash. O. 1927:2940	Eogan, (1983a), 51:1.	20.47
Antrim	Craighilly	Ash. O. 1927:2941	Eogan, (1983a), 51:2.	26.37
Antrim	Craighilly	Ash. O. 1927:2942	Eogan, (1983a), 52:3.	12.67
Antrim	----	B.M. 42.5–5.1	----	----
Armagh	Caddy (?Keady)	B.M. 62.6-17. 1	----	10.95
Clare	Gorteenreagh	N.M.I. 1948:330	Eogan, (1983a), 68:4.	42.24
Donegal	Glengad	N.M.I. R.2604	----	38.04
Down	Ballyculter Upper	U.M. A. L. 1.1979	Flanagan, *U.J.A.*, 43(1980), 23-4, Fig. 5.	25.1
Down	Downpatrick	U.M. A. 206:1913	Eogan, (1983a), 81:1.	37.2
Down	Loughbrickland	N.M.I. 1975:234	Cahill, *U.J.A.*,48(1985),116.	23.73 (part only)
Down	Tamary	N.M.I. 1931:333	----	15.08

Dublin	----	U.M. A. 207:1913	----	7.3
Fermanagh	Inishmore	N.M.I. R. 1859	----	35.06
Fermanagh	Tallykeel	U.M. A. 26:1935	----	31.8
Galway	----	Melted down	----	----
Louth	nr. Newry	N.M.I. 1876:19	----	3.89
Mayo	----	Not Known	----	----
Mayo	----	Not known	----	----
Meath	Lawrencetown or Oakley Park	N.M.I. W. 132	----	21.32
Meath	nr. Tara Hill	B.M. 49.3-1.8	Eogan, (1983a), 114:1.	----
Meath	nr. Tara Hill	B.M. 49.3-1.9	Eogan, (1983a), 114:2.	----
Monaghan	Drumbanagher	N.M.I. S.A. 1928:716	----	38.93
Monaghan	nr. Scotstown	N.M.I. 1879:6	Eogan, (1983a), 115:2	12.70
Monaghan	nr. Scotstown	N.M.I. 1879:7	Eogan, (1983a), 115:1.	12.38
Sligo	Colooney	?Chicago Museum.	----	----
Tyrone	Arboe-Killycolpy	N.M.I. 1967:235	Eogan, (1983a), 159:4.	17.62
Tyrone	Arboe-Killycolpy	N.M.I. 1967:236	Eogan, (1983a), 159:3.	26.13
Tyrone	Arboe-Killycolpy	N.M.I. 1967:237	Eogan, (1983a), 158:1.	43.9
Tyrone	Arboe-Killycolpy	N.M.I. 1967:238	Eogan, (1983a), 158:2.	49.26
Tyrone	Trillick	Ash. O. 1927:2935	----	37.39
Westmeath	Athlone	B.M. W.G. 27	----	----
Westmeath	Killucan	Private	----	----
South of Ireland	----	N.M.S. F.E. 81	Eogan, (1983a), 175:1.	----
Ireland	----	N.M.I. P. 822	----	16.07
Ireland	----	N.M.I. P. 823	----	13.54
Ireland	----	N.M.I. R. 614	----	41.99
Ireland	----	N.M.I. R. 4040	----	11.01
Ireland	----	N.M.I. R.4042	----	24.3
Ireland	----	N.M.I. R. 4043	----	17.82
Ireland	----	N.M.I. R. 4044	----	36.09
Ireland	----	N.M.I. R. 4045	----	33.89
Ireland	----	N.M.I. W. 123	----	148.97
Ireland	----	N.M.I. W. 125	----	11.66
Ireland	----	N.M.I. W. 126	----	11.60
Ireland	----	N.M.I. W. 127	----	16.33
Ireland	----	N.M.I. W. 128	----	18.53
Ireland	----	N.M.I. W. 129	----	21.51
Ireland	----	N.M.I. W. 130	----	38.88
Ireland	----	N.M.I. W. 131	----	42.38
Ireland	----	N.M.I. W. 133	----	26.89
Ireland	----	N.M.I. W. 134	----	12.83
Ireland	----	N.M.I. W. 135	----	12.89
Ireland	----	N.M.I. W. 136	----	6.67
Ireland	----	N.M.I. 1874:2	----	76.92
Ireland	----	N.M.I. 1881:106	----	13.41
Ireland	----	N.M.I. 1892:31	----	19.38
Ireland	----	N.M.I. S.A.1928:696	----	104.20

Ireland	----	N.M.I. 1946:395	----	30.71
Ireland	----	N.M.I. 1990:77 ex. Northumberland Coll.	Sotheby, (1990), 55.	16
Ireland	----	N.M.I. 1990:78 ex. Northumberland Coll.	Sotheby, (1990), 55.	14
Ireland	----	U.M. A. 3536	----	15.9
Ireland	----	U.M. A. 675:1910	----	12.8
Ireland	----	B.M. A.F. 409	----	61.2
Ireland	----	B.M. 39.1-25.1	----	16.2
Ireland	----	B.M. 47.11-26.5	----	52.3
Ireland	----	B.M. 71.4-1.7	----	43.2
Ireland	----	B.M. 71.4-1.8	----	9.00
Ireland	----	B.M. 74.3-3.6	----	7.71
Ireland	----	U.M.A.E.C. Z.15080 c	----	----
Ireland	----	U.M.A.E.C. 1924. 985	----	----
Ireland	----	Ash. O. 1924:985	----	----
Ireland	----	Ash. O. 1927:2943	----	35.65
Ireland	----	N.M.S. F.F.2	----	----
Ireland	----	N.M.S. F.F.3	----	----
Ireland	----	N.M.S. F.F.4	----	----
Ireland	----	N.M.S. F.F.28	----	----
Ireland	----	N.M.S. L 1963.31	----	----
Ireland	----	Royal Ontario Mus. Toronto. 918.3.100	----	----
Ireland	----	Detroit Institute of Arts. 54:240	----	----
Ireland	----	Metropolitan Museum, New York, 47.100.10.(139047 t f)	----	----
Ireland	----	Private	----	----
Ireland	----	Private	----	----
Ireland	----	Not known	----	----
Ireland	----	Not known	----	----
Ireland	----	Not known	Eogan, (1983a), 200:1.	----
Ireland	----	Not known	----	----
Ireland	----	Not known	----	----
----	----	Not known	----	----
----	----	Not known	----	----
----	----	----	N.M.I. IA/L/1968	----

STRIATED RINGS (Figure 43)

COUNTY	FIND PLACE	COLLECTION	PRINCIPAL REFERENCES. AFTER EOGAN 1972, WITH ADDITIONS	WEIGHT Grammes
		IRELAND		
Antrim	nr. Belfast	U.M. A. 208:1913	----	5.9

Down	Barmeen, Drumgath	N.M.I. 1931:334	----	5.88
Dublin	nr. Dublin	B.M. 49.3-1.18	----	1.94
Fermanagh	Newtown Butler	B.M. 60.11-22.1	----	----
Limerick	----	N.M.I. 1881:107	Eogan, (1983a), 106:4.	3.43
Tyrone	Glenadrush	U.M. A. 281:1964	----	0.7
Ireland	----	U.M. A. D.F.3	----	----
Ireland	----	N.M.I. W.124	----	3.63
Ireland	----	N.M.I. W.137	----	4.21
Ireland	----	N.M.I. R.4035	----	5.44
Ireland	----	N.M.I. R.4036	----	7.78
Ireland	----	B.M. 38.7-18.5	----	7.97
Ireland	----	B.M. 71.4-1.9	----	3.82
Ireland	----	B.M. 74.3-3.3	----	5.83
Ireland	----	B.M. 74.3-3.4	----	4.28
Ireland	----	B.M. 74.3-3.5	----	3.855
Ireland	----	N.M.S. F.F.5	----	----

'HAIR RINGS' (Ring Money) (Figure 42)

COUNTY	FIND PLACE	COLLECTION	REFERENCES	WEIGHT Grammes
		IRELAND		
Antrim	Armoy	N.M.I. 1899:31	Armstrong, (1933), 82:304.	7.65
Antrim	Belfast	U.M. A.209:1913	----	10.9
Antrim	Belfast	U.M. A.210:1913	----	24.9
Antrim	Ballyboley	Ash.O. 1927:2949	----	11.30
Antrim	Attributed to Lisnacrogher	U.M. A. 633:1924	*Sotheby's Catalogue* 1924, 48, lot 707, Pl. 8. ex. *Knowles Coll.*	3.7
Antrim	----	N.M.I. R.1758	Armstrong, (1933), 80:275.	17.82
Armagh	nr. Armagh	N.M.I. 1908:17	Armstrong, (1933), 80:276.	17.50
Armagh	Creevekeeren Castle (Crifkeran Castle)	B.M.62.6–17.2	----	2.07
Armagh	----	N.M.I. 1884:1	Armstrong, (1933), 82:300.	9.33
Carlow	Muine Beag (Bagnalstown)	N.M.I. W.163	Armstrong, (1933), 84:322.	2.65
Carlow	----	Private	----	----
Cavan	Baileborough. 1–9 possibly ring-money or armlets.	Not known	Eogan, (1983a), p.61, No.48.	----
Clare	----	B.M. 49.3–1.10	----	19.05
Clare	----	Private	----	----
Down	Edenordinary, nr. Dromore	N.M.I. 1876:20	Armstrong, (1933), 82:299.	9.56
Down	nr. Greyabbey	N.M.I. 1936:3695	----	12.19
Fermanagh	Gardenhill, Belcoo	N.M.I. 1909:10	Armstrong, (1933), 81:288.	12.70
Fermanagh	Enniskillen	N.M.I. 1899:30	Armstrong, (1933), 79:270; Frazer, (1897b), 362, 370.	21.06

Galway/Roscom mon	Between Ballinasloe and Athlone	B.M. W.G. 29	*Archaeological Journal*, 5(1848), 218.	6.54
Galway	Ellagh, nr. Headford	N.M.I. 1882:245	Armstrong, (1933), 79:267.	24.04
Galway	----	N.M.I. R1669	Armstrong, (1933), 82:305.	6.87
Limerick	Kilmallock	N.M.I. 1929:1302	*Journal of the Limerick Field Club*, (1906), 36, pl.:fig.4.	13.49
Louth	Drogheda	Ash.O. 1927:2948	----	25.38
Mayo	nr. Ballina	N.M.I. 1935:879	Report on N.M.I. (1934–5), 23, Pl. I ,5.	21.62
Mayo	Castlebar	N.M.I. 1899:33	Armstrong, (1933), 83:312; Frazer, (1897b), 362, 370.	4.60
Meath	Clonard	B.M. W.G. 30	----	7.19
Monaghan/Meath	between Lough Fea and Drumconragh	N.M.I. 1965:178	*J.R.S.A.I.*, 98(1968), 120, Fig. 16.	21.43
Monaghan	----	N.M.I. 1919:11	Armstrong, (1933), 80:280.	16.04
Offaly	nr. Tullamore	B.M. W.G.24	----	----
Sligo	----	N.M.I. 1899:34	Armstrong, (1933), 81:294; Frazer, (1897b), 362, 370.	11.08
Tipperary	nth. of Cashel	B.M. W.G..28	*Archaeological Journal*, 5(1848), 218.	8.46
Tipperary	nr. Roscrea	Private	----	----
Tipperary	New Sun (?New Inn)	B.M. 49.3–1.15	----	1.81
Tyrone	Loughmacrory	N.M.I. 1897:17	Armstrong, (1933), 80:279; *P.R.I.A.*, 20(1896–98), Minutes of *Proc.*, 279.	16.65
Westmeath	Ballinderry	Ash. O. 1927:2950	----	5.05
Westmeath	----	N.M.I. 1934:492	----	7.31
Wexford	----	N.M.I. 1917:86	Armstrong, (1933), 81:289.	12.05
Wicklow	Rathgall	N.M.I. E84.6070	Raftery in Harding (ed), *Hillforts: Later Prehistoric Earthworks of Britain and Ireland* (1976), 342; Toupet, *La Necropole Protohistorique de Longuesse* (1982), 37.	----
Ireland	Thirty miles south west of Dublin (? Kildare)	N.M.I. 1899:32	Armstrong, (1933), 83:309; Frazer, (1897b), 362, 370.	5.80
"South of Ireland"	----	N.M.S. F.E.80	----	----
Ireland	----	N.M.I. 1893:9	Armstrong, (1933), 79:268.	23.07
Ireland	----	N.M.I. 1876:1671	Armstrong, (1933), 79:269.	21.51
Ireland	----	N.M.I. 1881:109	Armstrong, (1933), 79:271.	20.93
Ireland	----	N.M.I. 1909:5	Armstrong, (1933), 79:272.	20.80
Ireland	----	N.M.I. W.168	Armstrong, (1933), 79:273.	18.53
Ireland	----	N.M.I. W.158	Armstrong, (1933), 80:274.	18.34
Ireland	----	N.M.I. W.167	Armstrong, (1933), 80:277.	17.24
Ireland	----	N.M.I. W.159	Armstrong, (1933), 80:278.	16.91
Ireland	----	N.M.I. R.2610	Armstrong, (1933), 80:281.	16.00
Ireland	----	N.M.I. P.824	Armstrong, (1933), 80:282.	14.58
Ireland	----	N.M.I. 1883:195	Armstrong, (1933), 80:283.	14.26
Ireland	----	N.M.I. 1876:1672	Armstrong, (1933), 80:284.	13.58
Ireland	----	N.M.I. W.160	Armstrong, (1933), 80:285.	13.54

Ireland	----	N.M.I. W.169	Armstrong, (1933), 81:286.	13.38
Ireland	----	N.M.I. W.287	Armstrong, (1933), 81:287.	13.09
Ireland	----	N.M.I. 1920:30	Armstrong, (1933), 81:290.	12.05
Ireland	----	N.M.I. W.170	Armstrong, (1933), 81:291.	11.73
Ireland	----	N.M.I. W.157	Armstrong, (1933), 81:292.	11.15
Ireland	----	N.M.I. R.1816	Armstrong, (1933), 81:293.	11.11
Ireland	----	N.M.I. 1906:161	Armstrong, (1933), 81:295.	10.76
Ireland	----	N.M.I. W.156	Armstrong, (1933), 81:296.	9.78
Ireland	----	N.M.I. 1881:108	Armstrong, (1933), 82:297.	9.85
Ireland	----	N.M.I. 1876:21	Armstrong, (1933), 82:298.	9.56
Ireland	----	N.M.I. R.1822	Armstrong, (1933), 82:301.	18.1
Ireland	----	N.M.I. W.166	Armstrong, (1933), 82:302.	7.84
Ireland	----	N.M.I. W.178	Armstrong, (1933), 82:303.	7.78
Ireland	----	N.M.I. 1876:22	Armstrong, (1933), 82:306.	6.74
Ireland	----	N.M.I. R.4041	Armstrong, (1933), 82:307.	6.32
Ireland	----	N.M.I. 1892:32	Armstrong, (1933), 83:308.	5.96
Ireland	----	N.M.I. W.154	Armstrong, (1933), 83:310.	5.70
Ireland	----	N.M.I. W.155	Armstrong, (1933), 83:311.	5.38
Ireland	----	N.M.I. W.153	Armstrong, (1933), 83:313.	4.15
Ireland	----	N.M.I. W.164	Armstrong, (1933), 83:314.	3.95
Ireland	----	N.M.I. W.161	Armstrong, (1933), 83:315.	2.27
Ireland	----	N.M.I. R.4051 A.W.177	Armstrong, (1933), 83:316.	3.50
Ireland	----	N.M.I. R.4039	Armstrong, (1933), 83:317.	3.50
Ireland	----	N.M.I. W.162	Armstrong, (1933), 83:318.	3.50
Ireland	----	N.M.I. 1881:107	Armstrong, (1933), 83:319.	3.43
Ireland	----	N.M.I. R.4037	Armstrong, (1933), 83:320.	2.98
Ireland	----	N.M.I. W.152	Armstrong, (1933), 83:321.	2.59
Ireland	----	N.M.I. W.151	Armstrong, (1933), 84:323.	2.30
Ireland	----	N.M.I. P.826	Armstrong, (1933), 84:324.	2.04
Ireland	----	N.M.I. W.165	Armstrong, (1933), 84:325.	0.91
Ireland	----	N.M.I. 1932:6404	----	7.31
Ireland	----	N.M.I. 1975:2313	----	12.35
Ireland	----	B.M. 49.3–1.11	----	23.72
Ireland	----	B.M. 49.3–1.16	----	3.63
Ireland	----	B.M. 53.12–16.5	----	14.64
Ireland	----	B.M. 38.7–18.3	----	25.21
Ireland	----	B.M. 38.7–18.4	----	7.84
Ireland	----	B.M. 38.7–18.6	----	1.91
Ireland	----	B.M. 47.11–26.4	----	18.71
Ireland	----	B.M. 47.11–26.1	----	14.18
Ireland	----	B.M. 47.11–26.2	----	14.54
Ireland	----	B.M. 47.11–26.3	----	20.97
?Ireland	----	B.M. 49.3–1.12	----	----
Ireland	----	B.M. 49.3–1.13	----	----
Ireland	----	B.M. 49.3–1.14	----	----

Ireland	----	B.M. 53.12–16.6	----	4.86 (part only)
Ireland	----	B.M. 53.12–16.7	----	0.71
Ireland	----	B.M. 53.12–16.8	----	3.89
Ireland	----	N.M.I. 1990: 76 ex. Northumberland Collection	Sotheby 1990, 55	7.75
Ireland	----	B.M. 54.7–14.137	----	----
Ireland	----	B.M. 65.2–21.1	----	26.57
Ireland	----	B.M. 65.2–21.2	----	14.0
Ireland	----	B.M. 71.4–1.10	----	19.37
?Ireland	----	B.M. 71.4–1.11	----	9.59
?Ireland	----	B.M. 71.4–1.12	----	6.35
Ireland	----	B.M. 74.3–3.1	----	23.72
Ireland	----	B.M. 74.3–3.2	----	3.14
?Ireland	----	B.M. ?	----	----
?Ireland	----	B.M. ?	----	----
?Ireland	----	B.M. ?	----	----
?Ireland	----	B.M. ?	----	----
?Ireland	----	B.M. A.F.408	----	17.17
Ireland	----	N.M.S. F.E.7	----	----
Ireland	----	N.M.S. F.E.25	----	----
Ireland	----	N.M.S. F.E.27	----	----
Ireland	----	Detroit Inst. of Arts 65.66	----	----
Ireland	----	Detroit Inst. of Arts 53.242	----	----
?Ireland	----	Private (H.C. Wells in 1920's)	----	----
?Ireland	----	Private (H.C. Wells in 1920's)	----	----
?Ireland	----	Private (H.C. Wells in 1920's)	----	----
Ireland	----	B.M. 69.2–23.1	----	----
Ireland	----	N.M.S. L.1963.32	----	----
?Ireland	----	Israel Mus. Jerusalem	----	----
ENGLAND				
Cambridgeshire	Haddenham Fen, nr. Wilburton	U.M.A.E.C. 19.97. Pell Coll.	Ridgeway, *The origin of Metallic Currency and Weight Standards*, (1892), Appendix C, 394–406.	----
Dorset	Dorchester	B.M. 88. 12–12. 1	----	7.78
Dorset	New Buildings Farm, Milton Abbas	Dorchester 1932. 1.15	*Archaeological Journal*, 6 (1849), 56, fig.4.	----
Dorset	----	Dorchester (Charles Hall's Dorset Collection)	----	----
Dorset	----	Dorchester (Charles Hall's Dorset Collection)	----	----
Essex	'Bradwell', nr. Maldon	B.M. A.F. 407	----	9.91
Hampshire	Andover	Not known	Kendrick & Hawkes, (1932), *Archaeology in England and Wales 1914–1931*, (1932), 128–9.	----

Norfolk	nr. King's Lynn	Ash. O. 1927. 2962	----	4.46
Oxford	Bicester	Not known	*Journal of the British Archaeological Association*, 6(1851), 445–6.	----
Somerset	Bridgewater	B.M. 1889.10–17.	*Archaeological Journal*, 8(1853), 112; British Museum *Bronze Age Guide* (1920), 53.	7.9
Sussex	Bracklesham Bay, Selsey	B.M. 78.3–15.1–234	----	3.7
Sussex	Cuckmere Haven	B.M. 1928. 7–16	Kendrick & Hawkes *Archaeology in England and Wales 1914–1931* (1932), 128. Curwen (1937), 212;	----
Sussex	Rustington	B.M. 95.5 -21. 1	Curwen (1937), 212.	15.5
Sussex	Brighton Area	Brighton Mus.	----	----
Sussex	Bracklesham Beach	B.M. 55. 11– 22. 1	*Archaeological Journal* 8 (1851), 112, fig. facing 112.	6.67
Wiltshire	Amesbury	Not known	Wilson, *Prehistoric Annals of Scotland*, (1863), I, 456.	----
Wiltshire	Bishopstone, nr. Salisbury	South Australian Mus. A 50523	*Wiltshire Archaeological and Natural History Magazine* (1911), 156; Records of the South Australian Museum, 17 (1974), 23, Figs. 1–2.	----
Wiltshire	Bishopstone, nr. Salisbury	Salisbury Mus.	*Wiltshire Archaeological and Natural History Magazine*, (1911), 156.	----
Worcestershire	Tenbury	Ash. O. 1927:2961	----	3.77
Yorkshire	Cawood-on-the-Ouse	Not known	*Proceedings of the Yorkshire Geographical & Polytechnic Society*, (1889), 324.	----
WALES				
Caernarvonshire	Graianog	N.M.W. 1985.127H	Green, *Bulletin of the Board of Celtic Studies*, 35(1988), 87–91.	----
SCOTLAND				
Angus	Balmashanner, Forfar	N.M.S. D.Q.155	*P.S.A.S.*, 26 (1891–2), 174, 182–8.	----
Angus	Balmashanner, Forfar	N.M.S. D.Q.156	*P.S.A.S.*, 26 (1891–2), 174, 182–8.	----
Angus	Balmashanner, Forfar	N.M.S. D.O.157	*P.S.A.S.*, 26 (1891–2), 174, 182–8.	----
Banffshire	Fuaraig Glen, Chebat, Glenavon	B.M. W.G. 23	Benton, (1930–1), 181.	24.3
Galloway	Galloway	N.M.S. F.E. 58	*P.S.A.S.*, 26 (1891–2), 213.	----
Invernessshire	Skye Island	N.M.S. F.E. 9	Benton, (1922–3), 163.	----
Morayshire	Sculptor's Cave, Covesea	N.M.S. H.M.56–61	Benton, (1930–1), 181–4, fig. 5, No. 1.	----
Morayshire	Sculptor's Cave, Covesea	N.M.S. H.M. 56–61	Benton, (1930–1), 181–4, fig. 5, No. 2.	----
Morayshire	Sculptor's Cave, Covesea	N.M.S. H.M. 56–61	Benton, (1930–1), 181–4, fig.5, No.3.	----
Morayshire	Sculptors Cave, Covesea	N.M.S. H.M. 56–61	Benton, (1930–1), 181–4, fig.5, No.4.	----

Morayshire	Sculptor's Cave, Covesea	N.M.S. H.M. 56–61	Benton, (1930–1), 181–4, fig.5, No.5.	----
Morayshire	Sculptor's Cave, Covesea	N.M.S. H.M. 56–61	Benton, (1930–1), 181–4, fig.5, No.6.	----
Morayshire	Sculptor's Cave, Covesea	N.M.S. H.M. 56–61	Benton, (1930–1), 181–4.	----
Morayshire	Sculptor's Cave, Covesea	N.M.S. H.M. 56–61	Benton, (1930–1), 181–4.	----
Morayshire	Sculptor's Cave, Covesea	Elgin	Benton, (1930–1), 181–4.	----
Morayshire	Sculptor's Cave, Covesea	Elgin	Benton, (1930–1), 181–4.	----
Scotland	----	N.M.S. (?) F.E. 73	*P.S.A.S.*, 93(1959–60), 91; Wilson, *Prehistoric Annals of Scotland*, (1883), I, 460–1.	----
FRANCE				
Val d'Oise	Longuesse (cremation burial no. 199)	Centre for excavations Val d'Oise	Toupet, (1979), 35–39; Toupet, *La Necrople Protohistorique de Longuesse*, (1982), Fig. 3:1; Eluère, (1982), 280, Fig.64:3.	2.1
Aisne	Villeneuve Saint Germain (cremation burial no.189)	Centre for excavations, Aisne	Eluère, (1982), 248, Fig.64:4.	----
Aisne	Villeneuve Saint Germain (cremation burial no.189)	Centre for excavations, Aisne	Eluère, (1982), 248.	----
Aisne	Villeneuve Saint Germain (cremation burial no.201)	Centre for excavations, Aisne	Eluère, (1982), 248, Fig. 64:5.	1.351
Cher	Sainte-Thorette	Not known	Girault, *Congré. nat. des Soc. Savantes*, Dijon, (1984); *Archéologie*, 2, 221–26.	----
France	----	M.N. St. Germain 35.801	Eluère, (1982), 281, Fig.64:2, 65.	
BELGIUM				
Antwerp	Borsbeek	----	O'Connor, (1980), 573.	----
Liège	Herstal	----	O'Connor, (1980), 573.	----
Liège	Herstal	----	O'Connor, (1980), 573.	----
Limburg	? Neerharen	M.R.A.H.	O'Connor, (1980), 573.	----
Namur	Han (more than one example)	----	O'Connor, (1980), 573.	----
Namur	Marche-les-Dames	Musée Archeol. Namur	O'Connor, (1980), 573.	----
NETHERLANDS				
Vessem	Knegsel	----	O' Connor, (1980), 573.	----
Vessem	Knegsel	----	O' Connor, (1980), 573.	----

'DRESS-FASTENERS' (Figure 40)

COUNTY	FIND PLACE	COLLECTION	REFERENCES	WEIGHT Grammes
IRELAND				
Antrim	Ballymoney area	N.M.I. R. 1939	Armstrong, (1933), 70:175.	101.09
Antrim	Ballymoney area	Not Known	----	667.17
Antrim	Portnagh, Ballycastle	N.M.I. R. 1887	Armstrong, (1933), 69:165	98.24
Antrim	Ratlin Island	Not Known	Evans, *U.J.A.*, 7(1944), 62.	----

Armagh	Derryhale	N.M.I. 1906:121	Eogan, (1983a), p.57–60, No.44:5.	(BRONZE)
Cavan	Lattoon	N.M.I. 1920:24	Eogan, (1983a), p.64–5, No.53:3; Armstrong, (1933), p. 47–9, Fig. 17.	47.63
Cavan	Lattoon	N.M.I. 1920:25	Eogan, (1983a), p.64–5, No.53:4; Armstrong, (1933), p. 47–9, Fig. 17.	27.73
Clare	River Fergus	Not known	Scott, *Journal of the Limerick Field Club*, 10(1909), 28–30.	----
Cork	Ballymacotten	N.M.I. 1979:3	----	38.5
Cork	Cloyne	U.M. A. 205. 1913	Hawkes & Clarke, (1963), 244.	49.1
Cork	Fermoy	Not known	----	c.327.00
Cork	? Inchigeelagh	N.M.I. 1913:37	Armstrong, (1933), 70:177.	76.33
Cork	Mountrivers	N.M.I. 1908:8	Armstrong, (1933), 70:171, Fig. 13; Eogan, (1983a), p.77, No.65:5.	90.14
Cork	Mountrivers	N.M.I. 1908:9	Armstrong, (1933), 70:172, Fig. 13; Eogan, (1983a), p.77, No.65:6.	115.34
Cork	Youghal	Not known	----	(Possibly over 300.00)
Donegal	Clonleigh	Not Known	Eogan, (1983a), p.79, No.69:2.	(Possibly a dress-fastener)
Galway	----	Melted down in 1747.	Eogan, (1983a), p.90–1, No.86:1.	466.55
Galway	----	Not known	Vallancey, *Collectanea de Rebus Hibernicis*, (1804), 237–40.	c.436.16
Kerry	Kilmoyly North	N.M.I. 1940:2A	Eogan, (1983a), p.92–3, No.89:4.	57.79
Kerry	Templenoe, Dunkerron	N.M.I. R. 1900	Armstrong, (1933), 69:166.	94.09
Kildare	Kilrathmurry	N.M.I. 1898:138	Armstrong, (1933), 69:170.	89.81
Kildare	Knockpatrick	N.M.I. 1953:37	----	132.92
Laoghais	Iry	N.M.I. 1984:2	----	166.97
Limerick	Bruree	N.M.I. 1929:1303	Hawkes & Clarke, (1963), 244.	59.37
Limerick	Springfield	N.M.I. 1945:366	----	94.04
Limerick	----	N.M.I. W. 148	Armstrong, (1933), 68:159; Cahill, *North Munster Antiquarian Journal*, 33 (1991), 99–100.	79.96
possibly Limerick?	----	Not known	----	----
Louth/Meath	----	Not known. Acquired by the Lord Chancellor of the time.	Eogan, (1983a), p.107, No.106:1.	----
Louth/Meath	----	Melted down	Eogan, (1983a), p.107, No.106:2.	96.42
Louth/Meath	----	Melted down	Eogan, (1983a), p.107, No.106:3.	65.45
Mayo	Dooros	N.M.I. 1934:5600	----	67.90
Mayo	----	Not known	Hawkes & Clarke, (1963), 244.	----
Mayo	----	Not known	Hawkes & Clarke, (1963), 244.	----
Meath	nr. Dunboyne	Not known	----	c.1353.00
Monaghan	nr. Clones	N.M.I. IA.L 1963:1	----	1032.64
Offaly	Meenwaun, nr.Banagher	N.M.I. 1918:349	Armstrong, (1933), 70:173; Eogan, (1983a), p.115–6, No.117:2; Whitfield, *Archaeology Ireland*, 7(1993), 9–11.	70.63
Offaly	Tullamore	B.M. WG.24	British Museum, (1920), 109–10.	----
Roscommon	Ballindrumlea	N.M.I. 1874:90	Armstrong, (1933), 69:168.	118.19

Roscommon	Castlekelly	N.M.I. W.122	Armstrong, (1933), 68:155.	524.35
Roscommon	----	N.M.I. 1890:52	Armstrong, (1933), 69:169.	125.71
Roscommon\West meath	Possibly Athlone	Detroit Inst. of Arts 53:275	Eogan, (1983a), p.195, No.26:2.	----
Sligo (?)	----	N.M.I. 1886:84	Armstrong, (1933), 73:202.	54.30
Tipperary	Cloghernagh ('Pairc an Óir')	Melted down except for fragment in N.M.I. 1886:4025	Cahill, *North Munster Antiquarian Journal*, (1986), 3–6.	393.46
Tipperary	Cullen	Birmingham Mus. 283'64	Eogan, (1983a), p.154–6, No.135:5.	----
Tipperary	nr. Tipperary	B.M. 40.9–28.3	Cahill, (1993), *Tipperary Historical Journal*, 189–193.	124.74
Tipperary	----	N.M.I. R. 4025	Armstrong, (1933), 70:179.	19.76
Tyrone	Killymoon	N.M.I. 1967:234	Eogan, (1983a), p.160, No.140:1; Armstrong, (1933), 33, Fig. 15.	102.90
Waterford	nr. New Ross	N.M.I. 1896:2	Armstrong, (1933), 70:174; Eogan, (1983a), p.164–5, No.145:5.	142.69
Waterford	nr. New Ross	N.M.I. 1896:4	Armstrong, (1933), 72:196; Eogan, (1983a), p.164–5, No.145:4.	63.89
Westmeath	nr. Mullingar	N.M.I. 1874:89	Armstrong, (1933), 69:167.	68.62
Westmeath	nr. Mullingar	B.M. 1921. 6–21.1	----	22.87
Wexford	Ballinesker	N.M.I. 1990:62	----	280.13
Wexford	Ballinesker	N.M.I. 1990:63	----	77.97
Wexford	Ballinesker	N.M.I. 1990:64	----	160.40
North of Ireland	----	U.M. A. 147. 1933	----	77.8
Ireland	----	N.M.I. W. 119	Armstrong, (1933), 70:176.	31.82
Ireland	----	N.M.I. W. 120	Armstrong, (1933), 68:156.	164.33
Ireland	----	N.M.I. W. 121	Armstrong, (1933), 68:157.	141.65
Ireland	----	N.M.I. W. 139	Armstrong, (1933), 71:186.	27.28
Ireland	----	N.M.I. W. 146	Armstrong, (1933), 69:161.	87.15
Ireland	----	N.M.I. W. 147	Armstrong, (1933), 68:160.	122.53
Ireland	----	N.M.I. W. 149	Armstrong, (1933), 68:158.	103.42
Ireland	----	N.M.I. W. 150	Armstrong, (1933), 69:162.	135.36
Ireland	----	N.M.I. R. 615	Armstrong, (1933), 69:163.	156.75
Ireland	----	N.M.I. R. 1670	Armstrong, (1933), 69:164.	210.08
Ireland	----	N.M.I. R. 1840 ?	Armstrong, (1933), 70:178.	90.39
Ireland	----	N.M.I. R. 4025	Armstrong, (1933), 70:179.	19.76
Ireland	----	N.M.I. P. 821	Armstrong, (1933), 72:190.	25.66
Ireland	----	N.M.I. 1892:30	Armstrong, (1933), 72:192.	26.05
Ireland	----	N.M.I. 1990:81 ex. Northumberland Coll.	Sotheby, (1990), 57.	73.25
Ireland	----	N.M.I. 1975:230	----	100.37
Ireland	----	Ash. O. 1927:2932	----	182.29
Ireland	----	B.M. 34. 12. 22.1	----	73.68
Ireland	----	B.M. 54. 7–1.1	----	99.8
Ireland	----	U.M.A.E.C.	----	----
Ireland	----	U.M.A.E.C. 1899. 246	----	(BRONZE)

Ireland	----	Detroit Inst. of Arts 53.275	----	----
Ireland	----	Metropolitan Mus. 47. 100. 9	----	----
Ireland	----	Not Known	Eogan, (1983a), p.178, No.161:1.	----
Ireland	----	Not Known	Hawkes & Clarke, (1963), 243.	----
Ireland	----	Not Known	Hawkes & Clarke, (1963), 243.	----
Ireland	----	Not Known	Hawkes & Clarke, (1963), 243.	----
ENGLAND				
Cornwall	nr. Lizard	B.M. (Payne Knight Collection) 1824	Way, *Archaeological Journal*, 6(1849), 61; Hencken, *Archaeology of Cornwall & Scilly*, (1932), 92; Hawkes & Clarke, (1963), 243–5.	----
Kent	Aylesford	Maidstone Mus.	*Archaeologia Cantiana*, 5(1862), 43; *Victoria Co. History of Kent*, I(1908), 325.	48.73(only about half)
Norfolk	Fulmodestone Common	Norwich Cas. 5.947	Hawkes & Clarke, (1963), 213–14.	----
Yorkshire	Rippon	Not known	Way, *Archaeological Journal*, 6(1849), 61; Hawkes & Clarke, (1963), 243–5; Elgee, *Archaeology of Yorkshire*, (1933), 99; Elgee, *Early Man in N.E. Yorkshire*, (1930), 175, Fig. 56b.	(one weighed 14.0)
Yorkshire	Rippon	Not known	Way, *Archaeological Journal*, 6(1849), 61; Hawkes & Clarke, (1963), 243–5; Elgee, *Archaeology of Yorkshire*, (1933), 99; Elgee, *Early Man in N.E. Yorkshire*, (1930), 175, Fig. 56b.	----
Yorkshire	Swinton Park	Not known	Way, *Archaeological Journal*, 6(1849), 61; Elgee, *Archaeology of Yorkshire*, (1933), 99; Hawkes & Clarke, (1963), 243–5; Manby and Turnbull, *Archaeology in the Pennines*, BAR British Series, 158(1986), 119, no.9, 92, Fig. 14.	163.94
SCOTLAND				
Argyll	Island of Islay	B.M. 1920.3–16.1	British Museum, *Bronze Age Guide*, (1920), 101.	113.3
Argyll	Tullich (Glen Aray)	Inveraray Castle, Argyllshire	Royal Commission on the Ancient & Historical Monuments of Scotland, *Mid Argyll and Cowal*, (1988), 20, 25.	----
Argyll	Tullick (Glen Aray)	Inveraray Castle, Argyllshire	Royal Comission on the Ancient & Historical Monuments of Scotland, *Mid Argyll and Cowal*, (1988), 20, 25.	----
Arran	Whitefarland	Glasgow Mus. & Art Gall. 21–43.	Eogan, (1969), 133–4.	----
Galloway	Found on an 'Estate of the Earl of Stair'	Not known	Way, *Archaeological Journal*, 6(1849), 61; Wilson, *Prehistoric Annals of Scotland* (1863), 461.	466.55
Moray	Cromdale	Not known	Wilson, *Pre. Annals of Scot.*, (1863), 460, fig. 90.	----
Ross-Cromarty	Heights of Brae	N.M.S. F.E.94	Clarke & Kemp, (1984), 192, illus. 2–4.	112.6

Ross-Cromarty	Heights of Brae	N.M.S. F.E.95	Clarke & Kemp, (1984), 192, illus. 2–4.	66.2
Ross-Cromarty	Heights of Brae	N.M.S. F.E.96	Clarke & Kemp, (1984), 192, illus. 2–4.	83.3
Ross-Cromarty	Poolewe	Not Known	----	(BRONZE)
Wigtown	High Drummore (Kirkmaiden)	N.M.S. F.E.72	*P.S.A.S.*, 57(1922–23), 165, fig. 22.	----
North of Scotland	----	Not known	*Archaeological Journal*, 2(1709), 41; Wilson, *Prehistoric Annals of Scotland*, (1863), 460–61.	----
Scotland	----	N.M.S. F.E.64	Wilson, *Prehistoric Annals of Scotland*, (1863), 462–3.	----

'LOCK-RINGS' (Figure 41)

COUNTY	FIND PLACE	COLLECTION	PRINCIPAL REFERENCES. AFTER EOGAN 1969, WITH ADDITIONS	WEIGHT Grammes
		IRELAND		
Clare	Gorteenreagh	N.M.I. 1948:326	Eogan, (1983a), p.67–8, No.56:5.	95.31
Clare	Gorteenreagh	N.M.I. 1948:327	Eogan, (1983a), p.67–8, No.56:6.	95.25
Dublin	Rathfarnham	N.M.I. W.51	----	1.296
Limerick	Askeaton	Not known	Eogan, (1983a), p.101–2, No.99:1.	----
Limerick	Askeaton	Not known	Eogan, (1983a), p.101–2, No.99:2.	----
Limerick	----	N.M.I. 1880:62a	----	15.10
Limerick	----	N.M.I. 1880:62b	----	13.02
Limerick	----	N.M.I. 1881:94	----	24.36
Limerick	----	N.M.I. 1881:95	Eogan, (1983a), p.105–6, No.104:5.	21.77
Limerick	----	N.M.I. 1881:96	----	6.22
Limerick	----	N.M.I. 1881:97	Eogan, (1983a), p.105–6, No.104:6.	4.08
Meath	Harristown	N.M.I. 1953:45	----	3.48
South of Ireland	----	N.M.S. F.E.80	Eogan, (1983a), p.174–5, No.157:2.	----
Ireland	----	N.M.I. W.48	----	4.99
Ireland	----	N.M.I. W.49	----	11.79
Ireland	----	N.M.I. W.50	----	7.90
Ireland	----	N.M.I. 1881:79	----	4.92
		ENGLAND		
Buckinghamshire	Bodrington	----	----	----
Buckinghamshire	Bodrington	----	----	----
Cambridgeshire	Burwell Fen	U.M.A.E.C. Z. 15313	----	----
Cambridgeshire	Wimblington	Not known.	Pendleton, *Proceedings of the Cambridge Antiquarian Society*, 74 (1984), 85–6.	----
Durham	Heathery Burn	B.M. W.G.25	----	5.77
Lancashire	Portfield	B.M. 1966. 12–8. 1	----	8.1
Norfolk	Feltwell	B.M. W.G. 2097	----	----
Northumberland	Alnwick	Newcastle Mus. 1895:5	----	----

Northumberland	Alnwick	Newcastle Mus. 1895:5	----	----
Northumberland	Cheeseburn Grange	B.M. W.G.20	----	4.60
Somerset	Castle Cary	Taunton Mus. Cat. No.76b	----	3.25
Suffolk/Essex	Haverhill/Saffron Walden	Moyses Hall Mus. F.168	----	----
Suffolk/Essex	Haverhill/Saffron Walden	Moyses Hall Mus. F. 168	----	----
Sussex	Harting Beacon	B.M. (Loan)	----	----
Sussex	Harting Beacon	B.M. (Loan)	----	----
Sussex	Highdown Hill	Worthing Museum 51/092044	----	----
Yorkshire	Startforth	Bowes Mus. 1958:1864	----	----
WALES				
Anglesey	Gaerwen	B.M. W.G. 17	----	5.64
Anglesey	Gaerwen	B.M. W.G.18	----	7.48
Anglesey	Gaerwen	Not known	----	----
Caernarvonshire	Great Orme's Head	N.M.W. 54.82/1	----	5.9
Caernarvonshire	Great Orme's Head	N.M.W. 54.82/2	----	----
SCOTLAND				
Angus	Balmashanner	N.M.S. D.Q.158	----	----
Angus	Balmashanner	N.M.S. D.Q.159	----	----
Angus	Balmashanner	N.M.S. D.Q.160	----	----
Angus	Balmashanner	N.M.S. D.Q.161	----	----
Arran	Whitefarland	Glasgow Mus. & Art Gall. 21–44	----	----
Lanarkshire	Boghall	N.M.S. F.E.85	----	----
East Lothian	Traprain Law	N.M.S. G.V.B.30	----	----
Mid Lothian	Gogar	N.M.S. F.E.7	----	----
Wigtownshire	Glenluce	Glasgow Mus. & Art Gall. L.A. 5719b	----	----
'West Highlands'	----	N.M.S. F.E.6	----	17.11
ATTRIBUTED TO SCOTLAND				
****Perthshire	Monzie	N.M.S. L.1963:33	----	----
FRANCE				
Charente	Vénat	Mus. Soc. Hist. et Arch. de la Charante	Coffyn, Gomez, Mohen, *Le Dépôt de Vénat*, (1981), 1–7, 10, 19.	(BRONZE)
Charente	Vénat	Mus. Soc. Hist. et Arch. de la Charante	Coffyn, Gomez, Mohen, *Le Dépôt de Vénat*, (1981), 1–7, 10, 19.	(BRONZE)
Charente	Vénat	Mus. Soc. Hist. et Arch. de la Charante	Coffyn, Gomez, Mohen, *Le Dépôt de Vénat*, (1981), 1–7, 10, 19.	(BRONZE)
Loir-et-Cher	Choussy	Seminary at Issy	----	(BRONZE)
Marne	Saint-Martin-sur-le-Pré	Musée Préhistoire, Epernay	----	(BRONZE)
Marne	Saint-Martin-sur-le-Pré	Musée Préhistoire, Epernay	----	(BRONZE)
Marne	Saint-Martin-sur-le Pré	Musée Préhistoire, Epernay	----	(BRONZE)
Marne	Saint-Martin-sur-le Pré	Musée Préhistoire, Epernay	----	(BRONZE)

Marne	Saint-Martin-sur-le Pré	Musée Préhistoire, Epernay	----	(BRONZE)
Marne	Saint-Martin-sur-le Pré	Musée Préhistoire, Epernay	----	(BRONZE)
Marne	Saint-Martin-sur-le Pré	Musée Préhistoire, Epernay	----	(BRONZE)
Marne	Saint-Martin-sur-le-Pré	Musée Préhistoire, Epernay	----	(BRONZE)

** N.B. This 'Lock-ring' has been attributed to Scotland — Monzie, Perthshire — but its form and structure can only be paralled in Ireland. Therefore, it may have been a modern import from Ireland and acordingly is being classed as being an unprovenced Irish example (see p. 124).

IRISH TYPE PENNANULAR BRACELETS (Figure 39)

Penannular bracelets, rounded body, solid evenly expanded terminals

COUNTY	FIND PLACE	COLLECTION	REFERENCES	WEIGHT Grammes
IRELAND				
Antrim	----	Ash. O. 1927:2934	----	244.42
Carlow	Tullow	N.M.I. W.102	Armstrong, (1933), 74:213.	13.48
Cavan	Lattoon	N.M.I. 1920:26	Armstrong, (1933), 47–9, fig. 17; Eogan, (1983a), p.64–5, No.53:1.	21.51
Cavan	Lattoon	N.M.I. 1920:27	Armstrong, (1933), 47–9, fig. 17; Eogan, (1983a), p.64–5, No.53:2.	19.96
Clare	Lahardan	N.M.I. R.510	Eogan, (1983a), p.68–9, No.57:3.	(BRONZE)
Clare	Mooghaun	N.M.I. W.22–7, 91–2, 117–18, 1936:3696–7 B.M. 57.6–27.2–13	Eogan, (1983), p.69–72. (c. 153 examples)	It appears that the entire content of the hoard weighed in the region of 6,220
Clare	Kilconnell	N.M.I. R.2603	Armstrong, (1933), 77:246; Eogan, (1983a), p.179–80, No.3:3.	15.62
Clare	Kilconnell	N.M.I. R.2601	Armstrong, (1933), 77:244; Eogan, (1983a), p.179–80, No.3:1.	19.70
Clare	Kilconnell	N.M.I. R.2602	Armstrong, (1933), 77:245; Eogan, (1983a), p.179–80, No.3:2.	18.73
Cork	Aghinagh	B.M. 71.4–1.4	----	63.44
Cork	Ballyneen	B.M. 71.4–1.5	----	40.18
Cork	----	N.M.I. 1934:451	Eogan, (1983a), p.181–2, No.6:1.	(BRONZE)
Donegal	Pollen Shore	B.M. W.G. 10	----	6.89
Donegal	Conwal	N.M.I. 1886:43	Armstrong, (1933), 76:242.	85.66
Donegal	----	N.M.I. 1886:41	Armstrong, (1933), 76:241.	82.10
Kerry (?Cork)	nr. Bantry	N.M.I. 1885:359	Armstrong, (1933), 77:250.	82.41
Kerry	Carhan Upper	N.M.I. 1899:71	Armstrong, (1933), 76:232.	16.52
Kerry	Kilmoyly North	N.M.I. 1940:2D	Eogan, (1983a), p.92–3, No.89:1.	30.44
Limerick	Askeaton	Not known	Eogan, (1983a), p.101–2, No.99:3.	----
Limerick	----	N.M.I. 1881:98	Armstrong, (1933), 75:228; Eogan, (1983a), 105–6, No.104:2.	13.93

Limerick	----	N.M.I. 1881:99	Armstrong, (1933), 75:229; Eogan, (1983), p.105–6, No.104:1.	12.18
Limerick	----	N.M.I. 1881:100	Armstrong, (1933), 75:227; Eogan, (1983a), p.105–6, No.104:3.	13.67
Limerick	----	B.M. 49.3–1.5	----	----
Mayo	Kilmeena	N.M.I. 1932:7	----	20.26
Meath	Moate (Kells)	N.M.I. 1922:6	Armstrong, (1922), 137–8, Fig. V.	21.77
Meath (possibly)	----	N.M.I. 1876:1670	Armstrong, (1933), 76:238.	118.97
Offaly	Meenwaun, nr. Banagher	N.M.I. 1918:350	Armstrong, (1933), 77:243; Eogan, (1983a), p.115–6, No.117:1; Whitfield, *Archaeology Ireland*, 7(1993), 9–11.	19.50
Offaly (possibly)	Kilnaborris	Private in England	Whitfield, *Archaeology Ireland*, 6(1992), 28–30.	----
Offaly	----	N.M.I. 1969:749	*J.R.S.A.I.*, 102(1972), 190.	12.82
Roscommon	nr. Athlone	N.M.I. 1990:79a ex. Northumberland Coll.	Eogan, (1983a), Pl. 43–4, No. 122:1; Sotheby, (1990) 56.	19
Roscommon	nr. Athlone	N.M.I. 1990:79b ex. Northumberland Coll.	Eogan, (1983a) Pl. 43–4, No. 122:2; Sotheby (1990) 56.	26.5
Roscommon	nr. Athlone	N.M.I. 1990:79c ex. Northumberland Coll.	Eogan, (1983a) Pl. 43–4, No. 122:3; Sotheby (1990) 56.	24.5
Roscommon	nr. Athlone	N.M.I. 1893:7	Armstrong, (1933), 78:254; Eogan (1983a) P. 144, no. 123:1.	24.56
Roscommon	nr. Athlone	N.M.I. 1893:8	Armstrong, (1933) 78:255; Eogan, (1983a) p. 144, no. 123:2.	21.90
Tipperary	Cashel Area	Not Known	Eogan, (1983a), p.153–4, No.134:4.	----
Tipperary	nr. Tipperary	Not Known	Cahill, (1993), *Tipperary Historical Journal*, 189–193.	122.73
Tyrone	Drumnakilly	U.M. A. 203:1913	----	58.1
Westmeath	possibly Mullingar	N.M.I. 1884:10	Armstrong, (1933), 76:234.	19.50
Possibly Wexford	----	N.M.I. 1899:37	Armstrong, (1933), 75:226.	12.63
Wicklow	----	N.M.I. W.89	Armstrong, (1933), 78:256; Eogan, (1983a), p.174, No.156:2.	11.79
Ireland	----	N.M.I. P.818	Armstrong, (1933), 74:217.	22.42
Irelad	----	N.M.I. P.819	Armstrong, (1933), 74:218.	10.82
Ireland	----	N.M.I. P.820	Armstrong, (1933), 75:219.	39.33
Ireland	----	N.M.I. P.829	Armstrong, (1933), 75:220.	13.54
Ireland	----	N.M.I. W.93	Armstrong, (1933), 75:221.	31.56
Ireland	----	N.M.I. W.101	Armstrong, (1933), 74:214.	13.15
Ireland	----	N.M.I. W.103	Armstrong, (1933), 75:222.	14.19
Ireland	----	N.M.I. W.104	Armstrong, (1933), 75:223.	32.20
Ireland	----	N.M.I. W.105	Armstrong, (1933), 76:240.	25.53
Ireland	----	N.M.I. W.106	Armstrong, (1933), 77:248.	46.40
Ireland	----	N.M.I. W.108	Armstrong, (1933), 77:249.	49.38
Ireland	----	N.M.I. W.113	Armstrong, (1933), 76:236.	76.20
Ireland	----	N.M.I. W.116	Armstrong, (1933), 76:237.	141.71
Ireland	----	N.M.I. W.280	Armstrong, (1933), 77:251.	88.71
Ireland	----	N.M.I. R.616	Armstrong, (1933), 74:215.	14.19
Ireland	----	N.M.I. R.1837	Armstrong, (1933), 74:210.	70.82

Ireland	----	N.M.I. R.1838	Armstrong, (1933), 74:211.	35.44
Ireland	----	N.M.I. R.1839 ; W.100	Armstrong, (1933), 74:212.	11.53
Ireland	----	N.M.I. R.2600	Armstrong, (1933), 73:206.	142.49
Ireland	----	N.M.I. R.2608	Armstrong, (1933), 76:231.	32.98
Ireland	----	N.M.I. R.4032	Armstrong, (1933), 77:247.	12.89
Ireland	----	N.M.I. R.4033	Armstrong, (1933), 76:233.	47.95
Ireland	----	N.M.I. 1899 ; 36	Armstrong, (1933), 75:225.	12.89
Ireland	----	N.M.I. 1899:35	Armstrong, (1933), 75:224.	13.15
Ireland	----	N.M.I. 1899:37	Armstrong, (1933), 75:226.	12.64
Ireland	----	N.M.I. 1930:109	----	29.91
Ireland	----	N.M.I. 1960:675	Eogan, (1983a), p.203, No.41:1.	43.5
Ireland	----	N.M.I. 1960:676	Eogan, (1983a), p.203, No.41:2.	24.77
Ireland	----	N.M.I. 1960:677	Eogan, (1983a), p.203, No.41:3.	11.21
Ireland	----	N.M.I. 1960:678	Eogan, (1983), p.203, No.41:4.	9.66
Ireland	----	N.M.I. SA.5:189(?)	Armstrong, (1933), 78:257.	30.26
Ireland	----	N.M.I. SA.6:1898	Armstrong, (1933), 74:216.	18.34
Ireland	----	N.M.I. 1975:232	----	16.81
Ireland	----	Ash. O. 1927:2951	----	8.30
Ireland	----	Ash. O. 1927:2952	----	17.43
Ireland	----	Ash. O. 1927:2953	----	50.37
Ireland	----	U.M.A.E.C. Z.15080	----	----
Ireland	----	Boston Mus. B 11717	----	----
Ireland	----	R.O.M. 952.184,3	----	----
Ireland	----	Israel Mus. Jerusalem	----	----
WALES				
Anglesey	Beaumaris	B.M. 49.6–27.1	Lynch, (1970), 204–6, Fig. 67, 5–6.	66.7
Anglesey	Beaumaris	B.M. 49.6–27.2	Lynch, (1970), 205–6, Fig. 67, 5–6.	33.2
Anglesey	Gaerwen	B.M. W.G.15	Lynch, (1970), 205–6, Fig. 67, 5–6.	33.31
Anglesey	Gaerwen	B.M. W.G.16	Lynch, (1970), 205–6, Fig. 67, 5–6.	15.42
Montgomery-shire	Llanrhaiadr-yn-Mochnant	N.M.W. 21.24.33	Savory, (1980), 115.	(BRONZE)
SCOTLAND				
Argyll	Coul/Islay	Not known; N.M.S. F.E.52, may be from Coul board.	Clarke, *P.S.A.S.*, 107(1975–6), 307–9; Anderson, (1886), 213.	----
Argyll	Killeen	Not known	----	----
Argyll	Killeen	Buried with owner	----	----
Argyll	Tullich (Glenaray)	Inveraray Castle, Argyllshire.	Royal Commission on the Ancient & Historical Monuments of Scotland, *Mid Argyll and Cowal*, (1988), 20, 25, Fig.27:B	----
Bute (Arran)	Ormidale	N.M.S. F.E.11	Hartmann, (1982), 104–5, Taf. 22.	----
Bute (Arran)	Ormidale	N.M.S. F.E.12	Hartmann, (1982), 104–5, Taf. 21.	----
Bute (Arran)	Ormidale	N.M.S. F.E.13	Hartmann, (1982), 104–5, Taf. 22.	----
Caithness	Hillhead	N.M.S. F.E.69	Hartmann, (1982), 106–7, Taf. 23.	----
Caithness	Hillhead	N.M.S. F.E.70	Hartmann, (1982), 106–7, Taf. 23.	----
Inverness	nr. Kilmallie	Private in 1975	Close-Brooks, *P.S.A.S.*, 107(1975–6), 309–10.	----

Inverness	nr. Kilmallie	Private in 1975	Close-Brooks, *P.S.A.S.*, 107(1975–6), 309–10.	----
Moray	Tomnavien	Aberdeen City & Dist. Mus.	----	----
Ross - Cromarty	Heights of Brae	N.M.S. F.E.97	Clarke and Kemp, (1984), 192, 195, illus. 5–6.	34
Ross - Cromarty	Heights of Brae	N.M.S. F.E.98	Clarke and Kemp, (1984), 192, 195, illus. 5–6.	32.5
Ross - Cromarty	Heights of Brae	N.M.S. F.E.99	Clarke and Kemp, (1984), 192, 195, illus. 5–6.	41.4
Ross - Cromarty	Heights of Brae	N.M.S. F.E.101	Clarke and Kemp, (1984), 192, 195, illus. 5–6.	41.48
Wigtown	Kirkmaiden	Not known	*P.S.A.S.*, 82(1947–48), 293.	----
Western Highlands	----	N.M.S. F.E.4	Eogan, (1969), 134.	29.94
Western Highlands	----	N.M.I. F.E.5	Eogan, (1969), 134.	27.60
PORTUGAL				
North Portugal	----	----	Silva Da, (1986), 185, Fig.99:7.	(BRONZE)

Penannular bracelets, rounded body, hollowed evenly-expanded terminals

COUNTY	FIND PLACE	COLLECTION	REFERENCES	WEIGHT Grammes
IRELAND				
Clare	Gorteenreagh	N.M.I. 1948:328	Eogan, (1983a), p.67–8, No. 56:2; Raftery, *North Munster Studies*, (ed. E. Rynne, 1967), 61–71.	14.86
Clare	Gorteenreagh	N.M.I. 1948:329	Eogan, (1983a), p.67–8, No. 56:3; Raftery, *North Munster Studies*, (ed. E. Rynne, 1967), 61–71.	28.93
Cork	Gortnalicky	B.M. 40.9–28.1	----	64.8
Cork	Gortnalicky	B.M. 40.9–28.2	----	54.88
Dublin	Newtown, Castlebryn	N.M.I. 1972:172	----	15.58
Galway	Ballykeaghra	N.M.I. 1960:3	Eogan, (1983a), p.88, No.83:3.	(BRONZE)
Kerry	Kilmoyly North	N.M.I. 1940:2 b	Eogan, (1983a), p.92–3, No. 89:3.	50.45
Kerry	Kilmoyly North	N.M.I. 1940:2 c	Eogan, (1983a), p.92–3, No. 89:2.	123.85
Kerry	Staigue (In, or at, the outer wall of the fort.)	Private in England 1994. Formerly on loan to U.M.	Proudfoot, (1955), 38.	----
Kildare	Grange	U.M.A.E.C. M.C. 99. 246. 6	Eogan, (1983a), p.94–5, No. 92:3.	(BRONZE)
Limerick	----	B.M. 49.3–1.4	----	14.2
Mayo	Killbride	N.M.I. 1987:104	Cahill, *Cathair na Mairt*, 8 (1988), 26–29.	38.5
Mayo	Liverourd or Oldcastle	Not Known.	Eogan, (1983a), p.108–, No. 109:1.	---
Meath	Drissoge	N.M.I. 1953:2	Eogan, (1983a), p.112–13, No. 113:1.	16.2
Meath	Drissoge	N.M.I. 1953:3	Eogan, (1983a), p.112–13, No. 113:2.	18.69
Sligo	nr. Sligo?	N.M.I. 1874:105	Armstrong, (1933), 73:201;	111.91
Tipperary	Cashel Area	N.M.I. W.307 ; R.587	Armstrong, (1933), 73:207; Eogan, (1983a), p.153–4, No. 134:1.	34.80

Tipperary	Cashel Area	N.M.I. W.308 ; R.558	Armstrong, (1933), 74:208; Eogan, (1983a), p.153–4, No.134:2.	28.96
Tipperary	Cashel Area	N.M.I. W. 309 ; R.589	Armstrong, (1933), 74:209; Eogan, (1983a), p.153–4, No.134:3.	25.47
Tipperary	Kilcommon	N.M.I. R.2600	Armstrong, (1933), 73:206; Eogan, (1983a), p.196, 7, No.29:1.	142.49
Westmeath	Brockagh	N.M.I. 1876:1640	Eogan, (1983a), p.166–8, No.147:1.	(BRONZE)
Possibly Co. Wicklow	----	Glasgow Mus. of Art Gallery 348 (18/10)	Whitfield, Archaeology Ireland, 7(1993), 5.	----
Ireland	----	N.M.I. R. 4026	Armstrong, (1933), 73:200.	34.34
Ireland	----	N.M.I. W. 107	Armstrong, (1933), 76:239.	36.09
Ireland	----	N.M.I. W. 109	Armstrong, (1933), 73:198.	31.17
Ireland	----	N.M.I. W. 110	Armstrong, (1933), 72:197.	18.34
Ireland	----	N.M.I. W.111	Armstrong, (1933), 72:189.	44.97
Ireland	----	N.M.I. W.112	Armstrong, (1933), 73:199.	34.67
Ireland	----	N.M.I. W. 114	Armstrong, (1933), 73:204.	30.26
Ireland	----	N.M.I. W. 115	Armstrong, (1933), 76:235.	31.23
Ireland	----	N.M.I. W. 138	Armstrong, (1933), 71:188.	72.77
Ireland	----	N.M.I. 1881:100	Armstrong, (1933), 75:227.	13.67
Ireland	----	B.M. 34. 12–22.2	----	48.3
Ireland	----	B.M. 38. 7–18.2	----	70.83
Ireland	----	B.M. 38. 1–28.1	----	231.6
Ireland	----	B.M. 74. 3–3.7	----	16.78
Ireland	----	Boston Mus. of Fine Arts B. 11717	----	----
SCOTLAND				
Berwickshire	----	N.M.S. F.E.84	Hartmann, (1982), 104–5, Au.2306.	----
Clackmannan	nr. Alloa	Private	P.S.A.S., 61(1926–27), 192	----

Thick penannular bracelets

COUNTY	FIND PLACE	COLLECTION	REFERENCE	WEIGHT Grammes
IRELAND				
Antrim	nr. Ballymoney	Not known	Armstrong, (1933), 17.	----
Armagh	Lurgan	N.M.I. 1875:54	Armstrong, (1933), 72:191.	398.38
Cavan	----	Ash. O. 1907:2903	Evans, (1881), 387, fig.484.	(BRONZE)
Clare	Faunrusk	N.M.I. W. 142	Armstrong, (1933), 71:184.	68.75
Cork	Brahalish	B.M. 49.3–1.3	British Museum, Bronze Age Guide (1920), fig. 114.	101.67
Cork	Mountrivers	N.M.I. 1908:10	Eogan, (1983a), p.77, No.65:4.	(BRONZE)
Donegal	Clonleigh	Not known	Three gold ornaments, possibly ornaments of this class, Donegal Annual, 11 (1975–6), 206–8.	----
Kerry	Headford	Not known	Vallancey, Collectanea de Rebus Hibernicis, 237, pl. XIII.	----
Kerry	----	U.M. A. 204 . 1913	----	22.6
Limerick	Castletroy	Not known	----	----

Mayo	nr. Castlebar	N.M.I. W. 141	Armstrong, (1933), 71:185.	102.38
Mayo	Kilbride	N.M.I. 1987:105	Cahill, *Cathair na Mairt*, 8(1988), 26–9.	49
Meath	Drissoge	N.M.I. 1953:1	Eogan, (1983a), p.112–3, No.113:3.	50.99
Roscommon/ Westmeath	Athlone	Detroit Institute of Arts. IA. 53.274	Eogan, (1983a), p.195, No.26:1.	----
Tipperary	Kilcommon	N.M.I. R.2599	Armstrong, (1933), 73:205; Eogan, (1983a), p.197, No.29:2.	878.22
Waterford	nr. New Ross	N.M.I. 1896:1	Armstrong, (1933), 72:193; Eogan, (1983), p.164–5, No.145:1.	542.50
Waterford	nr. New Ross	N.M.I. 1896:3	Armstrong, (1933), 72:195; Eogan, (1983), p.164–5, No.145:3.	65.06
Waterford	nr. New Ross	N.M.I. 1896:5	Armstrong, (1933), 72:194; Eogan, (1983a), p.164–5, No.145:2.	42.83
Westmeath	----	Detroit Institute of Arts. IA 53.274	----	----
Ireland	----	N.M.I. P. 821	Armstrong, (1933), 72:190.	25.66
Ireland	----	N.M.I. W.111	Armstrong, (1933), 72:189.	44.97
Ireland	----	N.M.I. W. 138	Armstrong, (1933), 71:188.	72.77
Ireland	----	N.M.I. W. 140	Armstrong, (1933), 71:187.	85.92
Ireland	----	N.M.I. W. 143	Armstrong, (1933), 71:183.	53.65
Ireland	----	N.M.I. W. 144	Armstrong, (1933), 71:182.	87.41
Ireland	----	N.M.I. W. 145	Armstrong, (1933), 71:181.	37.84
Ireland	----	N.M.I. 1881:101	Armstrong, (1933), 73:203.	9.65 (Part only)
Ireland	----	U.M. A. 3535	----	24.9
Ireland	----	B.M. 54. 12–27.1	----	27.34
Ireland	----	B.M. 37. 11–27.1	----	61.56
Ireland	----	B.M. 49. 3–1.7	----	34.54
Ireland	----	B.M. 53. 9–26.1	----	71.41
Ireland	----	B.M. AF 14	----	51.4
Ireland	----	Detroit Institute of Arts	----	----
ENGLAND				
Cornwall	Morvah	B.M. 85.6–13.1	Hawkes & Clarke, (1963), 230–31.	87.22
Cornwall	Morvah	B.M. 85.6–13.2	Hawkes & Clarke, (1963), 230–31.	92.73
Cornwall	Morvah	B.M. 85.6–13.3	Hawkes & Clarke, (1963), 230–31.	69.85
Kent	Wanderslade	B.M. 1965.10–10.2	Longworth, *British Museum Quarterly*, 31(1966–67), 131–3.	----
Norfolk	Caister-on-sea	Norwich Castle	Hawkes & Clarke, (1963), 210–15.	----
Norfolk	Caister-on-sea	Norwich Castle	Hawkes & Clarke, (1963), 210–15.	----
Northumberland	Whittingham	----	Hawkes & Clarke, (1963), 242.	(BRONZE)
GERMANY				
Lower Saxony	Gahlstorf	Folke Museum, Bremen	Hawkes and Clarke, (1963), Pl. VIII, 2, 3, 195–97, 204–5.	475

PENANNULAR BRACELETS, TERMINAL FORM UNCERTAIN
(could be either Irish or British) (Figures 38–39)

COUNTY	FIND PLACE	COLLECTION	REFERENCES	WEIGHT Grammes
IRELAND				
Cavan	Baileborough	Not known	Eogan, (1983a), p.61.	one weighed 19.31
Mayo. 11 examples. One had evenly-expanded terminals but whether solid or hollow cannot be determined.	----	Not known	Eogan, (1983a), p.111–2.	One weighed 143.08
Ireland	----	N.M.I. W. 281	Armstrong, (1933), 78:259.	5.44
Ireland	----	N.M.I. 1875:105	Armstrong, (1933), 79:265.	77.17
Ireland	----	N.M.I. 1881:103	Armstrong, (1933), 71:180.	48.47
SCOTLAND				
Angus	Gallow Hill	Not known	Anderson, (1886), 211. [Possibly hoard of five examples].	----
Bute (Arran)	South Kascadle	Not known	Callander, *P.S.A.S.*, 59(1922–23), 319; Wilson, *Prehistoric Annals of Scotland* (1863), 458–9.	----
East Lothian	Galla Law	Not known	Anderson, (1886), 213. [Possibly more than one example].	----
Perthshire	nr. Fingask	Not known	*P.S.A.S.*, 27(1892–93), 367.	----
Perthshire	Shieldhill	Not known	Anderson, (1886), 213.	----
Perthshire	Shieldhill	Not known	Anderson, (1886), 213.	----
Perthshire	----	Not known	----	----
Wigtown	Boreland (Old Luce)	Not known	----	----

BRITISH TYPE PENANNULAR GOLD BRACELETS (Figure 38)

1. Flat Body, solid terminals generally evenly-shaped

COUNTY	FIND PLACE	COLLECTION	REFERENCES	WEIGHT Grammes
ENGLAND				
Cambridge	Reach Fen	Ash. O. 1927:2957	----	45.30
Cheshire	Henwall	Private	Williams, *Cheshire Archaeological Bulletin*, 9(1983), 98.	----
Cornwall	Morvah	B.M. 1885.6–13.4	Hencken, *Archaeology of Cornwall and Scilly*, (1932), 92, fig.26.	78.73
Cornwall	Rosemorran	Private	----	----
Cornwall	Scilly (St. Martins)	Private	----	----
Kent	Bexley, No. 2	B.M. 1907.3–12.4	*Victoria Co. History of Kent*, I (1908), 338. Plate opposite is incorrectly labelled 'first hoard'.	23.46

Kent	Bexley, No.2	B.M. 1907.3–12.7	*Victoria Co. History of Kent*, I (1908), 338. Plate opposite is incorrectly labelled 'first hoard'.	24.75
Kent	Folkstone	Dover Mus.	----	----
Lincolnshire	'Fens'	B.M. W.G.7	----	28
Lincolnshire	'Fens'	Ash. O. 1927:2956	----	26.23
Norfolk	Caister-On-Sea	Norwich Mus. 210.955(2)	Hawkes & Clarke, (1963), 210–15, Pl. VII.	----
Somerset	Brean Down	Taunton Cas.Mus.	Needham in Bell, (1990), 146–51.	25.461
Somerset	Brean Down	Taunton Cas. Mus.	Needham in Bell, (1990), 146–51.	25.382
Stafford	Stanton	Stoke-on-Trent-Mus.	Vince, *The Neolithic and Bronze Age Cultures of the Middle and Upper Trent Basin*, BAR British Series, 105(1982), No.897.	----
Wiltshire	Potterne	Devizes Mus.	Taylor, *Wiltshire Archaeological and Natural History Magazine*, 78(1984), 35–40.	----
Wiltshire	Tisbury	B.M. A.F.405	Hawkes & Clarke, (1963), 231–5, Pl.XI, 6.	12.05
WALES				
Denbighshire	Llanarmon-yn-Lâl	N.M.W. 82.93H	Green, *Antiquaries Journal*, 63(1983), 384–7.	28.5
SCOTLAND				
Bute (Arran)	Ormidale	N.M.S. F.E.10	Anderson, (1886), 210; Hartmann, (1982), 104–5, Taf.20.	----
IRELAND				
Cork	Aghinagh	B.M. 71.4–1.6	----	21.32
Westmeath	Fore Abbey	N.M.I. W.97	Armstrong, (1933), 94:420.	25.92

2. Flat body, ends coiled to form terminals

COUNTY	FIND PLACE	COLLECTION	REFERENCES	WEIGHT Grammes
ENGLAND				
Buckingham	Milton Keynes	Bucks. Museum, Aylesbury	----	----
Cornwall	Morvah	B.M.85.6–13.5	Hencken, *Archaeology of Cornwall & Scilly*, (1932), 92, fig. 26.	53.14
Cornwall	Rosemorran	Private	----	----
Kent	Bexley, No. 2	B.M. 1907.3–12.8	*Victoria Co. History of Kent*, I (1908), 338. Plate opposite is incorrectly labelled 'first hoard'.	13.15
Kent	Bexley, No. 2	B.M. 1907.3–12.9	*Victoria Co. History of Kent*, I (1908), 338. Plate opposite is incorrectly labelled 'first hoard'.	12.76
Sussex	Patcham	Royal Pavilion Art Gall. and Mus. 230557 (R.4318/1)	Way, *Archaeological Journal*, 6(1849) 59.	----
Wiltshire	Tisbury	B.M. A.F.402	Hawkes & Clarke, (1963), 231–5, Pl. XI, 3–5.	25.14
Wiltshire	Tisbury	B.M. A.F.403	Hawkes & Clarke, (1963), 231–5, Pl. XI, 3–5.	12.57
Wiltshire	Tisbury	B.M. A.F.404	Hawkes & Clarke, (1963), 231–5, Pl. XI, 3–5.	16.91
Yorkshire	Cottingham	B.M. W.G.6	Hartmann, (1982), Taf.26. Au.3079.	----
IRELAND				
Wexford	Dunbrody Abbey	B.M. 49.3–1.19	----	13.22

3. Large deeply-hollowed body, flat outwardly-projecting terminals

COUNTY	FIND PLACE	COLLECTION	REFERENCES	WEIGHT Grammes
ENGLAND				
Wiltshire	Tisbury	B.M. A.F. 400	Hawkes & Clarke, (1963), 231–5, Pl. XI, 1–2.	47.95
Wiltshire	Tisbury	B.M. A.F. 401	Hawkes & Clarke, (1963), 231–5, Pl. XI, 1–2.	55.40

4. Internally hollowed body, solid outwardly-expanding terminals

COUNTY	FIND PLACE	COLLECTION	REFERENCES	WEIGHT Grammes
ENGLAND				
Cornwall	Rosemorran	Private	----	----
Durham	Heathery Burn	B.M. W.G.26	*Inventaria* GB. 55, 9th set 10(1), 2.	34.15
Kent	Bexley, No. 1	B.M. 1906.7–9.1	*Victoria Co. History of Kent*, I (1908), 338. Plate opposite is incorrectly labelled 'second hoard'.	134.78
Kent	Bexley, No. 1	B.M. 1906.7–9.2	*Victoria Co. History of Kent*, I (1908), 338. Plate opposite is incorrectly labelled 'second hoard'.	132.58
Kent	Bexley, No. 1	B.M. 1906.7–9.3	*Victoria Co. History of Kent*, I (1908), 338. Plate opposite is incorrectly labelled 'second hoard'.	130.57
Kent	Bexley, No. 1	B.M. 1906.7–9.4	*Victoria Co. History of Kent*, I (1908), 338. Plate opposite is incorrectly labelled 'second hoard'.	86.18
Kent	Bexley, No. 2	B.M. 1907.3–12.2	*Victoria Co. History of Kent*, I (1908), 338. Plate opposite is incorrectly labelled 'first hoard'.	50.54
Kent	Bexley, No.	B.M. 1907.3–12.3	*Victoria Co. History of Kent*, I (1908), 338. Plate opposite is incorrectly labelled 'first hoard'.	47.43
Kent	Bexley, No.2	B.M. 1907.3–12.5	*Victoria Co. History of Kent*, I (1908), 338. Plate opposite is incorrectly labelled 'first hoard'.	24.3
Kent	Bexley, No. 2	B.M. 1907.3–12.6	*Victoria Co. History of Kent*, I (1908), 338. Plate opposite is incorrectly labelled 'first hoard'.	23.78
Lancashire	Portfield	B.M. 1966.12–8.2	Blundell & Longworth, (1967), 8–14.	14.2

5. Solid body of D-shaped cross-section, outwardly-expanded solid terminals

COUNTY	FIND PLACE	COLLECTION	REFERENCES	WEIGHT Grammes
ENGLAND				
Kent	Aylesford, No. 1	Maidstone Mus.	Roch Smith, *Archaeologia Cantiana*, 9(1874), 2, 11 ; pl.B:1; *Victoria Co. History of Kent*, I (1908), 325–6.	65.51
Kent	Aylesford, No. 2	Maidstone Mus.	Pretty, *Archaeologia Cantiana*, 5(1862), 43, pl.1:22; *Victoria Co. History of Kent*, I(1908), 325–6.	65.90
Kent	Aylesford, No. 2	Maidstone Mus.	Pretty, *Archaeologia Cantiana*, 5(1862), 43, pl.1:33.	80.54
Kent	Bexley, No. 1	B.M. 1906.7–9.5	*Victoria Co. History of Kent*, I (1908), 338. Plate opposite is incorrectly labelled 'second hoard'.	69.34
Kent	Bexley, No. 1	B.M. 1906.7–9.6	*Victoria Co. History of Kent*, I (1908), 338. Plate opposite is incorrectly labelled 'second hoard'.	69.34

Kent	Bexley, No. 1	B.M. 1906.7–9.7	*Victoria Co. History of Kent*, I (1908), 338. Plate opposite is incorrectly labelled 'second hoard'.	68.69
Kent	Bexley, No. 1	B.M. 1906.7–9.8/9	*Victoria Co. History of Kent*, I (1908), 338. Plate opposite is incorrectly labelled 'second hoard'.	33.04
Kent	Bexley, No. 2	B.M. 1907.3–12.1	*Victoria Co. History of Kent*, I (1908), 338. Plate opposite is incorrectly labelled 'first hoard'.	92.01
Kent	Wanderslade	B.M. 1965.10–10.1	Longworth, *British Museum Quarterly*, 31(1966–67), 131–3.	----
Somerset	Hope Wood, nr. Wookey Hole	? Private	Haldane, *Proceedings of the Somerset Archaeological and Natural History Society*, 113(1969), 99–101.	23.7
Sussex	Patcham	Royal Pavilion Art Gal. and Mus. 230558 (R.4318/2)	Way, *Archaeological Journal*, 6(1849), 59.	----
Yorkshire	Cottingham	B.M. W.G.5	Hartmann, (1982), Taf. 28.	----
Yorkshire	Wanlas, Cottinghan	B.M. 62.11–14.1	Hartmann, (1982), Taf. 26.	207.62
SCOTLAND				
Clackmannan	Alloa	N.M.S. E.Q. 119	Hartmann, (1982), 106–7. Taf. 23.	----
Galloway	Estate of Earl of Stair	Not known	Wilson, *Prehistoric Annals of Scotland* (1863), 456. Anderson, (1886), 213.	----

6. Solid body of lozenge-shaped cross-section, evenly-expanded solid terminals

COUNTY	FIND PLACE	COLLECTION	REFERENCES	WEIGHT Grammes
ENGLAND				
Cornwall	Morvah	B.M. 85.6–13.6	Hencken, *Archaeology of Cornwall and Scilly*, (1932), 92, fig. 26.	86.51
Kent	Aylesford, district No. 1	Maidstone Mus.	Roch Smith, *Archaeologia Cantiana*, 9(1874), 2, 11:pl.B:2.	88.19
Kent	Aylesford, district No. 1	Maidstone Mus.	Roch Smith, *Archaeologia Cantiana*, 9(1874), 2, 11:pl.B:3.	124.93
Kent	Little Chart	B.M. 69.9–20.1	Gordan, *Archaeologia Cantiana*, 80(1965), 200–4.	138.9
Kent	Little Chart	Ash. O. 1927:2954	Gordan, *Archaeologia Cantiana*, 80(1965), 200–4.	----
Kent	Little Chart	Ash. O. 1927:2955	Gordan, *Archaeologia Cantiana*, 80(1965), 200–4.	----
Norfolk	Caister-on-sea	Norwich Cas. 210.955(1)	Hawkes & Clarke, (1963), 210–15, Pl. VII	----
Yorkshire	nr. Catterick	B.M. ?	----	----
SCOTLAND				
Lanarkshire	Stonehill	N.M.S. L.1978.4	Anderson, (1886), 211–2, Fig. 228, 229.	169.12
Lanarkshire	Stonehill	N.M.S. L.1978.5	Anderson, (1886), 211–2, Fig. 228, 229.	----
Lanarkshire	Stonehill	N.M.S. L.1978.	Anderson, (1886), 211–2, Fig. 228, 229.	32.01

7. Solid body of rounded cross-section, outwardly-expanded solid terminals

COUNTY	FIND PLACE	COLLECTION	REFERENCES	WEIGHT Grammes
SCOTLAND				
Berwickshire	Kirkhill	N.M.S. F.E.78	Hartmann,(1982), 106–7. Taf. 22; *P.S.A.S.*, 66 (1931–2), 26, Fig. 9.	----

8. Solid body of rounded cross-section, elongated evenly-expanded solid terminals

COUNTY	FIND PLACE	COLLECTION	REFERENCES	WEIGHT Grammes
ENGLAND				
Sussex	Beachy Head	B.M. F.K.3	*Archaeologia*, 16(1812), 363, Pl. 68; *Britsih Museum Guide*, (1920), 46, Pl. IV.	25.2
WALES				
Cardigan	Llan Fair	B.M. W.G.9	----	11.99
SCOTLAND				
Wigtown	Penninghame	N.M.S. F.E.57	Hartmann, (1982), 104–5. Taf. 22; *P.S.A.S.*, 25(1890–91), 417.	----

9. Solid body with almost rounded cross-section but normally with slight flattening along inner circumference, evenly-expanded solid terminals

COUNTY	FIND PLACE	COLLECTION	REFERENCES	WEIGHT Grammes
ENGLAND				
Cambridge	Ickleton	B.M. P. 1973.11–1.1	Longworth, *Antiquaries Journal*, 52 (1972), 358–63.	40.7
Cumberland	Aspatria	B.M. 1904.11–2.1	*Archaeologia*, 22(1829), 439; Way, *Archaeological Journal*, 6(1849), 59.	170.1
Durham	Gretna Bridge	B.M. W.G.8	----	113.01
Sussex	Beachy Head	B.M. F.K.1	*Archaeologia*, 16(1812), 363, Pl. 68; British Museum Guide, (1920), 46, Pl. IV.	94.9
Sussex	Beachy Head	B.M. F.K.2	*Archaeologia*, 16(1812), 363; British Museum Guide, (1920), 46.	28.2
Sussex	Beachy Head	B.M. F.K.4	*Archaeologia*, 16(1812), 363; British Museum Guide, (1920), 46.	34.1
Sussex	Beachy Head	B.M. F.K.5	*Archaeologia*, 16(1812), 363; British Museum Guide, (1920), 46.	12.5
Sussex	Patcham	Royal Pavilion Art Gal. and Mus. 230559 (R.4318/3)	Way, *Archaeological Journal*, 6(1849), 59.	----
Sussex	Selsey	B.M. 1926.1–12.1	*Antiquaries Journal*, 6(1926), 308–9.	144.3
Sussex	Selsey	B.M. 1937.5–5.1	*Antiquaries Journal*, 17(1937), 321–2.	78.41
Sussex	Selsey	B.M. 1957.7–1.2	----	5.1
Wiltshire	Tisbury	B.M. A.F.406 (missing)	Hawkes & Clarke, (1963), 231–5, pl. 11.	----
Yorkshire	Wanlas, Cottingham	B.M. 93.10–17.1	Hartmann, (1982), Taf. 28. (near Hull)	124.09
SCOTLAND				
Berwickshire	Kirkhill	N.M.S. F.E.79	Hartmann, (1982), 106–7. Taf.22.	----
Clackmannon	Alloa	N.M.S. E.Q.118	Hartmann, (1982), 106–7. Taf.22.	----

Plates

PLATE 1

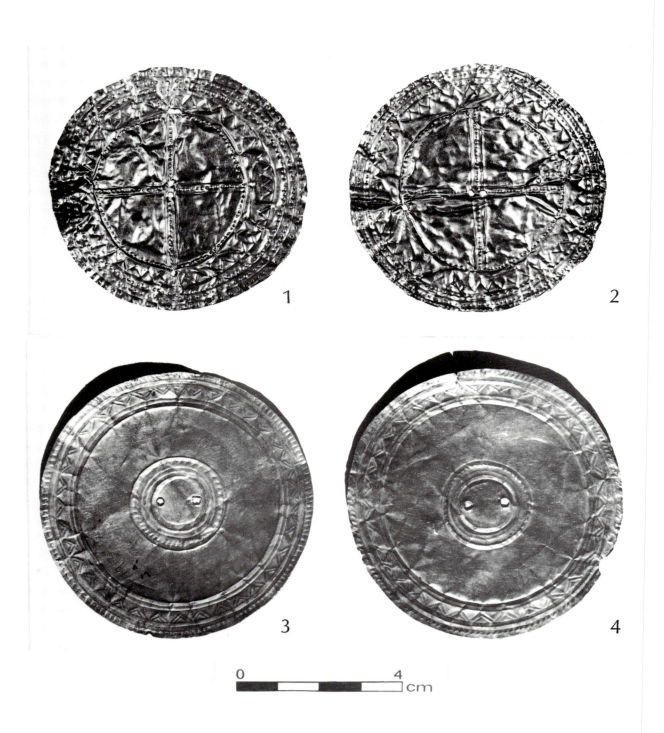

Discs. No locality, Ireland (1–2). Cloyne, Co. Cork (3–4).
Photo: National Museum of Ireland

PLATE 2

Details of lunulae horns. Nairn, Co. Donegal [Unaccomplished] (1); Trillick, Co. Tyrone [Classical] (2); nr. Killarney, Co. Kerry [Classical] (3).
Photo: National Museum of Ireland.

PLATE 3

Hoard. Kerivoa, Côtes-du-Nord, Brittany.
Photo: Musée des Antiquitès Nationale, Saint Germain-en-Laye

163

PLATE 4

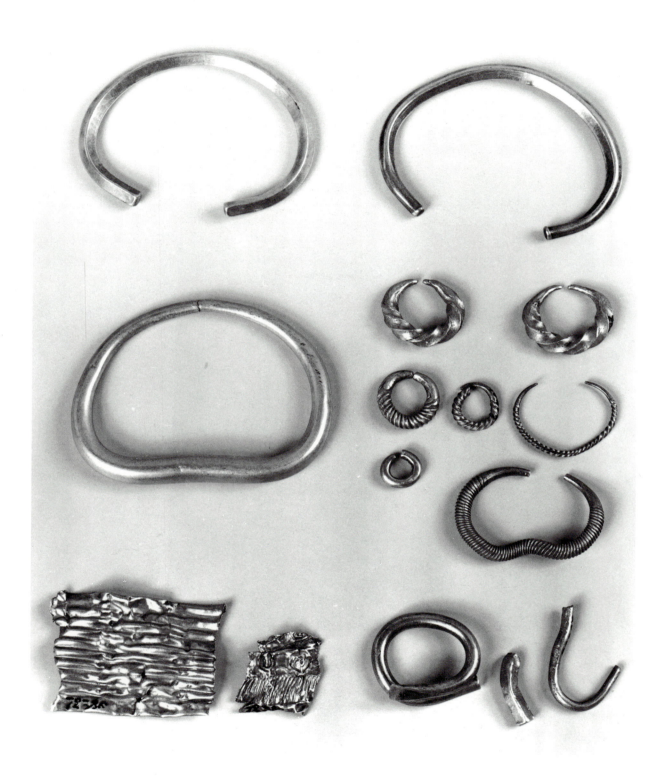

Hoard. Lanrivoaré, Finistère, Brittany.
Photo: Musée des Antiquitès Nationale, Saint Germain-en-Laye

PLATE 5

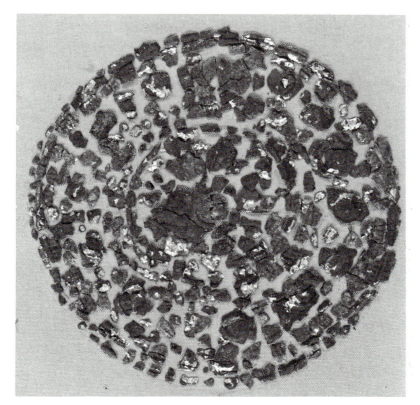

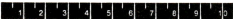

Disc. Lansdown, Avon (Somerset). Surviving remains (top); Reconstruction (bottom).
Photo: British Museum.

PLATE 6

Reconstruction of Mold cape, Flintshire. (After Powell 1953).

PLATE 7

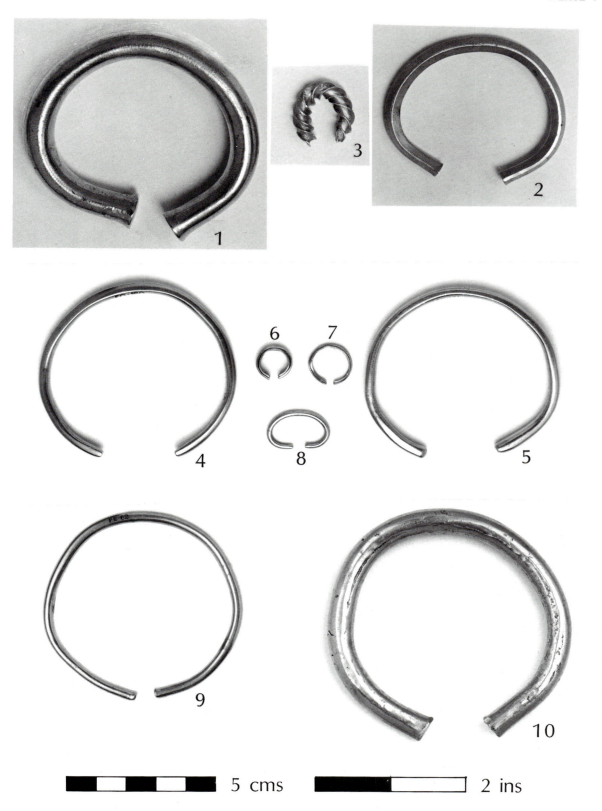

5 cms   2 ins

Gold ornaments from Sporle, Norfolk (1–3); bracelets and rings,Duff House, Banffshire (4–8);
bracelets from Briglands, Kinross (9) and Bonnyside, Stirling (10).
Photos: Norfolk Museum Services (top) and National Museum of Scotland (remainder).

167

PLATE 8

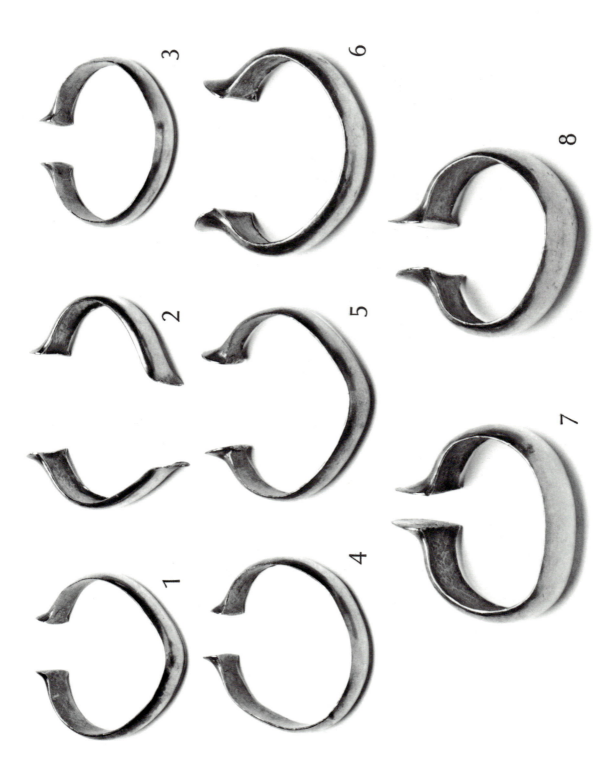

Hoard No. 1. Bexley Heath, Kent (1–8). Photo: British Museum.

PLATE 9

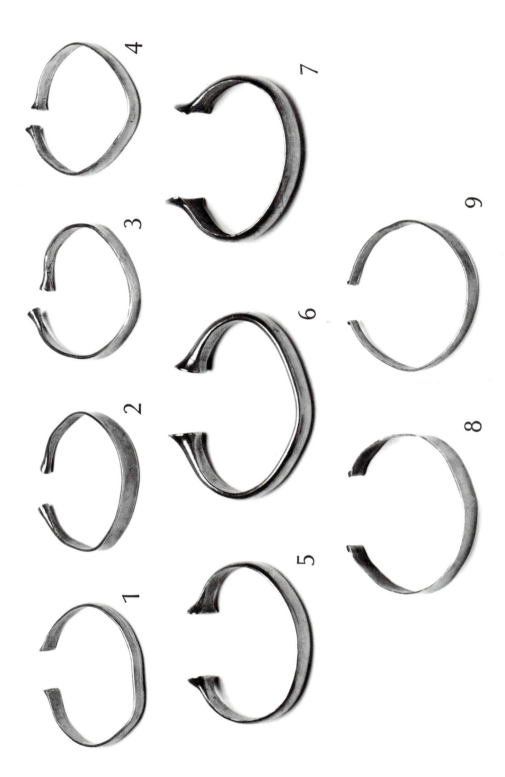

Hoard No. 2. Bexley Heath, Kent (1–9). Photo: British Musuem.

169

PLATE 10

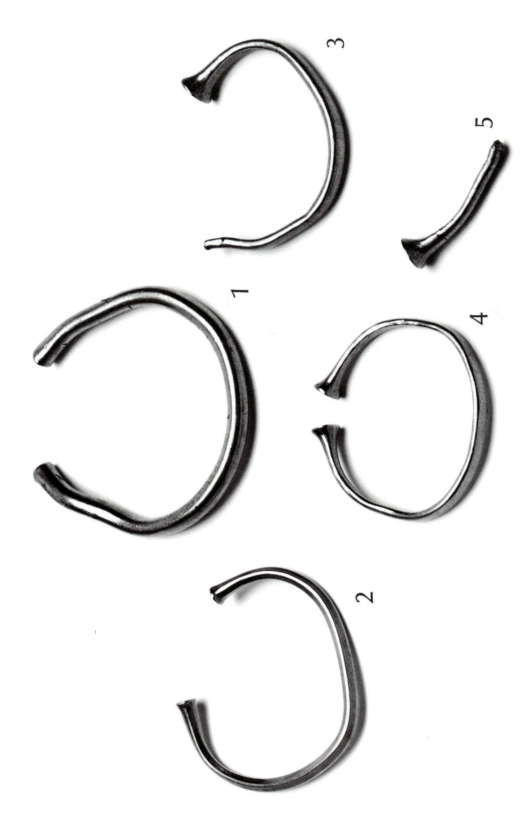

Gold bracelets, part of hoard from Beachy Head, Sussex (1–5). Photo: British Museum.

PLATE 11

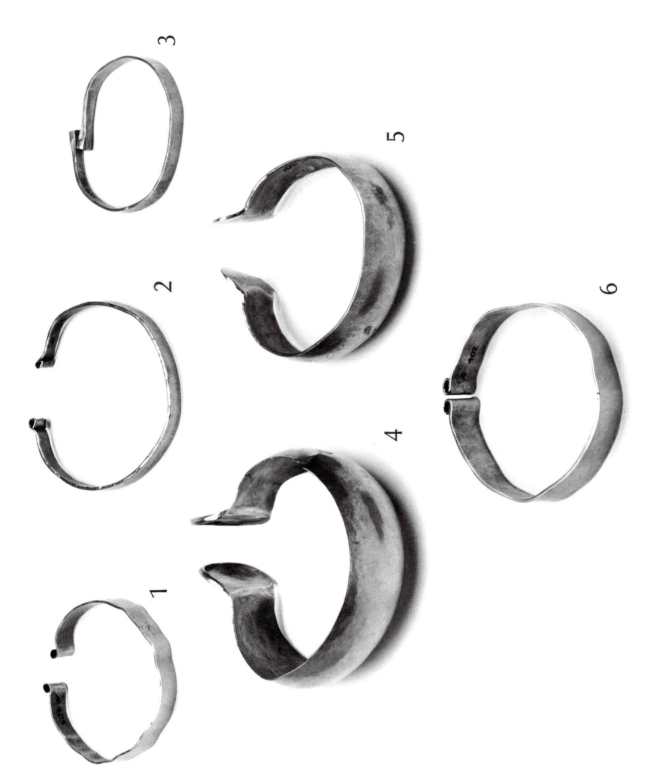

Hoard. Tisbury, Wiltshire (1–6). Photo: British Museum.

PLATE 12

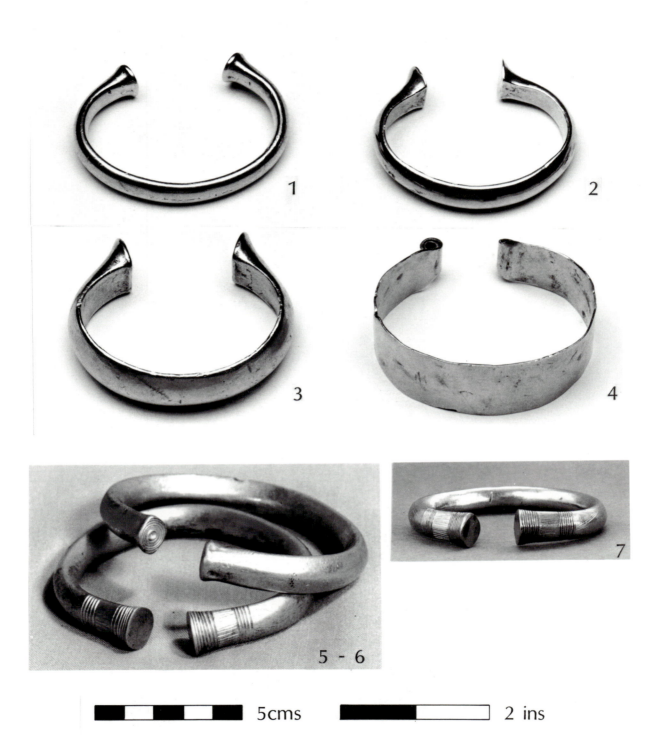

*Bracelets. Cottingham (Wanlas) area, Yorkshire (1-4). Hoard. Little Chart, Kent (5-7).
Photos: Ashmolean Museum and British Museum.*

PLATE 13

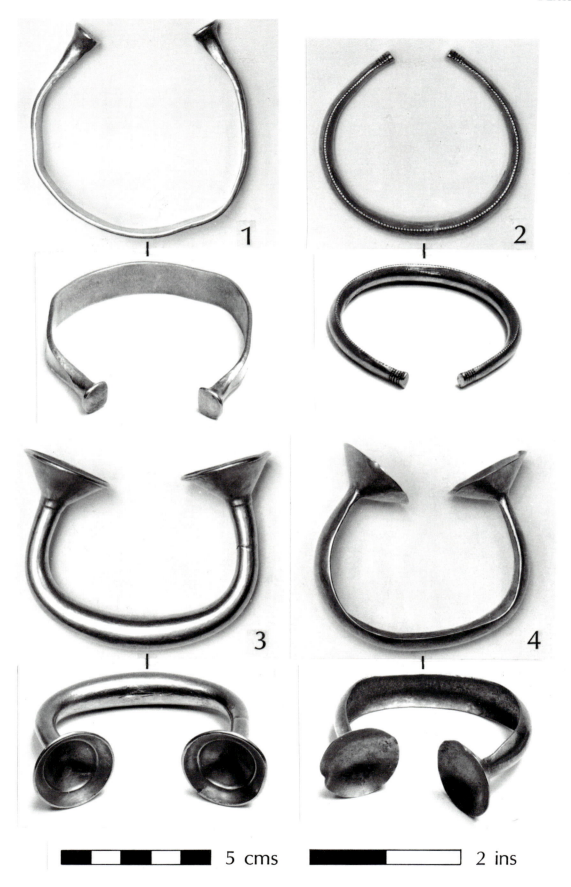

Hoard. Caister-on-Sea, Norfolk. Vertical (top) and oblique view of each object (1–4).
Photo: Norfolk Museum Services.

PLATE 14

Hoard, bronze except for 'hair-rings', 'lock-rings' and beads. Balmashanner, Angus. Photo: National Museum of Scotland.

National Museums of Scotland

PLATE 15

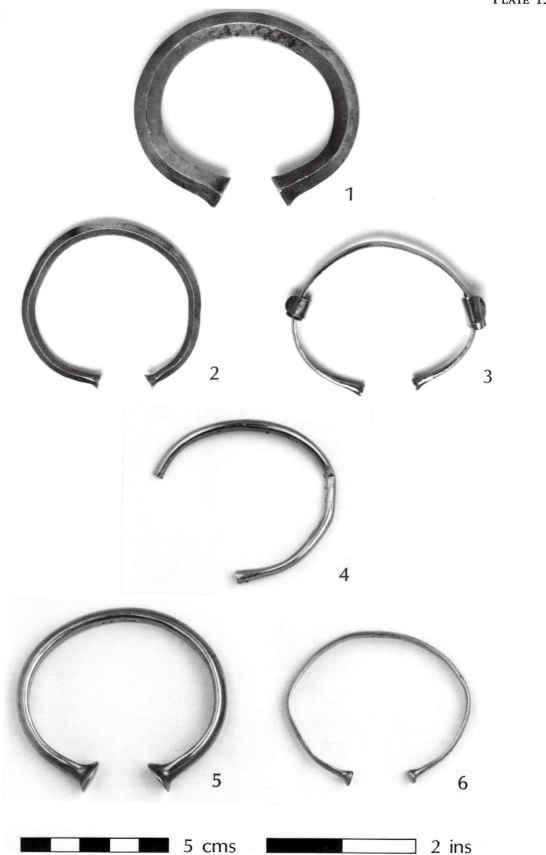

5 cms   2 ins

*Hoard. Stonehill, Lanark (1–3), single bracelet, Penningham, Wigtownshire (4), hoard Kirkhill, Berwickshire (5–6).
Photo: National Museum of Scotland.*

175

PLATE 16

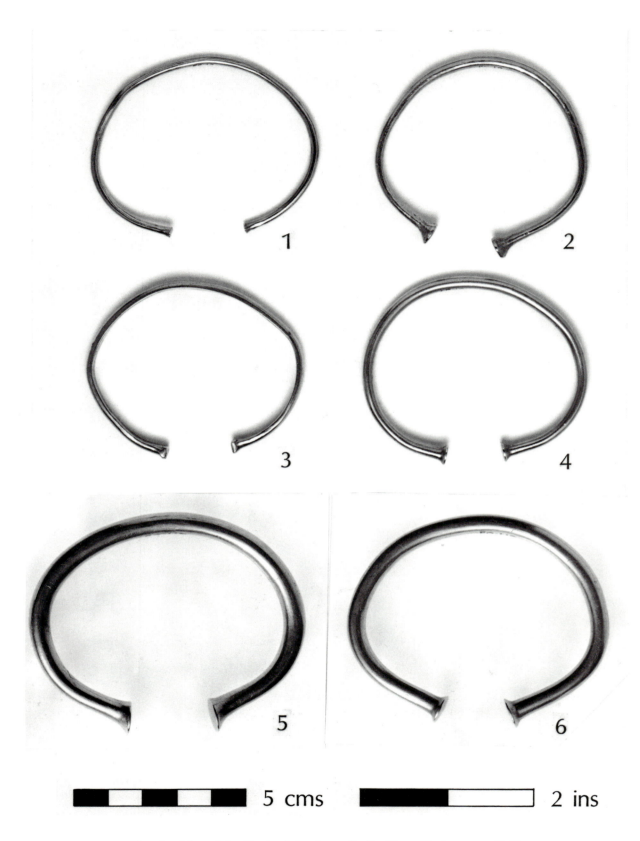

*Hoards of bracelets. Ormingdale, Arran (1–4); Alloa, Clackmannon (5–6).
Photo: National Museum of Scotland.*

PLATE 17

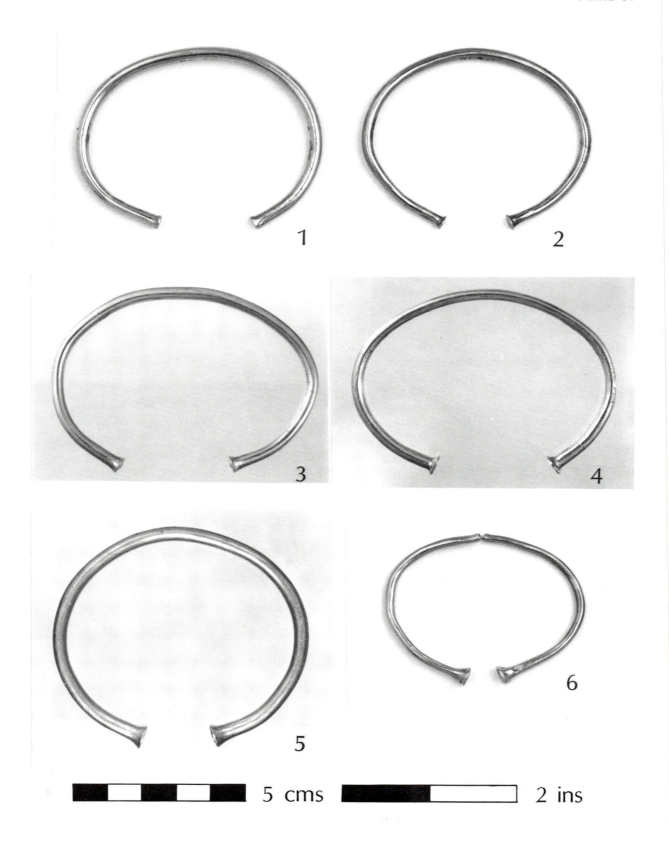

Hoards of bracelets. Hillhead, Caithness (1–2) and Kilmallie, Inverness-shire (3–4). Individual bracelets. Tomnavien, Morayshire (5) and Islay, Argyll (6). Photo: National Museum of Scotland.

PLATE 18

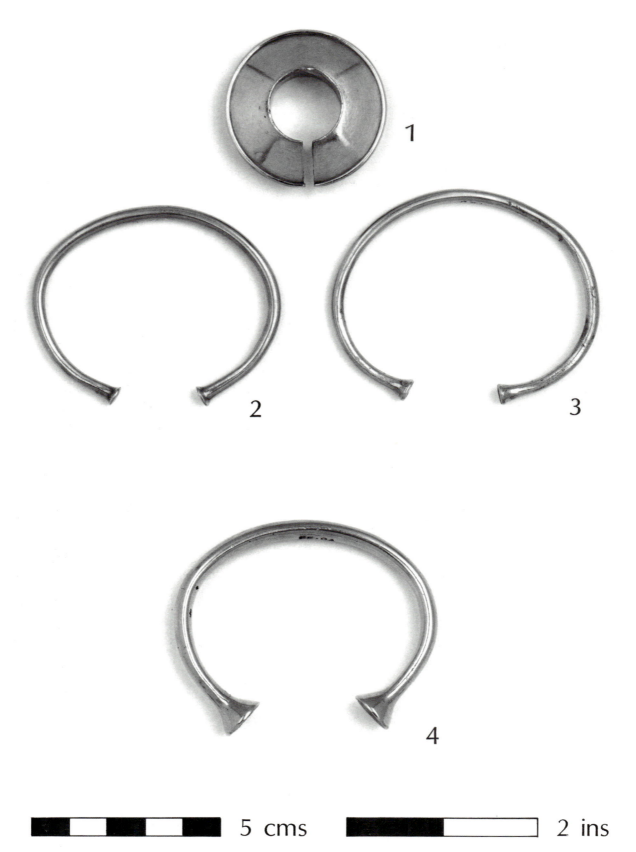

Hoard. West of Scotland (1–3). Individual bracelet. No location, Berwickshire (4).
Photo: National Museum of Scotland.

PLATE 19

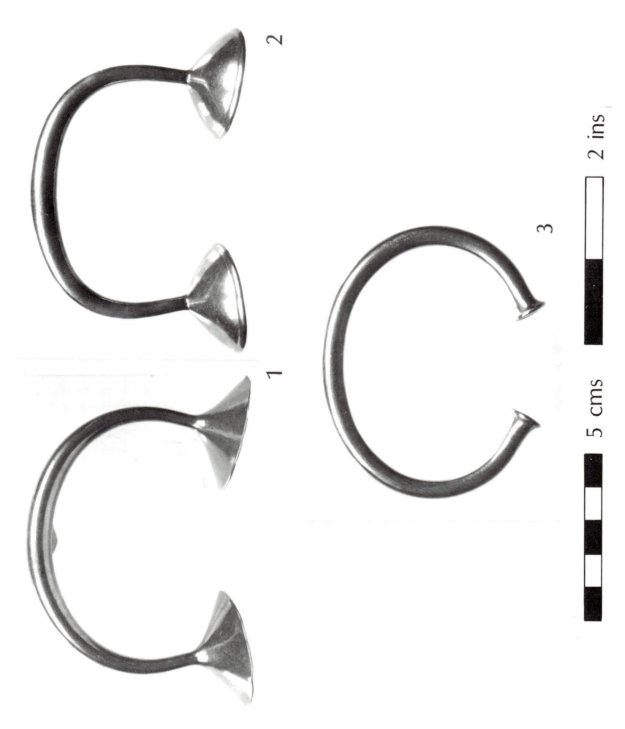

2

1

3

5 cms

2 ins

Hoard. Tullich, Glenaray, Argyll (1-3). Photo: National Museum of Scotland.

PLATE 20

Amber necklace. Derrybrien, Co. Galway.
Photo: National Museum of Ireland.

PLATE 21

Amber neckalce. Kurin, Co. Derry.
Photo: Ulster Museum.

PLATE 22

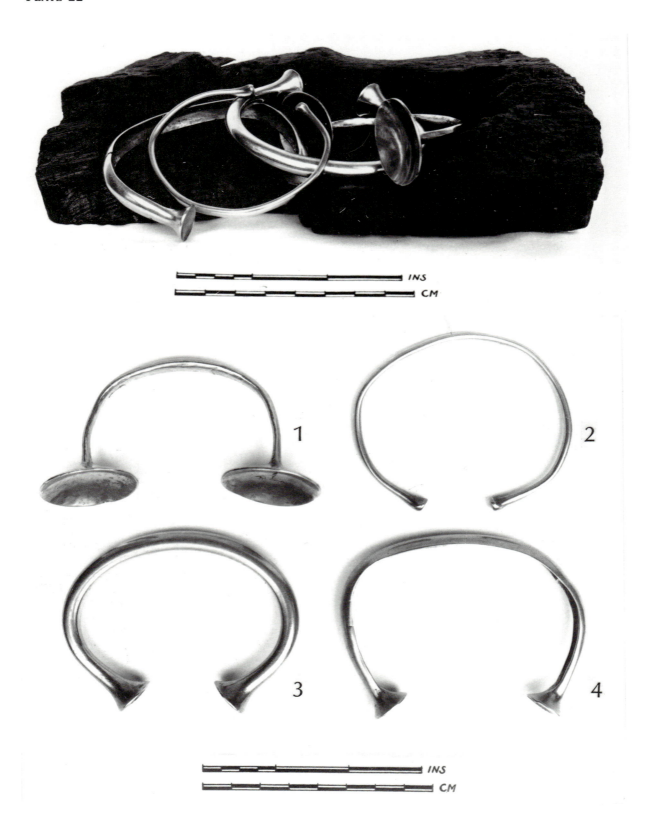

Wooden container with its contents of 'dress-fastener' and bracelets, Kilmoyley North, Co. Kerry (top). General view of the objects (1–4). Photo: National Museum of Ireland.

PLATE 23

├─────┼─────┼─────┼─────┤ 3 cm

Hoard. "South of Ireland" (1–3).
Photo: National Museum of Scotland.

PLATE 24

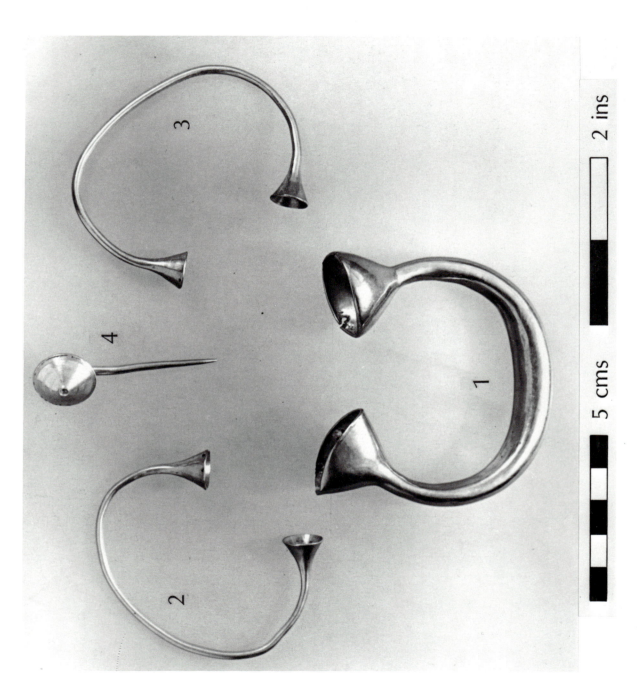

Hoard. Drissoge, Co. Meath (1–4). Photo: National Museum of Ireland.

PLATE 25

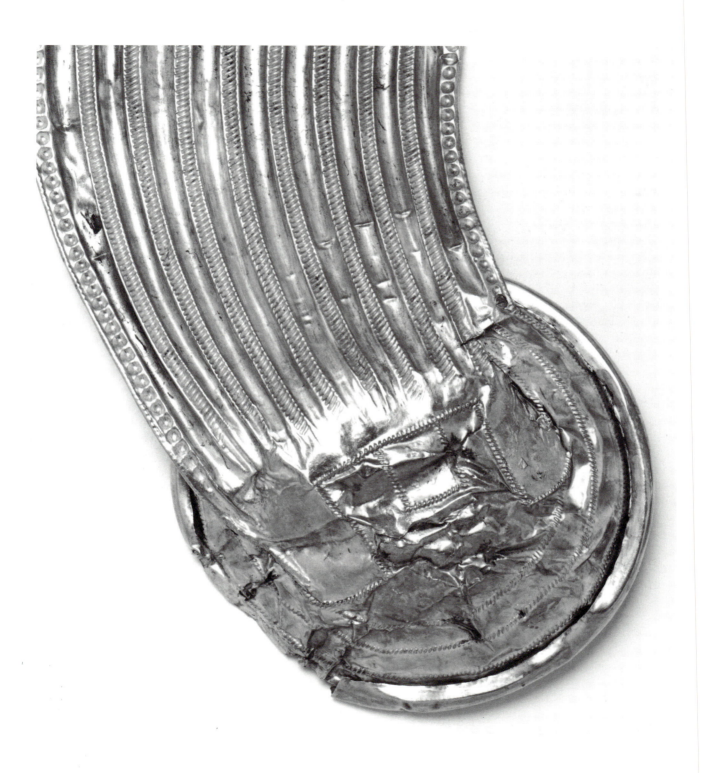

Detail of back of terminal and adjoining part of body of gorget from Shannongrove, Co. Limerick.
Photo: Victoria and Albert Museum, London

PLATE 26

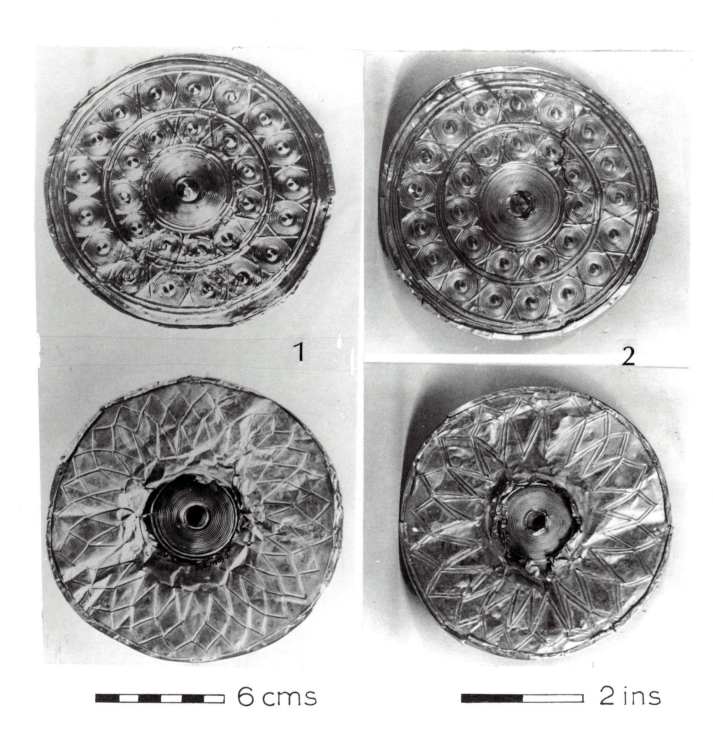

Disc-mounts. Enniscorthy, Co. Wexford. Front and back views.
Photos: National Museum of Ireland and Metropolitan Museum, New York

PLATE 27

Box. Ballinclemesig, Co. Kerry. Photo: National Museum of Ireland.

PLATE 28

Box. No location, Ireland. Photo: National Museum of Ireland.

PLATE 29

Bowl. No location, Ireland. Photo: National Museum of Ireland.

Index

gold encasing 83
gold incision 84
gold repoussé 84
gold tracer 84
gold wire 83, 84
gold, sheet 74
Tedavnet, Monaghan 19, 28
Thawley, J. E. 23
Thevenot, Jean-Paul 41
Thick penannualar ring 96
Thirsk, Yorkshire 51, 81
Thrane, Henrik. 46, 80
Thwing, Yorkshire 81
Tiers Cross, Pembrokeshire 3, 55
Tin 106
Tipperary 5, 10
Tisbury, Wiltshire 91
Tocík, Anton. 42
Todd, J.H. 6
Toggle 96
Tools 18, 82
Tooradoo, Limerick 89
Topped Mountan, Fermanagh 2, 41
Torbrügge, Walter 45, 59, 69, 72
Torcs
    bar 50, 53–57, 69, 70, 74, 76–77, 9, 91, 96
    bronze 69
    ribbon 53, 77, 79
Toupet, C.H. 95
Towednack, Cornwall 3, 4, 50, 51, 77, 79
Trackways 82
Trade route 107
Treasure Trove 4
Tréboul stage 66
Tremblestown, Meath 50, 78
Tress-rings 59, 74, 109
Trindhøj, Denmark 99
Trinity College, Dublin 4
Trundholm, Denmark 46
Tully, Roscommon 72
Tumulus Culture 42, 43, 44, 45, 69, 74
Tweed river, Scotland 10
Tweezers, bone 39
Twohig, Elizabeth Shee v
Ty Mawr, Anglesey 97, 106
Tylecote, R. F. 10
Tyrone County 10

Uenze, Hans P. 45, 59, 70, 72, 95
Ulster 57, 77, 97, 102
Ulster Museum V
Unĕtice (Aunjetitz) Culture 23, 27
University College Dublin v
University Museum of Archaeology & Ethnology, Cambridge 4
Unstrut-Saale Complex 38
Urn 40, 41, 75
Urnfields 41, 80, 91, 92, 95, 107
USA 6

Vandkilde, Helle 38
Vases 66
Velem-Szentvid, Hungary 8
Vessel 66, 107
Vessels, bronze 80
Villena, Spain 8
Villeneuve-Saint-Vistre, France 66
Voltofte, Denmark 80
Von Brunn, W. A. 38
Von Merhart, G. 42

Waggons, wheeled 46, 47, 81, 105
Wales 37, 53, 57, 70, 77, 79, 92, 106
Wallace, C. R. 37
Wallace, J. N. A. 5
Wallace, Patrick. V
Wallington Phase 81
Wanderslade, Kent 107
Warner, Richard. V
Wealth-Centre 28
Wedge-Tombs 21
Wedmore, Somersetshire 53
Wessex 1, 2, 4, 11, 18, 24, 27, 28, 38, 39, 40, 95, 109
Wessex Early Bronze Age Gold 2, 4, 13, 24, 28
Wessex I 'Culture' 38
Wessex II 'Culture' 40
West, Jones. 6
West, Mathew. 6
Western Asia 73
Westmeath County 78
Westow, Yorkshire 81
Wexford County 10, 19, 28
Wheeled vehicles 42, 43
Whetstone 40
Whitegates, Meath 88
Whiteway, Edward 5
Whitfield, Waterford 37, 38
Wicklow 10, 11, 12, 37, 77
Wig-rings 95
Wilburton Complex 81, 82, 91
Wilde, W.R. 3, 6, 7, 21, 83
Wilsford, Wiltshire 24, 38, 40
Wilson, B.C.S. 37, 59
Wilson, Daniel. 4
Wiltshire 2, 4, 92
Wiltshire Archaeological Society Museum, Devizes 4
Winterhay Green, Somersetshire 53
Winterslow, Wiltshire 18
Wood-working 99
Wood-Martin, W. G. 3, 7, 10, 36
Wright, E.P. 4, 7

Yeovil, Somerset 79
Yorkshire 18, 23, 33, 38, 92, 106

Zealand, Denmark 80, 96
Zelené, Bohemia 43